Faithbuilders

The Gospel of Matthew

by Mathew Bartlett & Derek Williams

The Gospel of Matthew by Mathew Bartlett & Derek Williams

First Published in Great Britain in 2015

FAITHBUILDERS PUBLISHING www.biblestudiesonline.org.uk

An Imprint of Apostolos Publishing Ltd,
3rd Floor, 207 Regent Street,
London W1B 3HH
www.apostolos-publishing.com

British Library Cataloguing-in-Publication Data

A catalogue record for this book is available from the British Library

ISBN: 978-1-910942-06-2

Cover Design by Blitz Media, Pontypool, Torfaen, UK

Printed and bound in Great Britain by Marston Book Services Limited, Oxfordshire.

Dedicated to all those who are hungry for God's Word.

More from Faithbuilders Bible Studies

Faithbuilders Bible studies: Mark

Esther – Queen of Persia

The Prophecy of Amos – A Warning for Today

Zechariah – Prophet of Messiah

Faithbuilders Bible Studies

The Faithbuilders Bible study series has been developed a useful resource for today's students of God's Word and their busy lifestyles. Pastors, home or study group leaders and indeed for anyone wishing to study the Bible for themselves will benefit from using Faithbuilders studies.

Each volume is the result of many years of group Bible study, and has been revised again and again to be relevant, challenging and faith building whilst remaining clear and easy to understand, helping more people to discover the blessings of God's Word.

Mathew Bartlett holds a Master's Degree in Biblical Studies from the University of Chester, England. Derek Williams is now retired, having been a pastor and preacher for over 40 years.

Contents

Matthew Chapter 1

The Genealogy of Christ

1:1 This is the record of the genealogy of Jesus Christ, the Son of David, the son of Abraham.

Matthew's purpose in writing his gospel is clear from the very beginning: he intends to reveal Jesus as the Christ, the long awaited anointed one promised by God. He demonstrates this fact by showing how all the promises of Scripture relating to the coming of Christ are fulfilled in him. The titles "Son of David" and "son of Abraham" describe Christ in this way, for God both to Abraham and to David that one of their descendants would be the Christ.

To David, God said "I will set one of your seed upon your throne" (1 Chron. 17:11; Psa. 132:11).

To Abraham, God said "Through your seed shall all nations of the earth be blessed" (Gen. 22:18). The apostle Paul explained the meaning of this promise in Galatians, that "seed" is singular, referring to one of Abraham's offspring, not all of them (Gal. 3:16). Matthew's aim throughout his gospel is to reveal Jesus as the one God had promised.

The word "genealogy" means the line of natural descent. Although Jesus Christ is the eternal Son of God (who pre-existed his manifestation in the flesh), yet he became part of Abraham's family by his incarnation, and was born as a Jew (2 Tim. 2:8).

Christ's genealogy reveals how Christ truly became one of us by entering the human family and the Jewish family in particular. Of this family's history much could be said, which would be superfluous to our understanding of this gospel. But since the inspired writer particularly highlights several features of this genealogy, so we shall consider them in greater detail.

1:2 Abraham was the father of Isaac, Isaac the father of Jacob, Jacob the father of Judah and his brothers.

Christ's descent from Abraham through Isaac and Jacob made him a Jew. This was a vital qualification for the Christ, since Moses said "The Lord your God prophet like me from *among your own people*" (Deut. 18:15). God had made it clear that it would not be through Ishmael (Abraham's child born in natural way, albeit to a slave) but through Isaac (Abraham's child born by the power of the Spirit in fulfilment of God's promise) that the lineage of Christ would come. It was not by the works of the flesh but by his miracle working power that God brought Christ into the world; and it is through that same power that God brings salvation to our hearts by faith.

Furthermore, God later revealed that the Christ would be descended from Judah (Gen. 49:10).

1:3 Judah the father of Perez and Zerah (by Tamar), Perez the father of Hezron, Hezron the father of Ram.

The devil had many times tried to frustrate God's purpose of bringing Christ into the world. One such occasion was in the days of Judah. Judah's oldest son married a girl named Tamar, but died without leaving children. Judah's younger son, Onan, according to custom, was to take her as his wife and raise up children who would inherit his brother's estate. But Onan knew that the child would not be his heir, so whenever he had sex with Tamar, he tried to prevent getting her pregnant (Gen. 38:6–10).

This scripture was not intended to imply that contraception is wrong; what Onan did it was wicked because behind it was Satan's attempt to end the family line of Judah. Judah had still one son, Shelah, whom he promised to give to Tamar when he was old enough, but when Judah did not keep his promise, Tamar made her own plans. She dressed up with a veil and waited near Judah's place of work posing as a prostitute. Judah's wife had already died and he paid Tamar to let him have sex with her, and made her pregnant; he did not know that she was his daughter in law. Since he had no money with him at the time, Judah left his personal seal as a pledge that he would return with payment. But when he sent a friend to pay the girl and get his seal back, the girl had disappeared. (Read the whole story in Genesis 38).

Later it was told Judah that his daughter in law, although a widow, was pregnant. He was about to order her execution when the girl announced that she was pregnant by the owner of a seal that she showed. It was Judah's. So he did not execute her, but said "she is more righteous than I". Tamar had twins, and it is through one of them (Perez) that Jesus Christ is descended from Judah according to the flesh.

The reason why God's Word details this whole sordid history is to show how neither the devil nor the wickedness of men could prevent God bringing his only begotten son into the world in the way that he had promised.

1:4–5 Ram the father of Amminadab, Amminadab the father of Nahshon, Nahshon the father of Salmon, Salmon the father of Boaz (by Rahab), Boaz the father of Obed (by Ruth), Obed the father of Jesse.

Matthew notes that Boaz's mother was Rahab, who by the faith which she showed when she hid the spies was accounted as righteous before God (Heb. 11:31) and became not only numbered among the people of Israel, but included in the family tree of the Lord Jesus Christ. We too are accounted as righteous by God through faith in Jesus Christ, a faith which expresses itself in good works (Rom. 5:1).

Boaz married Ruth, the Moabitess, even though the law had said that a Moabite could not enter the congregation of the LORD until ten generations (Deut. 23:3). This highlights that Jesus Christ would become the one who would break down the middle wall of partition and makes it possible for both Jews and Gentiles to enter into God's kingdom (Eph. 2:14).

1:6 And Jesse the father of David the king. David was the father of Solomon (by the wife of Uriah).

If Jesus is truly the Christ then he must be a descendent of David, and Matthew is at pains to stress that this is the case. When David committed adultery with Bathsheba, the child born from that unholy union died. But later, her husband Uriah being dead and God having forgiven David's sin, David and Bathsheba were married. Solomon, the result of their legal union, was loved by God, and it is through him that the future kings of Israel came, even up to the time of Christ, for when God forgives, he forgives fully.

This inclusion of Bathsheba is Jesus' family tree reveals God's ultimate purpose in sending his son, for "Christ Jesus came into the world to save sinners" (1 Tim. 1:15).

It is at this point that the genealogy in Matthew begins to differ from the one given by Luke. Scholars have debated much about this. Some suppose that Luke's genealogy is actually that of Mary. What is clear is that Matthew wants to show how Christ fits into the royal line, and that Joseph was in line for the throne. When it comes to Jesus, of course, he is not merely *in line* for the throne, for the throne belongs to him absolutely.

All the names given in the following verses were kings of Judah, and their life histories are found in the books of 1 & 2 Kings and 1 & 2 Chronicles.

1:7–11 Solomon the father of Rehoboam, Rehoboam the father of Abijah, Abijah the father of Asa, Asa the father of Jehoshaphat, Jehoshaphat the father of Joram, Joram the father of Uzziah, Uzziah the father of Jotham, Jotham the father of Ahaz, Ahaz the father of Hezekiah, Hezekiah the father of Manasseh, Manasseh the father of Amon, Amon the father of Josiah, and Josiah the father of Jeconiah and his brothers, at the time of the deportation to Babylon.

These verses span the 400 years from the civil war in Israel to the carrying of Judah to Babylon. During this time the purposes of God concerning his people were not forgotten, nor was that greatest purpose of all—to bring Christ into the world, Throughout the history of Israel, God was working out his purpose for the salvation of mankind.

It is of note that such was the effect of the deportation to Babylon on the corporate mind-set of the nation that the Jews dated their history as being either the time before or after the deportation and return.

1:12–16 After the deportation to Babylon, Jeconiah became the father of Shealtiel, Shealtiel the father of Zerubbabel, Zerubbabel the father of Abiud, Abiud the father of Eliakim, Eliakim the father of Azor, Azor the father of Zadok, Zadok the father of Achim, Achim the father of Eliud, Eliud the father of Eleazar, Eleazar the father of Matthan, Matthan the father of Jacob, and Jacob the father of Joseph, the husband of Mary, by whom Jesus was born, who is called Christ.

God had promised that after 70 years in exile, Judah would return again and rebuild Jerusalem, which they did. Matthew points out that God who kept this promise to Israel has also kept his greater promise of spiritual restoration in Christ Jesus.

1:17 So all the generations from Abraham to David are fourteen generations, and from David to the deportation to Babylon, fourteen generations, and from the deportation to Babylon to Christ, fourteen generations.

God's plan to bring Christ into the world was not drawn up last minute, for the way of salvation in Christ was ordained before time. God had planned it to the smallest detail before he ever made the world. Notice the symmetry of the generations, which reveals that God is in charge of the flow of human history. Everything happens according to his time scale. God predicted the exact day and date of Christ's crucifixion, resurrection and ascension to glory (through the foreshadowing of the Passover and also through Dan. 9:25–26). It was written of the exodus from Egypt that God's promise was fulfilled "on the exact day" (Gen. 15:13 and Exod. 12:41), so all the details of our spiritual exodus through Christ came exactly on time.

The Birth of Christ

In order to further show that Jesus is the Christ, Matthew demonstrates that the manner of his birth fulfilled the scriptures.

1:18 Now the birth of Jesus Christ happened this way. While his mother Mary was engaged to Joseph, but before they came together, she was found to be pregnant through the Holy Spirit.

Through the birth of Jesus, God breaks into time. The Word became flesh to dwell among us, in order to fulfil all the promises of God. This is why Matthew devotes a whole section to Christ's birth. Whilst Mary was engaged to be married to Joseph, she was found with child through the Holy Spirit who formed within her womb this fusion of God and man—Jesus Christ. Matthew emphasizes that she had not had sexual intercourse with Joseph, or any other man.

1:19 Because Joseph, her husband to be, was a righteous man, and because he did not want to disgrace her, he intended to divorce her privately.

Joseph at this time knew nothing about the purpose of God being carried out in Mary's life. Supposing she had been unfaithful, he considered his position. The selflessness of Joseph is here revealed. He wished to spare Mary the shame of being found pregnant outside of marriage. So he decided to go ahead with the marriage to keep up appearances, but later to divorce Mary away from the public eye, for he did not wish to be united with (as he may have then thought) an immoral woman.

1:20–21 When he had contemplated this, an angel of the Lord appeared to him in a dream and said, "Joseph, Son of David, do not be afraid to take Mary as your wife, because the child conceived in her is from the Holy Spirit. She will give birth to a son and you will name him Jesus, because he will save his people from their sins."

God began to reveal his purpose to Joseph. God wanted him to marry Mary without fear, for the child within her was conceived of the Holy Spirit. The son she would bear would be born in fulfilment of long awaited prophecy. He would be the Saviour who would save his people from their sins—Jesus.

1:22–23 This all happened so that what was spoken by the Lord through the prophet would be fulfilled: "Look! The virgin will conceive and bear a son, and they will call him Emmanuel," which means "God with us."

Matthew again emphasizes that Christ's birth was in fulfilment of the scripture, that a virgin would conceive and bear a son who although fully man would be no less than fully God. He would be God manifested in the flesh. Jesus would have a unique birth, a unique name, and a unique mission.

1:24–25 When Joseph awoke from sleep he did what the angel of the Lord told him. He took his wife, but did not have marital relations with her until she gave birth to a son, whom he named Jesus.

Although nothing like this had ever been heard of before—a virgin pregnant—Joseph believed and acted obediently upon the word of God. What is more, out of reverence for the holy child she carried, even after they were married, Joseph had no intercourse with Mary until after Jesus was born.

Discussion Questions for Chapter 1

1. vv. 1–17. Why do you think the genealogy of Jesus is important?

2. vv. 18–25. What was unique about Jesus' birth?

3. vv. 18–25. What impresses you most about the attitude of Mary and Joseph?

4. How do the genealogy of Christ and the account of his birth reveal God's sovereignty in human history?

5. What does this chapter say to you about the kind of God whom we worship?

You will find suggested answers to these questions on pages 306–323.

Matthew Chapter 2

The Time and Place of Jesus' Birth

2:1–2 After Jesus was born in Bethlehem in Judea, in the time of King Herod, wise men from the East came to Jerusalem saying, "Where is the one who is born king of the Jews? For we saw his star when it rose and have come to worship him."

Matthew (as Luke in Luke 1:5) dates the time of Jesus' birth as being in the days of Herod the Great, King of Judea, which leads scholars to believe that Christ was born in approx. 4BC. Traditionally, the term "Anno Domini" was used to denote the number of years from the date of Christ's birth; but these early estimates are inaccurate to the tune of 3–4 years.

It is of vital importance that Matthew records the place of Jesus' birth as Bethlehem, since this was long since prophesied and understood by the Jews to be the birth place of the coming Messiah (John 7:42; Micah 5:2).

Little is told us of the scholars which came from the East to Jerusalem, except that they had seen a sign which indicated to them that the Messiah King of the Jews had been born. The words "wise men" denote scientists, or learned men. They were clearly in possession of the prophetic Scriptures, and had observed a sign in the heavens as being the omen of the fulfilment of a prophecy concerning Christ's coming.

Balaam son of Beor prophesied that "a star will march forth out of Jacob, and a sceptre will rise out of Israel" (Num. 24:17).

Isaiah wrote, "and the Gentiles shall come to thy light, and kings to the brightness of thy rising" (Isa. 60:3).

To indulge in speculation as to the nature of this star is actually pointless. It served merely as a sign to these wise men, and afterward had no purpose. It is possible that the sign was supernaturally produced, or even that it was literally a new star, showing forth the glory of a creator.

Having read of his coming, these devout men travelled long distances in order to worship and pay him homage.

The Rejection of Christ

2:3 When King Herod heard this he was alarmed, and all Jerusalem with him.

The word "alarmed" is too weak. We are often told in Christmas nativities that Herod did not wish to lose his throne. Such may be the case, and yet this is not the only possible meaning of this verse. Perhaps Herod was not so much afraid of a new king taking his place as he was averse to God's king coming to reign in his heart and life; he would not submit to him. On hearing of the coming of Christ, Herod and all Jerusalem were stirred and agitated in opposition to the coming one, thus revealing the enmity in the heart of sinful people against God. To think that such antipathy was provoked merely by the mention of the coming king! Many today share this irrational enmity against God which is the result of sin.

2:4 After assembling all the chief priests and experts in the law, he asked them where the Christ was to be born.

Herod himself was not entirely in the dark concerning the prophecy of a divine king who would reign over all the earth and demand perfect submission from every man. He knew enough to know that the place of his birth was predicted in the scriptures, as the scribes may have reminded him.

2:5–6 "In Bethlehem of Judea," they said, "for it is written this way by the prophet: "And you, Bethlehem, in the land of Judah, are in no way least among the rulers of Judah, for out of you will come a ruler who will shepherd my people Israel." "

All the kings from David onwards might have been said in one sense to arise out of Bethlehem, for that was their ancestor David's family home. Yet the prophecy was specific that the Christ, the greatest of all kings, would himself be born in Bethlehem to shepherd and rule over God's people Israel. Matthew concentrates here on the fulfilment of this prophecy, and so does not elaborate on the rest of Micah's message which stated that the king's "goings forth" had been "from everlasting" (Micah 5:2).

2:7 Then Herod privately summoned the wise men and determined from them when the star had appeared.

In keeping with every evil work, Herod wanted his plans for the killing of the Christ child to be as secret as possible. No one does wrong openly, but secretly, behind closed doors. Pretending to show greater interest for some other reason, Herod found out by closely examining the wise men when the star had appeared, information which would enable him to roughly age the child.

2:8 He sent them to Bethlehem and said, "Go and look carefully for the child. When you find him, inform me so that I can go and worship him as well."

Originally it had only been Herod's intention to eliminate the Christ, so he asks the wise men to definitely locate the child and report back to him, so that he might find and destroy him.

Seeking, Finding and Worshiping

2:9–10 After listening to the king they left, and once again the star they saw when it rose led them until it stopped above the place where the child was. When they saw the star they shouted joyfully.

Since the hearts of the wise men were open to the guidance of God, they found that as they journeyed toward Bethlehem, the star "went before them" confirming that their direction of travel was correct, and they gave a shout of joy to think that they were now so near to completing their journey and finding their goal. Are we so enthusiastic about coming together to worship Jesus?

2:11 As they came into the house and saw the child with Mary his mother, they bowed down and worshiped him. They opened their treasure boxes and gave him gifts of gold, frankincense, and myrrh.

The worship of the wise men consisted of faith and homage. They sought him and bowed down to him. It consisted also of devotion, for they opened their treasures—it may well have been all they had to live on, it was certainly not cheap to them, this gold, frankincense and myrrh: gold the gift for a king, frankincense for the worship of God, and myrrh for burial and the priestly office.

Since by this time Matthew refers to Jesus as a "young child" (different word to "babe") we may assume that the arrival of the wise men came a while after Christ's birth and that Mary and Joseph had spent some time in Bethlehem. From what follows in this passage we assume that time to be approximately two years, and Jesus was anything up to two years old at this point.

2:12 After being warned in a dream not to return to Herod, they went back by another route to their own country.

Whether or not the wise men had been taken in by Herod's duplicity is unclear. Yet if they did harbour any suspicions, these were to be confirmed, for an angel of the Lord appeared to them in a dream, warning them about Herod's true purpose. They went back to their own country by a different route in order to escape and frustrate him.

Herod Tries to Kill Jesus

2:13–15 After they had gone, an angel of the Lord appeared to Joseph in a dream and said, "Get up, take the child and his mother and flee to Egypt, and stay there until I tell you, for Herod is going to look for the child to kill him." Then he got up, took the child and his mother during the night, and went to Egypt. He stayed there until Herod died. In this way what was spoken by the Lord through the prophet was fulfilled: "I called my Son out of Egypt."

God sent his angel also to warn Joseph of what was about to happen. "Herod is going to look for the child to kill him". God instructs Joseph to flee Bethlehem and remain in Egypt where he would be safe, until he once more received word from God. Joseph immediately obeyed, and through all of these circumstances another prophecy was fulfilled: "out of Egypt have I called my son" (Hosea 11:1).

2:16 When Herod saw that he had been tricked by the wise men, he became enraged. He sent men to kill all the children in Bethlehem and throughout the surrounding region from the age of two and under, according to the time he had learned from the wise men.

The opponent of Christ was angered when his plans were frustrated by the wise men, and so he sought to accomplish his evil plan in another way. This delay may be seen as God giving Herod an opportunity to turn from his evil purpose, but he did not do so. Instead, he ordered his soldiers to slaughter all children in Bethlehem and the surrounding districts who were aged two and under. It is worth remembering that the soldiers would not have asked to see evidence of age. They would have killed every child who looked two or under, and they would not have stopped to check the child's gender either, so many girls may have died too in Herod's efforts to rid the earth of the Christ child.

2:17–18 Then what was spoken by Jeremiah the prophet was fulfilled: "A voice was heard in Ramah, weeping and loud wailing, Rachel weeping for her children, and she did not want to be comforted, because they were gone."

This mindless slaughter, carried out in deliberate defiance of God, was predicted through the prophet Jeremiah. Barnes notes that Rama was a small town about 6 miles northwest of Jerusalem, and Rachel was buried near to Bethlehem (Gen. 35:16–19) which is about 10 miles from Rama.

The prophecy clearly indicates the extent of the "surrounding region" (v16) where the children were killed. One might easily understand why the parents refused to be comforted.

2:19–20 After Herod had died, an angel of the Lord appeared in a dream to Joseph in Egypt saying, "Get up, take the child and his mother, and go to the land of Israel, for those who were seeking the child's life are dead."

The one comfort we can take from this passage is that Herod died, as all tyrants will. It was time then for God to call his son back into Israel; which is what the angel instructed Joseph to do.

2:21–23 So he got up and took the child and his mother and returned to the land of Israel. But when he heard that Archelaus was reigning over Judea in place of his father Herod, he was afraid to go there. After being warned in a dream, he went to the regions of Galilee. He came to a town called Nazareth and lived there. Then what had been spoken by the prophets was fulfilled, that Jesus would be called a Nazarene.

Joseph immediately obeyed. But as he journeyed, he learned that Archelaus was reigning in Judea in place of his father Herod. Knowing the son to be as evil as his father, and perhaps worried that the story of the Christ child might endanger Jesus there, and with divine confirmation of this being given, Joseph decided to return to Nazareth, which was a different jurisdiction, where he and Mary had become engaged, and where no one was looking for Jesus. This once again caused the fulfilment of scripture, where the coming Messiah was foreshadowed by the oath of the Nazarite, the one from Nazareth. Thus the Messiah would be a Nazarene. Nazareth was a despised city, and so it was fitting that he who was despised and rejected by men should live there.

Discussion Questions for Chapter 2

1. vv. 1–12. In what ways might we describe the actions of the wise men as an example for all Christians to follow?

2. vv. 3, 16–18. Why do you think Herod rejected Christ?

3. What can we learn from the way that God warned the wise men and Joseph of Herod's evil intentions?

4. How did Herod's rejection of Christ have an effect on others?

5. Try to describe the effect on the life of Jesus Christ of this early rejection.

You will find suggested answers to these questions on pages 306–323.

Matthew Chapter 3

John's Call to Repentance

3:1 In those days John the Baptist came into the wilderness of Judea proclaiming,

Matthew does not record the details of John's birth; in fact it is only Luke who does so. Matthew begins his account of John at the commencement of his ministry. "In those days" is clearly not a reference to the birth narrative of the previous chapter, as John was only six months older than Jesus. Barnes suggests that Matthew was referring to the time when Jesus still lived in Nazareth (from 2:23). John took as his pulpit the desert area of Judea to proclaim his message.

3:2 "Repent, for the kingdom of heaven is near."

His message consisted of two headings, repent and the kingdom of heaven is near. The call to repentance is fundamental to the message of salvation. At the time of John's ministry, salvation had not been provided since Christ had not yet died for the sins of the world; nevertheless, the people needed to repent. The word "repent" simply means to "think differently" to "reconsider" (Strong's Dictionary); that is, to have a change of heart or direction, to be sorry for our sins against God (2 Cor. 7:10). Indeed, it is only against God that we sin (Psalm 51:4), although it is by the action of our sin that we cause others to suffer. But it is not only a turning away from sin but a looking to God as the only one who can save (Isaiah 45:22; Heb. 7:25). The kingdom of heaven does not refer to the kingdom of glory that is in the heavenly places but to the coming of the Messiah into the world. It was near at hand, because Jesus Christ was about to commence his ministry on earth; a ministry that would culminate in his death on the cross as an atonement of sin and thus open the door of the kingdom of heaven for all that believe.

3:3 For he is the one about whom Isaiah the prophet had spoken: "The voice of one shouting in the wilderness, 'Prepare the way for the Lord, make his paths straight."

The coming of John and the message he proclaimed had been prophesied in the Old Testament (Isaiah 40:3). John was the forerunner, the herald who went before the Christ to announce that he was on his way. Therefore, the people had to get themselves ready for his coming.

3:4 Now John wore clothing made from camel's hair with a leather belt around his waist, and his diet consisted of locusts and wild honey.

John was unmistakable; he was distinct from everybody else of his day. The clothes that he wore were woven of course camel hair tied with a leather belt around the waist. His diet consisted of locusts for meat and the honey of the wild bees that made their home in the desert.

3:5 Then people from Jerusalem, as well as all Judea and all the region around the Jordan, were going out to him,

John had no problem getting the people to come out to hear his message; they came from the city of Jerusalem and from all over Judea to the banks of the River Jordan.

3:6 and he was baptizing them in the Jordan River as they confessed their sins.

They not only came and heard the word but responded to it with repentance and were baptized confessing their sins.

3:7 But when he saw many Pharisees and Sadducees coming to his baptism, he said to them, "You offspring of vipers! Who warned you to flee from the coming wrath?

There were sceptics who came too: the Pharisees and Sadducees. John knew that they did not come to listen, repent or be baptized; they had come to criticize. John told them plainly that they were a bunch of snakes. Jesus later said the same of them (Matt. 12:34) and that they were of their father the devil (John 8:44). John was fully aware that these people were self-righteous hypocrites who considered themselves to be the elect of God and without sin; that is why they rejected his message. So he asked them who had warned them to escape from the impending wrath of God.

3:8 Therefore produce fruit that proves your repentance,

John appealed to the people to prove that they had repented of their sins by yielding their lives to God and living a godly life (Matt. 7:20).

3:9 and don't think you can say to yourselves, 'We have Abraham as our father.' For I tell you that God can raise up children for Abraham from these stones!

The biggest boast of the scribes, Pharisees and Sadducees was that they were descended from Abraham and they thought that this guaranteed them acceptance with God. John the Baptist made it clear that since God is able to raise up children from the very stones around them, their natural descent—apart from repentance—was of no worth in his eyes.

3:10 Even now the axe is laid at the root of the trees, and every tree that does not produce good fruit will be cut down and thrown into the fire.

Already the hand of God was outstretched in judgment against those to whom he had entrusted his word and whom he had separated to Himself, the people of Israel. Everyone who did not produce the fruits of righteousness would be destroyed.

The Greater One

3:11 "I baptize you with water, for repentance, but the one coming after me is more powerful than I am – I am not worthy to carry his sandals. He will baptize you with the Holy Spirit and fire.

John's commission from God was to baptize with water those who repented and turned to God. The one who came after him would be mightier, having greater ability and the power to do anything. In comparison to him, John was not worthy to be his slave, the one who carried his sandals. This coming one, the Messiah, would baptize with the Holy Spirit and fire (Acts 1:5).

3:12 His winnowing fork is in his hand, and he will clean out his threshing floor and will gather his wheat into the storehouse, but the chaff he will burn up with inextinguishable fire."

To separate the chaff from the wheat a winnowing fork, or fan, was used. Jesus Christ is pictured here as having a winnowing fan in his hand with which he will sort out the real from the false. The wheat, those who are truly his people, he will gather to Himself but those that are not his will be cast into the never ending fire (Revelation 20:15).

The Baptism of Jesus

3:13 Then Jesus came from Galilee to John to be baptized by him in the Jordan River.

While John was still by the banks of the Jordan Jesus also came to be baptized by him.

3:14 But John tried to prevent him, saying, "I need to be baptized by you, and yet you come to me?"

John had the witness within him that Jesus was the Christ. In John 1:29 it says "the next day John saw Jesus coming toward him, and

35

said, 'Behold! The Lamb of God who takes away the sin of the world!'" John, knowing who Jesus was, strenuously objected to baptizing him for he saw his own need of being baptized by Jesus.

3:15 So Jesus replied to him, "Let it happen now, for it is right for us to fulfil all righteousness." Then John yielded to him.

Although Jesus had no need to repent or be baptized in water (1 Peter 2:22), he asked John to baptize him in order to show that they were carrying out what God required of them. So John baptized Jesus in the River Jordan. In this act Jesus, although sinless, was identifying himself with the sinners whom he came to save.

3:16 After Jesus was baptized, just as he was coming up out of the water, the heavens opened and he saw the Spirit of God descending like a dove and coming on him.

After he was baptized Jesus came up out of the water. It is quite clear from this that John's baptism was by full immersion and not sprinkling. As he was coming up out of the water the heavens opened and the Holy Spirit descended in the form of a dove; settling on him, before entering him. This was the sign that God had given to John in order to reveal to him who the Christ was (John 1: 33).

3:17 And a voice from heaven said, "This is my one dear Son; in him I take great delight."

At the same time the voice of God spoke from heaven declaring that Jesus to be his beloved Son in whom he delighted (Psalm 2:7).

Discussion Questions for Chapter 3

1. vv. 1–3. In what ways did the ministry of John the Baptist prepare the people to meet with and accept Jesus?

2. vv. 13–17. The baptism of Jesus is referred to in all four gospels—what do you think is so important about it?

3. vv. 11–12. John referred to Jesus as the "one greater than I". In what ways do you think Jesus was greater than John?

4. vv. 16–17. What do you think is significant about the way the Holy Spirit came on the Lord Jesus Christ?

5. Have you—as Jesus was—been baptised? Take a moment to describe your own experience.

You will find suggested answers to these questions on pages 306–323.

Matthew Chapter 4

Jesus Tempted by Satan

4:1 Then Jesus was led by the Spirit into the wilderness to be tempted by the devil.

Having been baptised with the Holy Spirit of God, Jesus was immediately led by the Spirit into the wilderness of Judea to "be tempted by the devil". God's purpose was for his son to face Satan head on. Satan knew who Christ was, the seed of the woman who would come to destroy him, and so in various ways attempted to cause Jesus to fail in his mission.

We may find it difficult to understand how Christ was tempted, for whereas we are sinful and prone to fall into temptation, Christ was without sin. It is because our Lord Jesus Christ overcame all sin and went to the cross spotless for us that we can be forgiven. His word to believers who fall into sin is "if we confess our sins, he is faithful and just to forgive us our sins and to cleanse us from all unrighteousness." This cleansing makes us right with God again, just as fully as when we were made right with God initially by receiving Christ as Saviour and Lord. Moreover, Jesus Christ has the power to enable us to overcome temptations—even those which we were once helpless to resist—but only as we recognise that it is not we who can resist temptation; the living Christ within us will strengthen and enable us to share in *his* victory over sin.

4:2 After he fasted forty days and forty nights he was famished.

Christ was led into the wilderness to fast and pray for forty days and nights. The similar fasts of Moses and Elijah merely pointed forward to this event. Jesus deliberately starved his natural life in order to concentrate on that which is spiritual. This is the principle of fasting.

Christians should fast only as they are led by the Spirit of God; for ill-advised fasting leads only to health problems, not spiritual blessing.

4:3 The tempter came and said to him, "If you are the Son of God, command these stones to become bread."

Another name is used for the devil in this verse, describing his nature, as the tempter. He is the one who opposes and resists all that is of God or is godly. Satan's tempting of Christ was more than a temptation of his weak human nature. Satan primarily tempted Christ's divinity. "If you are the Son of God", he says. The devil knew very well that Jesus was the Son of God, and yet rebelliously resisted and opposed him. The devil is a liar from the beginning, and since it appears that he is confident of his own power, then he must be lying to himself also. To ask God for a demonstration of his power to prove that he exists is to test him in a sinful way. To allure a hungry man with food is to appeal to human weakness. Yet on both points of temptation, Jesus was victorious. The sin of Adam and Eve was to obey Satan rather than God; but Jesus remained faithful and obedient to his Father.

4:4 But he answered, "It is written, 'Man does not live by bread alone, but by every word that comes from the mouth of God.' "

Jesus used the word of God to good effect against the devil. The same scriptures which Satan twisted to tempt Jesus' deity, Christ uses correctly to justify his obedience to God and overcome the devil. The human soul needs to be fed by something more than bread (which only feeds the body). Although the human body cannot live without the soul, the human soul will live on eternally even without the body. It is the word of God which feeds the soul, and gives it life. It is this word which has brought us life, keeps us in life, and preserves us to eternal life. And it is this same word which Jesus successfully used to resist temptation.

4:5 Then the devil took him to the holy city, had him stand on the highest point of the temple.

The power of the devil may here be seen. By his power he bodily took Jesus, without the need of time or transport, to the highest point of the temple in Jerusalem. It is perhaps strange that Jesus allowed this to be done to him, but he wished to face Satan fully in all his evil power for our sakes. Christ's was no half-hearted battle or mock war. The word of God does not diminish the power of our enemy, but it assures us that the infinitely greater power of God is within us (1 John 4:4).

4:6 And said to him, "If you are the Son of God, throw yourself down. For it is written, 'He will command his angels concerning you' and 'with their hands they will lift you up, so that you will not strike your foot against a stone.'"

For the second time the devil tempts Christ's divinity. "If you are the Son of God," says Satan, "then prove your indestructability". Throw yourself down, and experience the fulfilment of scripture; God will not allow you to be hurt. But Christ had voluntarily humbled himself to become a servant and was committed to doing God's will, not forcing God's hand with impetuous actions of his own. So once again the lies of Satan fell on deaf ears. Someone has said that Christ was such a stranger to evil, and the ways of the devil, that he could pass sin by on the street without so much as a familiar look of recognition; for he knew no sin.

4:7 Jesus said to him, "Once again it is written: 'You are not to put the Lord your God to the test.'"

Jesus knew that the devil was asking him to test God, and he refused to do so in obedience to God's word, which he once again used like a sword to defeat Satan's purposes. The Bible says that believers also have access to this "sword of the spirit which is the word of God"

(Eph. 6:17) and that we can use it to overcome all the works of the devil. Since Christ has overcome, we too can overcome in union with him (Rev. 12:11).

4:8–9. Again, the devil took him to a very high mountain, and showed him all the kingdoms of the world and their grandeur. And he said to him, "I will give you all these things if you throw yourself to the ground and worship me."

In a similar way to that employed in verse five, the devil transported Jesus to a very high mountain and in a single instant showed him all the kingdoms of the world and their glory. This may at first sight be regarded as a temptation to the pride of the human heart, but since Christ was absolutely without pride, such a temptation would have proved useless. Rather, the tempting is again of Christ's divinity. All that glory which man presumes to possess was being offered to God, who himself should be man's glory. Offering the creator his own world, on condition of his abdicating his throne and bowing down to Satan, was certainly tempting his godhead, and is reminiscent of that earlier sin which Satan committed in heaven, when he sought to take God's place upon his throne.

4:10 Then Jesus said to him, "Go away, Satan! For it is written: 'You are to worship the Lord your God and serve only him.' "

On this occasion, Jesus ordered Satan away, upholding the very first commandment, to worship God and have no other gods before him.

4:11 Then the devil left him, and angels came and began ministering to his needs.

The hollowness of the devil's conceit is now revealed; for although he had offered Christ all the world's glory, and put himself forward as his superior, yet he has no choice but to obey the command of Jesus and leave. Christ's victory over Satan is overwhelming, but it is by no means complete. Jesus could no doubt carry on defeating the devil in this way forevermore, even as one day he shall order him to be cast into the lake of fire. But it was in order to save us that he confronted Satan in this way, for only by conquering him who had the power of death could Christ release all those who were held captive by the devil. So Christ is now ready to leave the desert and continue his victorious march to the cross (Heb. 2:14).

But first, after the physical rigours of fasting in the desert, and the expending of spiritual power in resisting Satan, Christ receives the ministry of angels to strengthen and renew him. It is thought by some that the angels brought food and water, as they did in the case of Elijah, but perhaps they also brought a more spiritual ministry, resulting in the supernatural quickening of Christ's mind and body.

4:12 Now when Jesus heard that John had been imprisoned, he went into Galilee.

From scripture we discern that both John and Jesus realised that the diminishing of the one would lead to the public ministry of the other, and both were content with this; it being God's will. Knowing that the time had come to begin his earthly ministry, Jesus returned from Judea to Galilee.

Jesus Begins His Ministry

4:13 While in Galilee, he moved from Nazareth to make his home in Capernaum by the sea, in the region of Zebulun and Naphtali.

Commencing his ministry, Jesus left his home town of Nazareth to take a house in Capernaum near the Sea of Galilee.

4:14–16 So that what was spoken by Isaiah the prophet would be fulfilled: "Land of Zebulon and land of Naphtali, the way by the sea, beyond the Jordan, Galilee of the Gentiles — the people who sit in darkness have seen a great light: and on those who sit in the region and shadow of death a light has dawned."

Matthew is keen to point out that by Christ's seemingly unimportant action the Scripture was again fulfilled. Galilee of the New Testament was the inheritance of the tribes of Zebulon and Naphtali, and Isaiah had predicted the day in which the people living there—being in the darkness of sin and death—might come face to face with the one who would bring them out of spiritual darkness to the light of eternal life (Col. 1:13; Acts 26:18).

4:17 From that time Jesus began to preach this message: "Repent, for the kingdom of heaven is near."

Christ had come to seek and to save the lost, and so begins his ministry by calling people to repent and return to God. Their repentance would not be in vain, for God was at this time offering full amnesty, pardon and forgiveness to guilty sinners; reconciling his enemies to himself by taking as his own children those who were once children of wrath. Such fullness of grace and blessing is implied whenever Jesus refers to "the kingdom of heaven". That kingdom had come near in as much as the king who inaugurated it was standing among the people.

The Call of the First Disciples

4:18–19 As he was walking by the Sea of Galilee he saw two brothers, Simon (called Peter) and Andrew his brother, casting a net into the sea (for they were fishermen). He said to them, "Follow me, and I will turn you into fishers of people."

The call of Peter, Andrew, James and John is referred to in all four gospels. Christ knew these men before he met them, and called them first to follow him. The life of every Christian is a personal walk and relationship with Jesus Christ. God has a will for every individual life, and our responsibility is to seek to do his will. Yet in God's wise plan his will for each individual coincides with his will for the whole church, and so God's servants are seen to serve him within the body of the church. In this way, whilst believers are called to a personal walk with God, no one ever walks alone.

This was not Christ's first meeting with Peter and Andrew; but it was this is the point at which they forsook all to follow him (just after the miraculous catch of fish). Christ's purpose for their lives was made clear from the start—they would be fishers of men, leading others to know Jesus Christ.

4:20–22 They left their nets immediately and followed him. Going on from there he saw two other brothers, James the son of Zebedee and John his brother, in a boat with Zebedee their father, mending their nets. Then he called them. They immediately left the boat and their father and followed him.

Having been prepared by earlier encounters with Christ, and having received such a meaningful and personal call, Peter, John, James and Andrew did not hesitate to give up their jobs and everything else to follow him.

4:23 Jesus went throughout all of Galilee, teaching in their synagogues, preaching the gospel of the kingdom, and healing all kinds of disease and sickness among the people.

This was the beginning of Jesus' ministry. His disciples accompanied him as he set out on an itinerant preaching tour across the region of Galilee, proclaiming the gospel both in the synagogues and in the open; healing every kind of sickness and malady in all those who were brought to him. Matthew later refers to this healing ministry of Christ as being in fulfilment of Scripture (Matt. 8:17).

4:24 So a report about him spread throughout Syria. People brought to him all who suffered with various illnesses and afflictions, those who had seizures, paralytics, and those possessed by demons, and he healed them.

Such a message, accompanied as it was by a demonstration of authority over sickness, spread Christ's fame throughout the region of Syria, and all the sick from that province were brought to Jesus and all were healed.

4:25 And large crowds followed him from Galilee, the Decapolis, Jerusalem, Judea, and beyond the Jordan River.

This first year of Jesus' ministry is often referred to by commentators as "the year of popularity". Huge crowds followed Christ, perhaps more because of his ability to heal them than his message which would challenge and save their souls.

Discussion Questions for Chapter 4

1. vv. 1–11. In what ways did the devil tempt Jesus?

2. vv. 1–11. How did Jesus respond to the temptation?

3. vv. 18–19. What is a disciple? Why do you think they first had to "follow him" before they could become "fishers of men"?

4. vv. 13–17. Why do you think Jesus moved to Capernaum?

5. v. 17. "Repent, for the kingdom of heaven is near!" What does this proclamation mean to you?

You will find suggested answers to these questions on pages 306–323.

Matthew Chapter 5

The Beatitudes

The main characteristics of the way of life set out in the beatitudes can be summarised in four ways:

a) Inwardness—rightness of heart and spirit. If we are not right with God we cannot be right within ourselves or with anyone else.

b) Enthusiasm, earnestness, perseverance. The work done within the heart should not exclude action but should be the source of it; it should result in our expressing our love for God through the good works he has called us to do (Eph. 2:10).

c) Disregard for the world's prizes and honours in preference of seeking those things from above (Col. 3:1) and for the supreme and heavenly prize to which God in Christ is calling us (Phil. 3:14).

d) Love, not self-regard. That is, a love for God and for our neighbour that will seek the wellbeing of others rather than merely that of oneself. An Old Testament parallel of the Beatitudes is found in Deuteronomy chapters 28 and 33.

5:1–2 When he saw the crowds, he went up the mountain. After he sat down his disciples came to him. Then he began to teach them by saying:

It was not to the multitudes that Jesus spoke his Sermon on the Mount, but to his own disciples. In fact, he makes certain that only his disciples were there (all those who followed him, not necessarily just the twelve). He then sat down and prepared himself before commencing to teach them.

5:3 "Blessed are the poor in spirit, for the kingdom of heaven belongs to them.

Those who were considered commoners, who possessed little of this world's goods, heard Jesus gladly and responded to him more than most. Yet "poor in spirit" does not refer to this type of poverty; nor does it denote those who are poor-spirited, that is dejected or self-pitying. Rather, the person who is poor in spirit knows that he has nothing to offer God except his own sin-stained soul; and that without God he is unprofitable.

The poor in spirit are the opposite of the proud. Goodspeed says "blessed are those who feel their spiritual need." This realisation of being poor in spirit is not just something we should have before coming to Christ, but is something we should retain throughout our Christian life. In Revelation 3:17–18 Jesus challenges the Laodicean church which, failing to acknowledge that they were still poor in spirit, had become proud and arrogant.

Only the poor in spirit receive the "kingdom of heaven". They live in the realm where God rules, where his name is holy. They are citizens of his kingdom and can therefore enjoy all the benefits that heaven offers; not only in this life, but also in the next (Rom. 14:17).

5:4 "Blessed are those who mourn, for they will be comforted.

"Those who mourn" may be those who display a sorrow for their sins and for the grief which these have caused God. It could also stand for those who are bereaved of loved ones, or for those who are grieved by the testing and trials of life. In Isaiah 53:3 we read that Jesus Christ was a man of sorrows and acquainted with grief. Since he has borne our griefs and carried our sorrows, he is able to comfort us; and it is as we receive comfort, support and encouragement from him so we in turn can comfort others (2 Cor. 1:3–5). Hugh Martin says that this beatitude has a deeper meaning—it is a blessing upon those who mourn for the needs of others, whose hearts are full of sympathy for their fellow beings. "Mourning is indeed but another and deeper side of loving" (G.M. Trevelyan). This is the love that Jesus Christ has for us and is the reason why his succour is so comforting (Heb. 4:15).

5:5 "Blessed are the meek, for they will inherit the earth.

The word "meek" is generally misunderstood to refer to a person who is weak, but in fact the opposite is true. There can only be meekness where there is strength. Jesus called himself "meek and lowly" (Matt. 11:29) and yet he spoke with authority and demonstrated his power. When a person with such power is, all the same, kind and gentle, that is meekness. Vine says "the Lord was meek because he had the infinite resources of God at his command".

The meek person denies self, not making selfish demands. Their concern is not for their own interests but for those of others. The story of the Good Samaritan provides us with a picture of a meek man who laid aside his own concern when required to assist a fellow human being in distress. "They will inherit the earth" says Jesus. In the Old Testament this phrase was used concerning the Israelites literally possessing the land of promise (Psalm 37:11). In the New Testament the inheritance of the Christian is usually spoken of as eternal life, but here Jesus speaks of possessing the earth. It is not to the strong and mighty that the world belongs, but to those who exhibit a Christ-like meekness. The earth does not belong to man anyway, for "the earth is the Lord's and the fullness thereof" (Psa. 24:1) but he will one day share his rule over it with those who are "joint heirs with Christ" (Rom. 8:17).

5:6 "Blessed are those who hunger and thirst for righteousness, for they will be satisfied.

Those who "hunger and thirst after righteousness" have a burning desire to fulfil the will of God in their lives and to grow more like Christ. "They shall be filled," for God will feed and satisfy their souls with spiritual things (Isaiah 55:1–2). They shall be filled with the fullness of God (Eph. 3:19); with the Holy Spirit and power (Acts 2:4); with the fruits of righteousness (Phil. 1:11); and with the knowledge of his will in all wisdom and spiritual understanding (Col. 1:9). Remember that before God can feed your soul in this way, you must hunger and thirst after righteousness.

5:7 "Blessed are the merciful, for they will be shown mercy.

"The merciful" referred to are those manifest pity. "[Mercy] assumes need on the part of him who receives it and resources adequate to meet the need on the part of him who shows it" (Vine). Mercy is one of the attributes of God who is declared to be rich in mercy (Eph. 2:4) and to be the Father of all mercies (2 Cor. 1:3). In the Old Testament the word "love" is often translated as "mercy", for without love it is impossible to be merciful, since the two qualities work hand in hand. To be merciful is to have compassion, a feeling of distress for the suffering of others and the desire to relieve it. God has revealed his mercy to us in that while we were still sinners, deserving the penalty of eternal death in hell, Jesus Christ came and paid our penalty for us (Rom. 5:8). In light of this, the apostle Paul exhorts Christians to clothe themselves with tender mercies (Col. 3:12); for it is only as we show mercy to others that we shall obtain mercy from God.

5:8 "Blessed are the pure in heart, for they will see God.

"The pure in heart" are those with clean and sincere hearts. The heart represents our desires and affections, and it is these that must be clean. Whilst purity or holiness is the nature of God, we know that human beings are not pure. The inspired writer in Prov. 20:9 asks "who can say, I have made my heart clean, I am pure from sin?" and Jeremiah the prophet declares "the heart is deceitful above all things, and desperately wicked: who can know it?" (Jer. 17:9). So how can we be made pure or clean in God's sight? By being washed in the blood of the Lord Jesus Christ (Heb. 9:13–14; 1 Cor. 6:11) and being made clean through the word of God (John 15:3). Having been thus made pure in heart through Christ we are exhorted to keep ourselves pure (1 Tim. 5:22) and to think upon those things which are pure (Phil. 4:8). To help us in this we are told in 1 John 3:2–4 that if we retain the hope within us of the return of the Lord Jesus Christ, and of our being made like him at his coming, then we shall be kept pure by that hope, even as he is pure.

The pure in heart "will see God". The only other place in scripture where it is said that God will be seen is in Job 19:26–27. God is spirit and Jesus said that "no man has seen God at any time" (John 1:18). Yet he also said that whoever had seen and known him (that is Jesus Christ) had both seen and known the Father. Since the Lord Jesus Christ is God manifest in the flesh (1 Tim. 3:16), those who saw him whilst he was on earth certainly saw God, although few realised it. As we have already seen (1 John 3:2), all believers will one day see Jesus Christ, and so perhaps in this way "will see God".

5:9 "Blessed are the peacemakers, for they will be called the children of God.

"The peacemakers" are not those who try to keep the peace at any price, and certainly not at the expense of the truth of the word of God. But in so much as it is possible, they seek to make peace. Peacemakers are likened to God, who sent Jesus to make peace between himself and sinners. Only those who display elements of God's character in this way have the right to be thought of as his children.

5:10 "Blessed are those who are persecuted for righteousness, for the kingdom of heaven belongs to them.

Doing the work of a peacemaker and bringing the message of reconciliation to sinners will bring persecution from a world which is at enmity with God. This persecution comes as a result of our doing what is good and right and does not refer to the trouble we bring on ourselves by our own bad behaviour (1 Pet. 2:19–20, 3:17). But to those who suffer opposition for doing the will of God, this beatitude promises the "kingdom of heaven".

5:11 "Blessed are you when people insult you and persecute you and say all kinds of evil things about you falsely on account of me.

Three forms of suffering are described here: insult, persecution and false accusation—all for Christ's sake. To be insulted is to be reviled with abusive and scornful language for the sake of Christ; to be persecuted is to be oppressed, harassed or maltreated in any way for Christ; and to be falsely accused means to be the victim of malicious slander, having lies told about you deliberately to incriminate or get you into trouble.

This time, the persecution is not "for righteousness" but on account of Christ. Yet since we have no righteousness outside of Christ, the two ideas might be taken together. Jesus himself suffered all these forms of ill-treatment and Isaiah tells us that he was oppressed, afflicted and led as lamb to be slaughtered; but even then he did not speak a word against his tormentors (Isa. 53:7 and 1 Pet. 2:21–23).

5:12 Rejoice and be glad because your reward is great in heaven, for they persecuted the prophets before you in the same way.

In all that we suffer for Christ we are to be glad and rejoice. When Jesus speaks of a great reward in heaven he is not offering compensation for suffering; rather he means that the things which we have received by the sovereign act of God's grace are kept eternally for us in heaven, and the sufferings of this present time are not worthy to be compared with them (Rom. 8:18). Through the beatitudes, Jesus has outlined the characteristics he wishes to see in all who believe in him. In the next part of his sermon, he will proceed to show how the work of grace he accomplishes in our souls should be evidenced by good and righteous living.

What Believers are in the World

5:13 "You are the salt of the earth. But if salt loses its flavour, how can it be made salty again? It is no longer good for anything except to be thrown out and trampled on by people.

"Salt of the earth"; in eastern countries salt is a symbol of loyalty and friendship. To eat of a person's salt and so to share his hospitality is still regarded in this way among the Arabs. Similarly, in the scriptures it is a symbol of the covenant between God and his people (Num. 18:19).

In the Lord's teaching, salt is a symbol of the spiritual health and morality of the Christian; the counter effect to the immorality of a corrupt world. All the offerings made to God by the children of Israel were to contain salt (Lev. 2:13). W.E. Vine says that "this was symbolic of the holiness of Christ and suggests the reconciliation provided for man by God on the ground of the death of Christ".

The following properties of salt illustrate the potential that every believer has through Jesus Christ:

1. Food is seasoned with salt to bring out its full flavour.

2. It is a preservative—it keeps things from decaying.

3. It has antiseptic qualities, therefore it heals.

4. It cleanses or purifies.

5. In small quantities it is also used to fertilize soil.

Applying these ideas to believers, we observe that:

1. Believers are the seasoning that is sprinkled throughout a sinful world to makes it a more pleasant and beautiful place to live in.

2. Our presence in the world keeps it from falling into utter decay and from being completely ruled by wicked men, as indeed it will be when the day of grace ends and believers are taken to be with the Lord.

3. As Jesus healed the broken hearted and the sick so we too are called to do this work through preaching the gospel, the ministry gifts of Christ and the gifts of the Holy Spirit (Matt. 24:19–20; Mark 16:17–18).

4. While it is only the blood of Christ that cleanses from all sin, believers can function as cleansing agents in the world because they have been made clean and pure in Christ. The presence of a Christian among other people can silence foul and blasphemous mouths, and prevent other evil deeds from being carried out.

5. Before planting seeds the gardener prepares the soil so that it will be fertile enough to help the seeds grow. We too are able to prepare the hearts of people to receive the word of God by praying that they may be saved. In Colossians 4:6 we are told that everything we say as Christians should be with grace and seasoned with salt, that we may know how we ought to answer every man. Jesus concludes this verse by stating that if salt loses its properties, or if a Christian loses his Christ given life and character, how can he regain it? It is impossible, for it then becomes worthless (Heb. 6:1–6).

5:14 You are the light of the world. A city located on a hill cannot be hidden.

The "light of the world" in the truest sense is the Lord Jesus Christ (John 8:12). Because Christ indwells every believer they are too the "light" as he radiates from them so that all men should know they are his disciples and that they are walking in that "light". Light is as essential in the world as salt, it cannot be dispensed with. Natural light is needed for production and growth; it is needed to give sight and colour. As the light of the world the children of God are:

1. To so shine as to produce fruit in bringing many to receive Christ as Saviour and to instruct them in the ways of the Lord so that they will grow in his grace.

2. To reveal the truth that all people are in darkness, dead in trespasses and sins, but that Jesus Christ has come to deliver and bring them out of darkness into light and to give them eternal life. "A city set on a hill"— Christ has lifted his church to a place of prominence and given it gifts which make it effective, so that all may see that he is in the midst of her; because of this she cannot hide herself away.

5:15 People do not light a lamp and put it under a basket but on a lampstand, and it gives light to all in the house.

Believers are not made partakers of the "light" to go and hide themselves in a monastery or cut themselves off from the world; this would be as idiotic as lighting a candle and sticking it under a basket where it would be of no benefit to anyone.

5:16 In the same way, let your light shine before people, so that they can see your good deeds and give honor to your Father in heaven.

We are to let the light that is in us to blaze forth in the good works that we are called to do (1 Tim. 6:18; Tit. 2:7; Matt. 25:35–36). In so doing we shall bring glory and honour to God our Father for we will be a reflection of him.

Christic the Fulfilment

5:17 "Do not think that I have come to abolish the law or the prophets. I have not come to abolish these things but to fulfil them.

Many of the people who had heard the teachings of Jesus were by now wondering if he had come to replace the law given by God (the first five books of the Old Testament) as well as the things revealed by the prophets. His sayings seemed to be so different to them. Jesus therefore corrects them and says he has not come to destroy the law but to teach the "spirit" of the law; for up to now they had become bound by the letter of it. In other words, they had endeavoured to live by the do's and don'ts of the law, but Jesus came to show them that it was a new spirit and the law written in their hearts which they needed (Ezek. 36:26–27; Heb. 8:10; Rom. 7:6). Jesus came to accomplish and to fulfil all the righteous requirements of the law; and because he was without sin, he was the only one who could do so

5:18 I tell you the truth, until heaven and earth pass away not the smallest letter or stroke of a letter will pass from the law until everything takes place.

Christ had not come to do away with the law; for not one of the least of the law's commandments will be nullified until heaven and earth have passed away (2 Pet. 3:10) and all has been accomplished according to the plans and purposes of God. Today, the law of God serves to give us the knowledge of sin (Rom. 3:20) and as a schoolteacher to bring us to Christ (Gal. 3:24).

5:19 So anyone who breaks one of the least of these commands and teaches others to do so will be called least in the kingdom of heaven, but whoever obeys them and teaches others to do so will be called great in the kingdom of heaven.

Whoever therefore breaks or tries to do away with the least important of these laws and teaches others to do the same, they will be of least importance in the kingdom of heaven. Those who practice them and teach others to do so will be great in the kingdom of heaven.

5:20 For I tell you, unless your righteousness goes beyond that of the experts in the law and the Pharisees, you will never enter the kingdom of heaven.

The Scribes and Pharisees considered themselves righteous according to their own standards, but they were not righteous in the sight of God. They deemed the many rules and regulations which they had added to the law of God to be more important than the law itself. Only a righteousness which exceeds theirs can gain us entrance into the kingdom of heaven—and that is the righteousness of Christ, which he gives to us (Phil. 3:9).

Spiritual Standards in Society

Anger, Discord and Murder
5:21 "You have heard that it was said to an older generation, 'Do not murder,' and 'whoever murders will be subjected to judgment.'

In the Law of Moses, murder was described as the unlawful premeditated killing of an innocent person (Ex. 20:13). The murderer was to be brought before the local judges (Deut. 16:18) and if found guilty was to be put to death (Ex. 21:12), usually by the sword. The interpreters of the law at that time applied this only to the actual act of murder.

5:22 But I say to you that anyone who is angry with a brother will be subjected to judgment. And whoever insults a brother will be brought before the council, and whoever says 'Fool' will be sent to fiery hell.

Yet Jesus declared that the action of murder begins in the heart, and that anger which is allowed to build up can become uncontrolled, leading to violence. Colossians 3:8 tells us to completely rid ourselves of anger against a Christian brother or sister. Jesus defines murder as being angry or harbouring malice without any real reason. Those who do so will be brought to judgement and pay the penalty of a murderer. The word "Raca" (AV), means empty-head, or idiot, and those who insulted a brother or sister with such words were to be brought before the ruling council, the high court of those days, who had the power to impose death by stoning. But if a man calls his brother or sister "a fool", which means a godless moral reprobate, such a person would be judged by God to be worthy of the punishment of hell.

5:23–24 So then, if you bring your gift to the altar and there remember that your brother has something against you, leave your gift there in front of the altar. First go and be reconciled to your brother and then come and present your gift.

Consequently, because of what Jesus has just said, if anyone remembers that he has any grievance against a brother or sister when he comes before God to offer his gift he should leave the gift there as a token of his sincerity and determination to put the matter right. Having done so he will be able to offer his gift, for it will be acceptable to God. The equivalent of the altar today would be the communion service (1 Cor. 11:26–28).

5:25–26 Reach agreement quickly with your accuser while on the way to court, or he may hand you over to the judge, and the judge hand you over to the warden, and you will be thrown into prison. I tell you the truth; you will never get out of there until you have paid the last penny!

The adversary referred to here is the legal term for an opponent in a lawsuit. If you are being taken to court by someone you owe a debt then you should come to a friendly agreement with them while you have the chance; otherwise you might end up in prison. If God has become your adversary, for you have turned against him in your heart, then judgment may go worse for you, too. The context of Jesus' teaching implies that to be right with God, you must be right with your brother also (1 John 3:15–16).

Marriage, Adultery and Divorce

5:27 "You have heard that it was said, 'Do not commit adultery.'

Adultery was forbidden by the law of God (Ex. 20:14 and Lev. 20:10). Lawyers of Jesus' time interpreted this to mean only the physical act of adultery, but Jesus applied this law to the heart.

5:28 But I say to you that whoever looks at a woman to desire her has already committed adultery with her in his heart.

It is not the passing glance, or the momentary impulse of desire, but the continued or regular looking at another woman with sexual intentions that arouses the evil desires which ultimately express themselves in bodily activity. The sin starts in the heart, before it is committed in body.

5:29–30 If your right eye causes you to sin, tear it out and throw it away! It is better to lose one of your members than to have your whole body thrown into hell. If your right hand causes you to sin, cut it off and throw it away! It is better to lose one of your members than to have your whole body go into hell.

To "offend" (AV) or "cause to sin" means to cause another to stumble or fall into a trap. The words used by Jesus "pluck it out" and "cut it off" were not meant to be literally applied, for even if these parts were destroyed it would not remove the inward corruption of sin. It means what Paul says in Colossians 3:5 to "mortify" the sinful nature; that is to account it as dead and "to put on the Lord Jesus Christ, and make no provision for the flesh, to fulfil the lusts thereof" (Rom. 13:14).

Jesus means us to deal with sin in a serious way, for it can lead us away from him and back into the world. In Corinth, when a man was living in an incestuous relationship with his stepmother, Paul had to intervene to impose strict discipline; but it worked, and the man's soul was saved. This is the idea behind the "cutting off your hand".

5:31 "It was said, 'whoever divorces his wife must give her a legal document.'

The law on divorce was given in Deuteronomy 24:1–4. The interpreters of this law said that a man could divorce his wife for any reason simply by issuing a certificate to her. But in Matthew 19:3–9 Jesus said that God has ordained that when a man and woman married they became as one flesh, which means inseparable. Hence it was only because of the hardness of their hearts Moses permitted them to divorce.

5:32 But I say to you that everyone who divorces his wife, except for immorality, makes her commit adultery, and whoever marries a divorced woman commits adultery.

Jesus states that the only grounds on which God will permit a man and wife to divorce is immorality (or fornication), meaning sexual intercourse outside of marriage. Note that in this verse Jesus really does mean the physical act of sex, not the thought of the heart. A man who marries a divorced woman (and by implication a divorced man remarrying) is committing adultery. Allowance is made in the Bible for separation, but this likewise involves the idea of continuing sexual faithfulness (1 Cor. 7:10–11).

Making Oaths

5:33 "Again, you have heard that it was said to an older generation, 'Do not break an oath, but fulfil your vows to the Lord.'

The word "forswear" (A.V.) actually means to swear falsely, to tell lies under an oath. Although oaths were not commanded by the law of God, it had become common practice to use oaths in every-day speech without really thinking, and it is this practise which Jesus condemns. Anyone who needs take an oath to prove that he is telling the truth is bringing their own honesty into question. To invoke the Lord's name in an oath is to use his name in vain and this was forbidden by the law (Ex. 20:7; Lev. 19:12).

5:34–35 But I say to you, do not take oaths at all — not by heaven, because it is the throne of God, not by earth, because it is his footstool, and not by Jerusalem, because it is the city of the great King.

Jesus tells us not to bind ourselves to oaths at all. To use heaven or earth as surety is to appeal to God, as it implies a reference to the one whose throne is heaven and whose footstool is earth. So also is an appeal to Jerusalem, the city of the king of kings, an appeal to that king (Isaiah 66:1). None of these things are ours to swear by, and so we have no right to use them.

5:36 Do not take an oath by your head, because you are not able to make one hair white or black.

Nor are we to swear by our own heads because we have no power to alter the colour of a single hair with our words.

5:37 Let your word be 'Yes, yes' or 'No, no.' More than this is from the evil one.

If we are living in the light of Christ then we should be confident that we are living a life of truth and honesty, and so our "yes" or "no" should be sufficient in dealings with others (James 5:12). Anything more than a "yes" or "no" comes from the devil. The Annotated Paragraph Bible Commentary says in fact that "the first recorded appeal to God was made by Satan in his support of the lie by which he tempted Eve" (Gen.

3:5). There are however examples of sacred vows that were made to God in the Bible (e.g. Acts 18:18 by Paul, and Acts 21:23 by four believers). According to the word of God such vows are to be kept (Num. 30:2; Deut. 23:21). In Hebrews 6:17 we read that God gave an oath to show beyond any shadow of a doubt to the heirs of his promises that he was unchangeable concerning his plans and purposes. So it could be said that the only one that we make our vows to is God and that they should be made concerning our commitment and service to him.

Revenge
5:38 "You have heard that it was said, 'An eye for an eye and a tooth for a tooth.'

This law was given in Exodus 21:24 "as a check on the wild justice of revenge" (Ellicott). The purpose of this law was not that the injured party should do exactly the same to the person who had injured him, but rather that the judges should make the punishment fit the crime, and not allow vengeance to go become disproportionate.

5:39 But I say to you, do not resist the evildoer. But whoever strikes you on the right cheek, turn the other to him as well.

In contrast, Jesus teaches us that we are not even to put up a fight against anyone who physically assaults us but to show a spirit of meekness and forgiveness.

5:40 And if someone wants to sue you and to take your tunic, give him your coat also.

If anyone should take us to court to obtain payment from us we are not to make a counterclaim but give them more than they ask for. (Note: the tunic was the undergarment worn next to the body and would have been of less value than the coat or cloak which was the heavier and more expensive top garment).

5:41 And if anyone forces you to go one mile, go with him two.

Jesus uses this illustration to show that we should not put a limit on our willingness to suffer wrongfully or to forgive. When wrong is done to us, we are not to retaliate but to leave the way open for God's wrath, for he declares that the right of vengeance belongs to him alone (Rom. 12:17–19).

5:42 Give to the one who asks you, and do not reject the one who wants to borrow from you.

The Amplified New Testament says "give to him who keeps on begging from you". This translation rightly suggests that if someone who is in need comes asking something from you then you may give according to your ability (Deut. 16:17; 2 Cor. 9:7). Or if someone comes to borrow from you, do not turn them away (Deut. 15:8). In Luke 6:35 Jesus says to "lend hoping for nothing again, and your reward shall be great." However, we need the wisdom of God in handling these matters, for we are stewards of all that he has given to us and are accountable to him to use our money wisely. For example, it would not be wise for a man to give money so another child can have food, when that money should have been used for his own children's food.

Christian Love

5:43 "You have heard that it was said, 'Love your neighbour' and 'hate your enemy.'

Only the first part of this verse is correct (Lev. 19:18) but the second part of "hate your enemy" is what the scribes added.

5:44 But I say unto you, Love your enemies, bless them that curse you, do good to them that hate you, and pray for them which despitefully use you, and persecute you; (KJV)

Jesus not only gives the correct spiritual interpretation of the law but also reverses the order, telling us to do something which is impossible in and of ourselves—to love our enemies. W.E. Vine says "Christian love has God for its primary object, and expresses itself generally, is not an impulse from feelings, it does not always run with the natural inclinations, nor does it spend itself only upon those for whom some relation is discovered—love seeks the welfare of all". We are able to love our enemies only with the love of God that is poured into our hearts by the Holy Spirit (Rom. 5:5). God loved us when we were still his enemies and so we ought to love likewise. We saw in verse 39 how we should react to those who physically abuse us; here we are told how we should treat those who verbally abuse us. Jesus says we are to bless them in return for their cursing, and not retaliate. The literal meaning of bless is to speak well of. Pray for those despitefully using you—those who are making false accusations against you and who persecute you.

5:45 So that you may be like your Father in heaven, since he causes the sun to rise on the evil and the good, and sends rain on the righteous and the unrighteous.

In loving, blessing and praying for them it shows that God is our Father, that the Lord Jesus Christ dwells in our hearts, and that we are truly his children, for God is impartial. He providentially provides for the good and evil.

5:46–47 For if you love those who love you, what reward do you have? Even the tax collectors do the same, don't they? And if you only greet your brothers, what more do you do? Even the Gentiles do the same, don't they?

The love of the heathen (which is what tax collectors were considered to be) is confined to those who give to them, whereas ours should be that universal love that God has: "for God so loved the world, that he gave his only begotten Son" (John 3:16).

5:48 So then, be perfect, as your heavenly Father is perfect.

The fulfilment of the standard set down in these verses can again only be accomplished as we allow the nature of Christ to be perfected in our hearts and lives. The word perfect signifies complete and mature. We know that God is perfect. When this word is applied to the believer it means that we are to become mature in our spiritual growth. It is in this way that Paul exhorts us to go on to maturity (Heb. 6:1) for he said concerning himself that he was not already perfect but that he was going on to perfection (Phil. 3:12). By the grace of God let us therefore go on to perfection.

Discussion Questions for Chapter 5

1. vv. 1–12. Which of the beatitudes do you most aspire to in your own life?

2. vv. 27–32. How might applying Christ's teaching on marriage, divorce and adultery alter your own view about these subjects?

3. vv. 33–37. Have you ever made a vow to God? Did you keep it?

4. vv. 21–48. Consider how the standards of behaviour discussed in these verses fulfil Christ's instruction for us to be the "light" and "salt" of the world.

5. vv. 43–48. What difficulties can you foresee in keeping Christ's command to "love your enemies"? How might these be overcome?

You will find suggested answers to these questions on pages 306–323.

Matthew Chapter 6

Giving

6:1 "Be careful not to display your righteousness merely to be seen by people. Otherwise you have no reward with your Father in heaven.

The word "righteousness" Jesus uses here means "righteous acts", or acts of mercy. The New King James Version reads "charitable deeds". The word is translated as "alms" in the AV, which suggests monetary giving only; but "charitable deeds, righteous acts, and acts of mercy" embrace all kinds of giving. Jesus accepts without question that the disciples were fulfilling their duty to give to the needy as prescribed in Leviticus 25:35 and which he further says in Luke 11:41 "give alms of such things as you have".

What Jesus is concerned about in this verse is the way that his disciples were to give. They were not to give in order to be seen as benevolent; for if they did so then they would receive no reward from their Father in heaven who knows the hearts of all people, and the motive behind their giving.

6:2–4 Thus whenever you do charitable giving, do not blow a trumpet before you, as the hypocrites do in synagogues and on streets so that people will praise them. I tell you the truth, they have their reward. But when you do your giving, do not let your left hand know what your right hand is doing, so that your gift may be in secret. And your Father, who sees in secret, will reward you.

The correct way to give is from a sincere heart with the pure motive of helping the one in distress without any thought of return (1 Cor. 13:3); and to do so in as secretive a way as possible. Do not take too long in deciding or considering the cost of giving (Rom. 12:8). Instead, give with regularity (1 Cor. 16:2) and with a cheerful heart (2 Cor. 9:7).

Jesus says "do not do as the hypocrites". The word "hypocrites" was original used to describe actors. In other words, Jesus is saying do not merely play the part of a giving person so that you may be known as such; honoured and praised by men. The Father who sees what is done from the heart will bless you in such a way that it will be seen by others.

Praying

6:5 "Whenever you pray, do not be like the hypocrites, because they love to pray while standing in synagogues and on street corners so that people can see them. Truly I say to you, they have their reward.

Jesus is not disparaging public prayer, but is stating that private prayer should not be conducted in the open air or church—there is a right place and time for it. The hypocrites he refers to prayed publicly in order to give the impression that they were very spiritual and had a good standing with God (Luke 18:11–12). They already had all the reward they will get—the adulation of men, which is worth very little. Jesus tells us of a better way to pray.

6:6 But whenever you pray, go into your room, close the door, and pray to your Father in secret. And your Father, who sees in secret, will reward you.

We are to find ourselves a place where no one can disturb us, where we can shut ourselves in alone with God. Personal prayer should be strictly private (Ellicott). Jesus went up on the mountain to pray and Peter up to the roof. As we pray in this fashion so our Father who hears the cry of our hearts will bless us openly.

6:7 When you pray, do not babble repetitiously like the Gentiles, because they think that by their many words they will be heard.

We are not to repeat over and over again the same phrases and words as if by doing so we will get God to hear us (this is not a reference to our being persevering in intercessory prayer), nor do we necessarily need to pray a long time in order to get an answer, as the heathen do (1 Kings 18:26).

6:8 Do not be like them, for your Father knows what you need before you ask him.

We have no need to be like them, for our God hears and answers prayer; he knows what we have need of but still requires us to come and make our requests known to him with thanksgiving (Phil. 4:6).

What should we pray for? The Lord gave his disciples this pattern prayer (often called the Lord's Prayer) to help them.

6:9 So pray this way: Our Father in heaven, may your name be honoured,

First of all we are to fully realise our relationship with God in our Lord Jesus Christ, which is that of a Father and his children (Rom. 8:15). He dwells in the heavenly places where we sit with Christ (Eph. 2:6). Therefore we do not have to reach up to bring him down for he is always present with us. Although we have this relationship with God as Father, he is still the Almighty and Everlasting God and so we must approach him with reverence and awesome fear of his very being (his name).

6:10 may your kingdom come, may your will be done on earth as it is in heaven.

We are to pray that his kingdom will be established on the earth. Although in one sense the kingdom has come into the hearts of those who have received Jesus Christ as their Saviour, God's desire is that his purpose will be fulfilled on the earth, especially in his people, as it always is in heaven by the angels.

6:11 Give us today our daily bread,

We pray for our physical needs to be met for each day.

6:12 and forgive us our debts, as we ourselves have forgiven our debtors.

Some translations read "forgive us our debts" and others "forgive us our trespasses". Debts are sins of omission (the things that we do not do and so are in debt to God for them) and trespasses are the sins we commit. It is only as we forgive what others have done or neglected to do for us, that we can ask God to forgive us.

6:13 And do not lead us into temptation, but deliver us from the evil one.

God does not tempt any man (James 1:13) the Amp. N.T. has "bring" not lead and would therefore suggest that we ask God to keep us from the paths that would be a temptation to us and cause us to fall, especially since the next part of the prayer is "deliver us from the hand of the evil one". The prayer finishes with a hymn of praise in acknowledgement that God is sovereign, he reigns over all. All power belongs to him and he is exalted above all. Amen—so it is.

6:14-15 "For if you forgive others their sins, your heavenly Father will also forgive you. But if you do not forgive others, your Father will not forgive you your sins.

In these verses Jesus enlarges on verse 12 by saying that our sins will only be forgiven by God as we forgive those who have wronged us.

Fasting

Jesus accepts that the disciples fasted. Although while he was with them they did not do so, this was no grounds for an accusation against them (Matt. 9:14–15). Under the law there was only one great fast for the Day of Atonement (Lev. 23:27). Other than that they were only held in times either of distress or penitence (Joel 1:14, 2:15). By the time of our Lord it had become common practice to fast religiously twice a week as a way to obtain self-control; unfortunately, this had become a mechanical ritual (Luke 18:12). The Lord still recognises fasting as important however, and on one occasion referred to a demon possessed person who was only able to be delivered by prayer and fasting (Matt. 17:21). In 1 Corinthians 7:5 Paul talks about "giving yourselves to fasting", in 2 Corinthians 6:5 "proving ourselves in fasting" and in 2 Corinthians 11:27 he speaks about "fasting often".

6:16 "When you fast, do not look sullen like the hypocrites, for they make their faces unattractive so that people will see them fasting. I tell you the truth, they have their reward.

Jesus does not give much instruction concerning this subject; only to say that when we fast it should not be apparent to anyone that we are doing so. The Amplified N.T. has "do not look gloomy, sour and dreary". In other words do not just play the part so that everybody can see that you are suffering a fast.

6:17 When you fast, put oil on your head and wash your face,

Instead, during our fast we should refresh ourselves by washing our faces and perfume (anoint) our head; dressing and appearing as usual.

6:18 so that it will not be obvious to others when you are fasting, but only to your Father who is in secret. And your Father, who sees in secret, will reward you.

This is because our fasting should be between our Father and us, and should be seen only by him. And again Jesus says that as God sees in secret so he will bless us before all men.

Seek Those Things which are from Above

6:19 Do not accumulate for yourselves treasures on earth, where moth and rust destroy and where thieves break in and steal.

The things which we hoard for ourselves on earth are of little value compared to heavenly and eternal things, which Jesus called true riches (Luke 16:11). Why amass that which does not keep its value, when we can possess that which is of everlasting worth? Why accumulate what may be stolen from us when we can have what will never be taken away? If we want to receive the things of God in full measure then we must seek them and not those things that belong to this world. We are not to set our affection on earthly things (Col. 3:1–2), or put our trust in them (1 Tim. 6:17), and we should consider them of little value in the light of eternity.

6:20 But accumulate for yourselves treasures in heaven, where moth and rust do not destroy, and thieves do not break in and steal.

The eternal things of God are not subject to decay, and are the source of real happiness and joy. The God who provides us with them also guarantees that they shall never be taken from us (Col. 1:5).

6:21 For where your treasure is, there your heart will be also.

If what is most important to us (our treasure) is in heaven then our whole heart will be taken up with it and our focus will be heavenward—for it is where our love, affection, hope and trust will be. The greatest treasure that we can possess is the Lord Jesus Christ, a treasure we possess in our frail human bodies (2 Cor. 4:7).

6:22–23 The eye is the lamp of the body. If then your eye is healthy, your whole body will be full of light. But if your eye is diseased, your whole body will be full of darkness. If then the light in you is darkness, how great is the darkness!

Jesus uses this illustration to show that we must have single vision, our eyes being focused on him and our desires fixed on heavenly things. By the help of our natural eyesight, we can properly identify and understand things. If there is any defect in the eye then we are not able to receive sufficient light to give clear vision. The spiritual eye is the spirit within man (Prov. 20:27) for it is there that God has commanded the light of his glorious gospel to shine (2 Cor. 4:6), giving us an understanding of his truth. If there is anything in our lives that distracts us from God then our spiritual eyesight will be defective. If we hinder the light of God from entering our spirit by not responding to the truth of his word then we will not be able to receive that full knowledge of the glory of God as it is revealed in Jesus Christ.

6:24 No one can serve two masters, for either he will hate the one and love the other, or he will be devoted to the one and despise the other. You cannot serve God and money.

We cannot have one foot in the world and one in Christ. We cannot we divide ourselves between serving God and serving mammon (that is, whatever this world has to offer). It must be one or the other. Serving God half-heartedly will result in our going away from God altogether; for a double minded man is unstable in all his ways (James 1:6–8).

Do not Worry

As we serve God fully, so he will take full care of us. So, we have no cause for worry (Phil. 4:6 and 1 Pet. 5:7).

6:25 Therefore I tell you, do not worry about your life, what you will eat or drink, or about your body, what you will wear. Isn't there more to life than food and more to the body than clothing?

We are not to charge ourselves with the care of obtaining enough food and drink to live, or clothes to wear; for God will take the responsibility of caring for his children on Himself. In any case, these are not things we should concern ourselves with, for the kingdom of God "is not meat and drink; but righteousness, and peace, and joy in the Holy Spirit" (Rom. 14:17) and it is these spiritual things that we should concern ourselves with. Jesus has already been quoted as recalling God's declaration that man shall not live by bread only, but by every word that comes from God (Deut. 8:3).

6:26 Look at the birds in the sky: They do not sow, or reap, or gather into barns, yet your heavenly Father feeds them. Aren't you more valuable than they are?

The birds of the air do not concern themselves with the work of growing and harvesting their own food, for although they are not as valuable in God's sight as we are, yet he feeds them. They do not make provision for themselves, but allow God to take care of them.

6:27 And which of you by worrying can add even one hour to his life?

By this deliberately ridiculous question Jesus illustrates how senseless it is for us to worry. How ridiculous to worry when by doing so we cannot alter our own circumstances one bit!

6:28–29 Why do you worry about clothing? Think about how the flowers of the field grow; they do not work or spin. Yet I tell you that not even Solomon in all his glory was clothed like one of these!

The flowers of the field do no work, nor do they make their own clothes and yet the richest king who ever lived, Solomon, was not as splendidly clothed as they.

6:30 And if this is how God clothes the wild grass, which is here today and tomorrow is tossed into the fire to heat the oven, won't he clothe you even more, you people of little faith?

We are challenged by Christ to see that if God takes care of meadow flowers which are here today and gone tomorrow, how much more will he care for us, his own dear children who shall live with him eternally? Christ chides our anxiety in that it reveals just how little we trust God. He not only provides clothing fit for our lives on earth, but with even more wonderful garments suitable for heaven (Isa. 61:10).

6:31–32 So then, don't worry saying, 'What will we eat?' or 'What will we drink?' or 'What will we wear?' For the unconverted pursue these things, and your heavenly Father knows that you need them.

Since we have witnessed God's provision in nature for the birds and flowers, and Jesus has told us of the much greater love and concern which God has for his own children, then we are not to concern ourselves with such things, as if God were not our father (as the unconverted do, the Gentiles). Their lives are completely taken up with the things of this world, for they do not know the spiritual blessings of the next world. God our Father is fully aware of what we lack and will "supply all our needs according to his riches in glory by Jesus Christ" (Phil. 4:19).

6:33 But above all pursue his kingdom and righteousness, and all these things will be given to you as well.

First and foremost we are to seek for the things that belong to the kingdom of God and do what is right in God's sight. Then we will have no cause to worry, for God has promised in return to give to us everything that we need.

6:34 So then, do not worry about tomorrow, for tomorrow will worry about itself. Today has enough trouble of its own.

We could paraphrase this, do not borrow tomorrow's worries and cares for tomorrow might never come; take one day at a time. Remember that Jesus was speaking to his disciples who had given up their means of living to follow him and we know that Peter at least, if not the others, was married and could very well have had children. So when he tells us not to worry, Jesus is fully aware of all our circumstances. What does worry rob us of? It robs us of faith, confidence, peace, joy, fruitfulness (Matt. 13:22), and a good night's sleep—but it gives nothing in return.

Discussion Questions for Chapter 6

1. vv. 1–4. Explain how Jesus intends us to give.

2. vv. 5–15. Highlight some of the major points in Jesus' teaching about prayer.

3. vv. 16–18. How do you think the practise of fasting might help when someone wishes to pray more effectively?

4. vv. 25–34. List several reasons why Jesus says it is foolish to worry.

5. vv. 19–24. What things would Jesus have us seek and focus our affections on?

You will find suggested answers to these questions on pages 306–323.

Matthew Chapter 7

Judging

7:1–2 "Do not judge so that you will not be judged. For by the standard you judge you will be judged, and the measure you use will be the measure you receive.

      The Lord exhorts his disciples not to be like the self-righteous Pharisees who put themselves above everyone else in the position of judges. People judge according to the outward appearance (1 Sam. 16:7) and the facts which present themselves. People can never hope to judge in absolute righteousness for only God knows the heart of all (Jer. 17:10); and his word is a discerner of the thoughts and intents of the heart (Heb. 4:12). The word "judge" as used here also suggests to condemn, pass sentence or to criticise. Jesus gives the reason why we are not to judge others: that we should not in turn be judged by God according to the same standards that we have used. In dealing with us God will use the same measuring stick that we have used in our condemnation of others. Matthew Henry comments "What would become of us, if God should be as exact and severe in judging us, as we are in judging our brethren; if he should weigh us in the same balance?"

Reproving

      To reprove is to rebuke, convict and expose. Although we are not to judge anyone, this does not mean that we are not to reprove for James 5:19–20 Amp. N.T. says "My brethren, if anyone among you strays from the truth and falls into error, and another person brings him back to God, let the (latter) one be sure that whoever turns a sinner from his evil course will save that one's soul from death and will cover a multitude of sins (that is, procure the pardon of the many sins committed by the convert)."

7:3–4 Why do you see the speck in your brother's eye, but fail to see the beam of wood in your own? Or how can you say to your brother, 'Let me remove the speck from your eye,' while there is a beam in your own?

We must, however, make certain that we are not guilty of the same faults as others before we seek to correct them. How is it that we make a big thing about the small faults (mote, splinter, speck) that we see in other people, and are quick to point them out and yet fail to see the larger faults (beam, plank) in our own lives? Jesus uses the word "consider" which would seem to suggest that we *are* aware of our own faults but are prone to ignore these whilst highlighting the faults of others.

7:5 You hypocrite! First, remove the beam from your own eye, and then you can see clearly to remove the speck from your brother's eye.

The matter of reproving a Christian brother or sister must be handled in the right way. First we have to consider our own faults and failings and seek to right these. Although this should not stop us offering a friendly reproof, it ought to keep us from being magisterial or condemnatory.

7:6 Do not give what is holy to dogs or throw your pearls before pigs; otherwise they will trample them under their feet and turn around and tear you to pieces.

This verse would seem to be out of place here but Matthew Henry ties it in by saying, "our zeal against sin must be guided by discretion, and we must not go about to give instructions, counsels, and rebukes, much less comforts, to hardened scorners".

Do not give what is holy to dogs. To the Jew the holy things were those that were separated for the service of God, the sacrifices and the word of God. These were not to be given as meat for the dogs. In the New Testament, believers in Christ are the temple of God, and the Spirit of God dwells in them (1 Cor. 3:16; 1 Cor. 6:19); therefore as Christians we are not to give ourselves over to anything that would defile (1 Cor. 3:17) but present our bodies as living sacrifices, holy and acceptable to God (Rom. 12:1). The Bible is the *Holy* Bible and we are to handle and use it correctly. To give its deep truth to those who despise and treat it as worthless would be just like giving pearls to pigs for food.

What is Prayer?

7:7 "Ask and it will be given to you; seek and you will find; knock and the door will be opened for you.

We have heard previously how to pray and what to pray for, and now Jesus tells us what prayer is. Prayer is asking that we might receive. When we know the will of God concerning a matter, we can ask in complete confidence for it and so receive it (1 John 5:14). Seeking to find—if we do not know the mind of God concerning any matter we are to seek him until we know what his will is and then having found out we can pray that his will be done (Proverbs 8:17; Hebrews 11:6). Knocking and opening—when we know the will of God and we find a closed door then we are to persist in prayer until God opens the way.

7:8 For everyone who asks receives, and the one who seeks finds, and to the one who knocks, the door will be opened.

The promise to receive, find and for the door to be opened is given only to those who ask, seek and knock (Luke 11:5–8).

7:9–11 Is there anyone among you who, if his son asks for bread, will give him a stone? Or if he asks for a fish, will give him a snake? If you then, although you are evil, know how to give good gifts to your children, how much more will your Father in heaven give good gifts to those who ask him!

If a son came to his parents and asked for something good to eat would they give him something that was bad? If we, although we are imperfect, know how to give good things to our children, how much more will our Father in heaven, who is perfect and good, give good things to his children from the abundance of his riches in glory when we ask him (James 1:17).

7:12 In everything, treat others as you would want them to treat you, for this fulfils the law and the prophets.

Therefore, considering all that we have heard in these verses, we should make it our principle that whatever we desire others to do for us then we should first do for them; for in so doing we fulfil the righteousness of God.

Two Ways

7:13–14 "Enter through the narrow gate, because the gate is wide and the way is spacious that leads to destruction, and there are many who enter through it. But the gate is narrow and the way is difficult that leads to life, and there are few who find it.

Jesus declared Himself to be the way to the Father (John 14:6) and he made clear that there is no other way to enter heaven except by the way that he has made by his atoning death on the cross. He said "I am the door if any man enters in by me, he shall be saved" (John 10:9). Peter in Acts 4:12 said "there is salvation in no one else, for there is no other name under heaven given among people by which we must be saved." So no matter what other religions or philosophies may claim, there is only one way to God.

Since the "narrow gate" is Jesus himself, it follows that the gate is the width of a man. In other words, people can only enter one at a time. A husband cannot take his wife through, a father his child, or a brother his sister. Every individual has to enter by their own choice and by personal faith in Jesus Christ.

If the gate is narrow then it follows that the way beyond it also is narrow. It is narrow, because it is the way of the cross (1 Cor. 1:18, 23). Because of this Jesus maintains that only a few that will be saved in comparison to the total world population, for many will refuse to walk this way. It is testing and difficult to walk the narrow way of Christian life; we will find that we are restricted and disciplined by the Holy Spirit through the work of grace being done in our lives. Moreover, there is no provision made for us to turn back on the narrow road, although on the way there will be many tempting side roads to take (as depicted by John Bunyan in "Pilgrims Progress").

If we were under the impression that once we are saved and on the road to heaven all our problems would be solved then Jesus corrects that view; for the word "narrow" in its fuller sense means "difficult". However, the good news is that we have Jesus to lead, guide, guard and keep us and the Holy Spirit as our comforter and helper.

The only alternative to the narrow way is the broad way which has a wide gate. It is so wide that it does not even have to be searched for, and people not only enter themselves but can lead others there too. There are no restrictions on the wide road, and in terms of our lives and behaviour anything goes. But there is only one place this road can lead to, and that is hell (Rev. 21:8).

False Prophets

7:15 "Watch out for false prophets, who come to you in sheep's clothing but inwardly are voracious wolves.

Jesus warns us to be on our guard against the false prophets that we will meet on our journey. They will be very difficult to recognise for they will be cleverly disguised and to all outward appearance will seem like fellow pilgrims. They will say and do the right things. They will participate in the fellowship, praise and worship, but inwardly their purpose is to destroy and tear apart the church of Christ and to cause division. They seek to undermine the truth and replace it by their own doctrines. How are we to recognise them?

7:16 You will recognize them by their fruit. Grapes are not gathered from thorns or figs from thistles, are they?

"By their fruit"—Jesus uses an illustration from nature. We do not expect to find grapes on thorn trees or figs from a thistle; it is impossible. Therefore no matter how well disguised these false prophets are, what is in their hearts will show (Prov. 23:7; Mark 7:21–22). Their fruits are well described by Paul in Galatians 5:20.

7:17–18 In the same way, every good tree bears good fruit, but the bad tree bears bad fruit. A good tree is not able to bear bad fruit, nor a bad tree to bear good fruit.

A good tree is a cultivated one that has been planted by the Lord Jesus Christ (Isaiah 61:3, Jer.17:8). New fruit trees purchased from a garden centre have usually been grafted on to an approved root stock so that they will bear good fruit. So it is with us, for we have been grafted into the new Israel of God, into the Lord Jesus Christ (Rom. 11:17). It is only as we abide in him that we can bring forth good fruit, the fruit of the Spirit (Gal. 5:22–23). The false prophets on the other hand are bad or wild trees. It is impossible for them to bring forth good fruit for they are not the planting of the Lord but tares (Matt. 13:24–29).

7:19–20 Every tree that does not bear good fruit is cut down and thrown into the fire. So then, you will recognize them by their fruit.

We will recognise false prophets by their speech and behaviour. For a little while they may be able to pretend to be what they are not, but it is impossible to keep up this charade forever. What is in their hearts will eventually reveal itself; and in the end they will be cut down and thrown into the fire (Rev. 21:8).

True Believers

In these verses Jesus shows that true believers are not those who *call* themselves Christians but those who live the Christ-like life.

7:21 "Not everyone who calls me, 'Lord, Lord,' will enter into the kingdom of heaven – only the one who does the will of my Father in heaven.

The key words here are "calls" and "does". It is not the ones who pay lip service to the Lord but those who are obedient and seek to carry out the will of the Father that shall enter the kingdom of heaven.

7:22–23 On that day, many will say to me, 'Lord, Lord, didn't we prophesy in your name, and in your name cast out demons and do many powerful deeds?' Then I will declare to them, 'I never knew you. Go away from me, you lawbreakers!'

Many who stand before the Lord when he comes to separate the goats from the sheep (Matt. 25:31–41) will try to escape judgement by making claims that they had prophesied, cast out devils and done many mighty works in the name of Jesus. But Christ will declare before everyone that he never knew them and banish them from his presence. These are "mock believers", the "false prophets".

Spiritual Foundation

Here Jesus uses the illustration of house building to show how those who truly belong to him are firmly established (2 Chron. 20:20; 2 Thess. 2:17; Col. 2:7).

7:24–25 (Therefore) "Everyone who hears these words of mine and does them is like a wise man who built his house on rock. The rain fell, the

81

flood came, and the winds beat against that house, but it did not collapse because it had been founded on rock.

In verse 24 we have the final "therefore" which is a reference to all that Jesus has said in the Sermon on the Mount. It is a blessed thing to hear the word of God, but it is far more blessed to allow the Lord to do the work of grace in our lives so that we can obey his words. Jesus Christ is the rock on which the foundation of our faith is laid (1 Cor. 3:11; 10:4), and we are being built upon the foundation of the apostles and prophets, Jesus Christ Himself being the chief corner stone (Eph. 2:20). Therefore when temptations, trials and persecution beat upon us like a mighty hurricane we shall not be moved (Psa. 46:5) but remain firm and steadfast.

7:26–27 Everyone who hears these words of mine and does not do them is like a foolish man who built his house on sand. The rain fell, the flood came, and the winds beat against that house, and it collapsed; it was utterly destroyed!"

On the other hand those who hear but do not carry out the words of the Lord are building their lives on the uncertain, unstable and shifting things of the world rather than eternal things. When the storms of life assail them, such people will collapse like a pack of cards with nothing left to show for all their wasted labours.

7:28-29 When Jesus finished saying these things, the crowds were amazed by his teaching, because he taught them like one who had authority, not like their experts in the law.

The things that Jesus spoke to the people in the Sermon on the Mount completely astounded them; for although they were used to the teaching of the Scribes and the Pharisees, no man ever spoke like Jesus. The words which he spoke were living and packed with genuine power and authority.

Discussion Questions for Chapter 7

1. vv. 1–5. Why is it important not to judge others?

2. vv. 7–11. In what ways does Jesus encourage us to pray?

3. vv. 13–14. How would you explain the difference between the wide and narrow way?

4. vv. 15–20. How are we to tell the difference between a true servant of Christ and a false prophet?

5. vv. 24–27. Consider the way in which you are building your life. How will you be able to stand the test Jesus describes in these verses?

You will find suggested answers to these questions on pages 306–323.

Matthew Chapter 8

Christ the Divine Healer

Cleansing the Leper

8:1 After he came down from the mountain, large crowds followed him.

After the Lord had finished his teaching in the Sermon on the Mount and came down from the mountain, large crowds followed him. It may have been that his teaching had awakened a sense of their need and they sought more from him. Once we have experienced Christ we will want to experience him more, for we have "tasted and seen that the Lord is good" (Psa. 34:8).

8:2 And a leper approached, and bowed low before him, saying, "Lord, if you are willing, you can make me clean."

It was news of Christ's healing power as much as his amazing teaching that drew many to him. This sufferer of leprosy had heard the report about Jesus and believed it (Isa. 53:1). He accepted that the Lord had power to heal him, but humbly inquired as to his willingness. This leper gives us an example of how to approach the Lord—in faith and humility. As he bowed low, this man was open and ready to receive anything from Jesus.

8:3 He stretched out his hand and touched him saying, "I am willing. Be clean!" Immediately his leprosy was cleansed.

In reply to the man's question Jesus declares "I am willing!" From the lips of the Son of God this statement is as powerful as the earlier "I am" declarations of God: "I am the Lord that heals you" (Exod. 15:26) and "I am the Lord, I change not" (Mal. 3:6). Since Jesus Christ does not change, the Lord who was willing to heal this leper is still willing to heal. Here is an eternal "I am" saying: *"I am willing"*.

Because of the leper's faith and petition, Jesus commanded the healing; notice he did not pray over him. "Be clean!" is the command of the creator, and as Jesus spoke, so the leper became clean (Gen. 1:2–3).

8:4 Then Jesus said to him, "See that you do not speak to anyone, but go, show yourself to a priest, and bring the offering that Moses commanded, as a testimony to them."

Christ did not want cheap advertising for his gospel campaign. He never looked for the fantastic in order to provide publicity. It was enough to Jesus that he had met the need of this man. He did, however, want the man to show the priest a testimony of his divine healing power, and to obey the command of Moses by presenting a thank offering. In this quiet way, Christ sought to win the hearts of the religious leaders, and not without success (Acts 6:7).

Healing the Centurion's Servant

8:5–7 When he entered Capernaum, a centurion came to him asking for help: "Lord, my servant is lying at home paralyzed, in terrible anguish." Jesus said to him, "I will come and heal him."

When a Roman centurion approached the Lord with a need, Jesus was willing to go to his home to heal the servant who was in terrible pain and paralyzed, possibly as the result of a recent accident.

8:8–9 But the centurion replied, "Lord, I am not worthy to have you come under my roof. Instead, just say the word and my servant will be healed. For I too am a man under authority, with soldiers under me. I say to this one, 'Go' and he goes, and to another 'Come' and he comes, and to my slave 'Do this' and he does it."

Like the leper, the centurion too was a man of humility and faith. Having heard of the works of Christ, he addressed him as Lord, and did not consider himself worthy for Jesus to come under his roof. He knew that his soldiers obeyed him because of the authority entrusted to him by the emperor. If he commanded them to do anything, it was done at once without demurring. How much more could Christ, who held authority as the representative of God, command that sickness depart? How could sickness refuse him?

8:10 When Jesus heard this he was amazed and said to those who followed him, "I tell you the truth, I have not found such faith in anyone in Israel!

Christ marvelled at the great faith shown by this Roman, a faith far greater than any he had encountered among the Jews. It gave Christ an opportunity to speak of the day, following his death and resurrection, when the gospel would be preached to the whole world. God's kingdom would be open to all men and the blessings promised to Abraham given to all who would believe in Christ and accept him as Lord and Saviour.

8:11–12 I tell you, many will come from the east and west to share the banquet with Abraham, Isaac, and Jacob in the kingdom of heaven, but the sons of the kingdom will be thrown out into the outer darkness, where there will be weeping and gnashing of teeth."

Those who reject Christ will not be part of the kingdom of God, even if they are the natural descendants of those to whom the promises were given (the sons of the kingdom—Israelites). Unbelievers of all races, including those from Israel, shall be cast into the everlasting darkness of hell; where there will be unending pain, anguish and sorrow (signified by the weeping and gnashing of teeth). Christ is the only one who can save us from our sin and its eternal consequences. Those who refuse Christ's salvation must face the punishment for their sin.

8:13 Then Jesus said to the centurion, "Go; just as you believed, it will be done for you." And the servant was healed at that hour.

As the word of the Lord is given, that which was asked and believed for in faith is granted. This is the way to receive from the Lord

Jesus Christ—by asking in faith (Mark 11:24). As soon as the centurion received the word of the Lord with faith, the servant was instantly healed.

The Healing of Peter's Mother in Law

8:14–15 Now when Jesus entered Peter's house, he saw his mother-in-law lying down, sick with a fever. He touched her hand, and the fever left her. Then she got up and began to serve them.

When Jesus came to Simon Peter's house in Capernaum, they informed him that Peter's wife's mother was in bed, sick with a fever. Jesus took her hand and rebuked the fever (Luke 4:38–39) and immediately she got up. She was completely well and began to cook and serve food to Jesus and his disciples.

Jesus Heals Many

8:16 When it was evening, many demon-possessed people were brought to him. He drove out the spirits with a word, and healed all who were sick.

The Lord Jesus Christ was and is the only one who can heal the sick. At evening, they brought those possessed by devils to him and he set them free. Notice that he did not lay hands or pray for these people but rebuked and cast out the devils by his word of command. Mark 1:21–26 gives us another example of his doing this, as does Mark 9:25–26. Paul learned to use this same method, as we see in Acts 16:16–18. Jesus healed so many that day that there were no sick people left in Capernaum (Mark 1:33–34). Yet evangelists take note of this—even then they did not repent (Matt. 11:23–24).

8:17 In this way what was spoken by Isaiah the prophet was fulfilled: "He took our weaknesses and carried our diseases."

Christ's healing ministry revealed him to be the Son of God and the promised Messiah, as he fulfilled the words of the prophet Isaiah—

"he himself carried our weaknesses" when we were too weak to bear them, and bore away our sicknesses. Only Christ could do this, and thank God he still can. It is of note that Matthew relates Isaiah's prophecy as a reference to Christ's healing ministry and not to his work on the cross.

8:18 Now when Jesus saw a large crowd around him, he gave orders to go to the other side of the lake.

Christ often had compassion on large crowds of people, but this verse reminds us that it was not crowds themselves that Jesus sought, but to do the will of God. As the crowds increased, Jesus gave instructions to his disciples in preparation to withdraw to the other side of Lake Galilee. There he would meet an individual, but that individual would reach another densely populated area with the good news.

Commitment Needed to Follow Jesus

8:19 Then an expert in the law came to him and said, "Teacher, I will follow you wherever you go."

As he was getting ready to leave, a doctor of the Mosaic Law approached Christ with a show of devotion. His words are almost without fault, but notice that he addressed Jesus as "teacher" and not as "Lord".

8:20 Jesus said to him, "Foxes have dens, and the birds in the sky have nests, but the Son of Man has no place to lay his head."

Jesus knows the hearts of all people (John 2:24–25). He knew that in reality, this lawyer was not prepared to forsake all he had and follow him into homelessness and hardship as his other disciples had done. Words do not count with God if words are all they are. God requires us to demonstrate our devotion by obedience (1 John 5:3).

8:21–22 Another of the disciples said to him, "Lord, let me first go and bury my father." But Jesus said to him, "Follow me, and let the dead bury their own dead."

The response of Jesus at first seems harsh. We are not sure whether the man's father was already dead awaiting burial, or what is more likely, that the man's father still lived and that this disciple wanted permission to stay and care for his father, whilst the Lord was clearly calling him elsewhere. Jesus was teaching that nothing and no one must come before him or before the call of God on our lives. We must put Jesus first (Matt. 10:37–38). Let the unsaved, the spiritually dead in sin, walk according to their carnal attachments, but let the child of God walk according to the Spirit. Even if a believer dies, he or she is not actually dead. The child of God does not need to linger by their grave to mourn; instead we press ever onwards to join them and God in glory.

Jesus Stills the Storm

8:23–24 As he got into the boat, his disciples followed him. And a great storm developed on the sea so that the waves began to swamp the boat. But he was asleep

After this exchange, the boat was ready and Jesus entered it. No doubt being exhausted from dealing with the crowds (John 4:6), he soon fell asleep in the stern. As he slept, an awful storm arose; producing great waves which threatened to overwhelm and sink the boat.

8:25 So they came and woke him up saying, "Lord, save us! We are about to die!"

The disciples were terrified, despite the fact that Jesus was with them. They had not yet understood who he really was. They considered that all was lost, but at least had the sense to cry out for the Lord to save them, which he did.

8:26 But he said to them, "Why are you cowardly, you people of little faith?" Then he got up and rebuked the winds and the sea, and it was dead calm.

But before he did so, he rebuked their lack of faith. Whether he was awake or asleep, they were in God's hands, and should have trusted that all would be well. Then Jesus arose and rebuked the winds and the sea, and immediately the sea and sky became placid and tranquil.

8:27 And the men were amazed and said, "What sort of person is this? Even the winds and the sea obey him!"

Still the disciples failed to recognize Christ as the creator of the universe, for they were amazed, not at his miracle working power, but that his authority extended even to the elements of nature. Later, after another experience on the lake, they finally understood (Matt. 14:33).

Jesus Delivers Two Demon Possessed Men

8:28 When he came to the other side, to the region of the Gadarenes, two demon-possessed men coming from the tombs met him. They were extremely violent, so that no one was able to pass by that way.

In other gospels only one of the two men is described, yet Matthew insists that there were two. They lived in the tombs—an unclean place for Jews—naked, cutting themselves with stones and crying out continually in the blackness of despair and torment that such possession brings. They were so dangerous and violent that no one dared to pass that way. It is quite possible that they had been guilty of the most hideous murders on more than one occasion.

8:29 They cried out, "Son of God, leave us alone! Have you come here to torment us before the time?"

Notice that it is the demons, not the men, which cry out, for even their speech organs were not under their own control; they were operated by the demons which possessed them. The clean, holy presence and unlimited, uncreated power of the Son of God tormented these unclean spirits greatly, and they cried out to be left alone. They understood Christ's purpose was to bring about their final undoing, and that their inevitable end would be in hell. They do not, for they could not, oppose this fact, but only ask if he were come to cast them into hell before the time appointed by God.

8:30–31 A large herd of pigs was feeding some distance from them. Then the demons begged him, "If you drive us out, send us into the herd of pigs."

Christ had come on this occasion to free men from the dominion of Satan; only later will he return to destroy Satan and cast him and his demons into the lake of fire. What happened to the demons was not of particular interest to him at this point—only what happened to the men. So the demons are given permission to enter the pigs, something which they found preferable to going straight into hell. Notice that they did not (for they could not) resist the word of Jesus to leave the men. Demons never can oppose the word of God. They recognize that they have no choice but to obey the higher authority.

The Bible says "greater is he that is in you than he that is in the world." We need not fear when called upon to handle demonic personalities (Luke 10:17–20).

8:32 And he said, "Go!" So they came out and went into the pigs, and the herd rushed down the steep slope into the lake and drowned in the water.

With the voice of command, Jesus ordered the unclean spirits to go, and they enter the herd of pigs, tormenting those poor beasts so much that they found drowning preferable to living. It appears that the demons gained nothing from this encounter but a bare escape from immediate incarceration in hell.

8:33 The herdsmen ran off, went into the town, and told everything that had happened to the demon-possessed men.

When those who kept the pigs saw what had happened, they ran into town to tell the news. Not only had they lost their jobs and their herds; they were also astonished, as the rest of the people were, to see the dangerous and violent madmen, sitting quietly at the feet of Jesus with their sanity restored.

8:34 Then the entire town came out to meet Jesus. And when they saw him, they begged him to leave their region.

The towns-people were so afraid of the supernatural authority which enabled Jesus to perform the impossible, that they begged him to leave, which he did. In other gospels we are told that one of the men wanted to go with him, but Jesus sent him to the neighbouring towns to share the testimony of his life. Although Christ was at this point turned away, through the faithful witness of this man, Christ was later accepted by many in this area. We should never give up witnessing and testifying for the Lord simply because people are not responding; for this situation may change in God's time.

Discussion Questions for Chapter 8

1. vv. 1–4. What does the healing of the leper teach you about how to approach or pray to God?

2. vv. 5–13. What was significant about the Centurion's approach to Jesus?

3. vv. 19–22. How would you describe what commitment to Jesus means from these verses?

4. vv. 22–27. What do you think is the most important lesson we can draw from the stilling of the storm incident?

5. vv. 28–34. Describe the difference which Jesus made in the lives of the demon-possessed men. Why do you think the towns-people initially rejected Jesus?

You will find suggested answers to these questions on pages 306–323.

Matthew Chapter 9

Jesus has Authority to Forgive Sin

9:1 After getting into a boat he crossed to the other side and came to his own town.

After casting out the demons from the men of Gadara, Jesus did what the people of the town had asked. He got back into the boat and went to Capernaum, where he seems to have been residing with Peter (Matt. 4:13; Matt. 8:14).

9:2 Just then some people brought to him a paralytic lying on a stretcher. When Jesus saw their faith, he said to the paralytic, "Have courage, son! Your sins are forgiven."

As he arrived some people brought to him a man on a stretcher who was paralysed. Jesus saw how much faith that they (and also the paralytic man) had, but said the most unexpected thing. Firstly, he encouraged the man to recognise himself as a "son" (teknon - the word used for child or young son), for we are all little children to God. Next, Jesus told the man that his sins were forgiven. Jesus knew, of course, that the man was paralysed, but he realised that the greatest need he had was of forgiveness; it is the greatest need we all have.

9:3 Then some of the experts in the law said to themselves, "This man is blaspheming!"

Some of the teachers of the religious law reacted immediately; for they knew that only God could forgive sin, and regarded Jesus as nothing but an ordinary man. Therefore, in their minds, he was blasphemer.

9:4 When Jesus saw their reaction he said, "Why do you respond with evil in your hearts?

Jesus knew what they were thinking (Heb. 4:12) and so addressed them, asking why they had such evil thoughts in their hearts.

9:5 Which is easier, to say, 'Your sins are forgiven' or to say, 'Stand up and walk'?

Neither of these two things is easy to do as far as man is concerned. Not one of Christ's opponents could heal the man or forgive his sin. By his atoning death on the cross Jesus has provided both forgiveness for sin and healing. In this sense, forgiving our sins was not easy for the Son of God, for only by his taking our sin on himself could our sin be forgiven (1 Peter 1:18–19; 1 Cor. 7:23).

9:6–7 But so that you may know that the Son of Man has authority on earth to forgive sins" – then he said to the paralytic – "Stand up, take your stretcher, and go home." And he stood up and went home.

In order to prove to them that as the Son of Man had the authority on earth to forgive sins, Jesus demonstrated his power by turning to the man and telling him to get up, pick up his bed and go home. And that is exactly what the man did.

9:8 When the crowd saw this, they were afraid and honoured God who had given such authority to men.

When the people saw what Jesus had done they were filled with awe and gave praise to God that he had given such authority to a man. So we see that although they attributed this miracle to God they still considered Jesus to be just another man and not God manifest in the flesh.

Jesus Came to Call Sinners to Repentance

9:9 As Jesus went on from there, he saw a man named Matthew sitting at the tax booth. "Follow me," he said to him. And he got up and followed him.

Our text says that as Jesus was walking he saw Matthew the tax collector; but this was no accidental encounter. Jesus purposed to go that way so that he could call Matthew to follow him. Jesus knew all about Matthew and what the people thought of him but still wanted him to be his disciple. Without hesitation Matthew left his job and went with Jesus, never looking back.

9:10 As Jesus was having a meal in Matthew's house, many tax collectors and sinners came and ate with Jesus and his disciples.

Sometime later Matthew invited Jesus to have dinner with him at his home. He had also invited many tax collectors and others who were branded as sinners to come and see the man for whom he had given up all things.

9:11 When the Pharisees saw this they said to his disciples, "Why does your teacher eat with tax collectors and sinners?"

As far as the Pharisees and scribes were concerned, Jesus couldn't do anything right. Here they made a complaint against him to his disciples about accepting an invitation from a tax collector to dine with him and his sinful friends. Were they being extra cautious in not complaining to Jesus directly because they knew that he would refute them again?

9:12–13 When Jesus heard this he said, "Those who are healthy don't need a physician, but those who are sick do. Go and learn what this saying means: 'I want mercy and not sacrifice.' For I did not come to call the righteous, but sinners."

Hearing what they said about him Jesus replied that a healthy person has no need of a doctor, only those who are ill. It is sinners who need a remedy for their sins and not those who consider themselves to be righteous. Jesus is the only one able to set sinners free from their sins (1 Tim. 1:15; Luke 19:10). God puts mercy before sacrifice for he is first and foremost a God of mercy (Eph. 2:4).

Jesus does not give the Pharisees an understanding of this scripture (Hosea 6:6) but tells them to go and learn the truth of it for themselves.

A Time for Fasting

9:14 Then John's disciples came to Jesus and asked, "Why do we and the Pharisees fast often, but your disciples don't fast?"

The disciples of John the Baptist came to Jesus to ask him why it was that they and the Pharisees often fasted (the Pharisees religiously fasted twice a week, see Luke 18:11–12) but his own disciple did not.

9:15 Jesus said to them, "The wedding guests cannot mourn while the bridegroom is with them, can they? But the days are coming when the bridegroom will be taken from them, and then they will fast.

In this simile, Jesus is the bridegroom (Rev. 21:2). While he is still with his disciples it is not a time for them to fast but to rejoice. But he forewarns that the day will come when he will be taken away from them and then they will fast. This is a reference to the time following his death on the cross, resurrection and ascension.

9:16–17 No one sews a patch of unshrunk cloth on an old garment, because the patch will pull away from the garment and the tear will be worse. And no one pours new wine into old wineskins; otherwise the skins burst and the wine is spilled out and the skins are destroyed. Instead they put new wine into new wineskins and both are preserved."

If you sew a new piece of cloth to patch up an old garment the new piece will shrink and rip away from the old, resulting in a bigger hole. If you put new wine into old wine skins, then as the wine continues to ferment it will expand and burst the skins, since they are no longer elastic. New wine is put into new, flexible skins so that both are preserved. Jesus used these illustrations to show that the new covenant which he would introduce was not a patch up of the old; it was completely new and different (Jer. 31:31; Matt. 26:28; Heb. 8:13; Heb. 9:15; 2 Cor. 3:6). It is only by being "born again" that we can enter in and receive the eternal blessings of the new covenant (John 3:3; 2 Cor. 5:17).

Jairus' Daughter Raised from the Dead and the Woman with the Issue of Blood

9:18 As he was saying these things, a ruler came, bowed low before him, and said, "My daughter has just died, but come and lay your hand on her and she will live."

The ruler is not named here as he is in other gospels, but it is Jairus the ruler of the synagogue in Capernaum. He initially comes to Jesus as his only child, a girl of twelve, is lying at the point of death (Luke 8:41–42). Jairus had faith that Christ could heal his daughter while she lived (Mark 5:22–23); but it was while he sought the help of Jesus that news reached him via his servants that his little girl had actually died. Jesus then challenges Jairus to keep on believing and she would live again (Mark 5:35–36). Matthew condenses this whole situation into one sentence.

9:19–21 Jesus and his disciples got up and followed him. But a woman who had been suffering from a haemorrhage for twelve years came up behind him and touched the edge of his cloak; for she kept saying to herself, "If only I touch his cloak, I will be healed."

As Jesus and his disciples went on their way with Jairus to his house, a woman came up behind him, no doubt pushing her way through the crowd. She had suffered with a gynaecological problem which meant that the bleeding from her womb was continuous, and had been so for twelve years. Such was her faith in Christ's power to heal that she said, "I have only to touch the hem of his cloak to be healed, and indeed she was. She was naturally modest about her situation and did not wish her condition or her healing to be made public.

9:22 But when Jesus turned and saw her he said, "Have courage, daughter! Your faith has made you well." And the woman was healed from that hour.

The woman had hoped to be healed without being noticed, but one can never go unnoticed as far as Jesus is concerned. He encouraged her to tell her story, as a testimony to God's goodness (Mark 5:33), and reassured her that because of her faith, she was fully and truly healed.

9:23–24 When Jesus entered the ruler's house and saw the flute players and the disorderly crowd, he said, "Go away, for the girl is not dead but asleep." And they began making fun of him.

On arriving at Jairus' house, Jesus and his disciples found a crowd of relatives, friends and neighbours gathered to mourn the dead girl. In hot eastern countries, funerals must take place quickly, because of decay. They mourned in the traditional way, with doleful music. Can you imagine anyone entering a funeral and telling the relatives not to worry, for their dead loved one is not dead but only asleep? The words "laughed at him" or "made fun of him" are really too weak. The word derided is more correct. The reaction of the crowd was intensely hostile.

9:25 But when the crowd had been put outside, he went in and gently took her by the hand, and the girl got up.

The crowd were persuaded to leave for a time, possibly by Jairus, (though Christ's authority would have been sufficient to compel them to leave, had he chosen to do so). In this way the Lord was given an opportunity to do his work.

Notice that Christ did not call on God or even pray for the girl. He himself is the resurrection (John 11:25) with power over life and death (Rom. 14:9). He took her by the hand and summoned her spirit back from the world of the dead, with the words recorded by Mark in Aramaic "Talitha Kumi" which mean 'Little girl, I say to you, get up" (Mark 5:41).

9:26 And the news of this spread throughout that region.

Mark tells us that he allowed only Peter, John and James with him into the child's bedroom, together with her father and mother (Mark 5:37). Yet no one can keep secret a dead girl being brought back to life. Such an occurrence shook the entire region.

The Healing of Two Blind Men

9:27 As Jesus went on from there, two blind men followed him, shouting, "Have mercy on us, Son of David!"

Christ had healed many blind people, and here two more came to him shouting out for mercy, calling him the Messiah, the promised Son of David.

9:28–31 When he went into the house, the blind men came to him. Jesus said to them, "Do you believe that I am able to do this?" They said to him, "Yes, Lord." Then he touched their eyes saying, "Let it be done for you according to your faith." And their eyes were opened. Then Jesus sternly warned them, "See that no one knows about this." But they went out and spread the news about him throughout that entire region.

It was not at the roadside, as in the case of Bartimaeus, but later in the house that the two men were brought to Jesus. Jesus questions them concerning their faith, to challenge them. Notice how

100

after this challenge they no longer call him Son of David but Lord. He touched their eyes, and by faith they received healing from Jesus.

Yet on this occasion, the Lord did not want their healing advertised. He sternly warned them not to give their testimony. Yet they did not heed this warning, and Mark tells us that it was a result of such instructions being unheeded that so many sought Christ for healing that he could no longer enter the cities, but carried on his ministry in the deserts (Mark 1:45). Christ did not want his ministry to be seen as a healing campaign. He longed for the crowds to gather to hear the teaching of his word and to receive eternal life; for healing was not as important as the mission he came to fulfil—to seek and to save the lost.

Deliverance of a Demon Possessed Man

9:32–33 As they were going away, a man who could not talk and was demon-possessed was brought to him. After the demon was cast out, the man who had been mute spoke. The crowds were amazed and said, "Never has anything like this been seen in Israel!"

This man who was brought to Jesus had been robbed of the power of speech by a demon which possessed him. It was when the demon was cast out that his power of speech returned—there had been nothing physically wrong with his speech organs. Indeed, the ministry of Christ was the first time that men had ever seen demons cast out, and it was a characteristic of Christ's ministry everywhere he went, fulfilling the scripture which says: "the spirit of the sovereign LORD is upon me, because the LORD has chosen me...to decree the release of captives, and the freeing of prisoners" (Isa. 61:1).

9:34 But the Pharisees said, "By the ruler of demons he casts out demons."

In a mere fit of jealousy, the religious leaders accuse Jesus with this ludicrous statement. Matthew 12:24–30 tells us how Christ answered them. Just as it is nonsense to suppose that an army would attack and destroy itself in battle, so it is ludicrous to suggest that Satan could drive out Satan. Jesus warns the Pharisees that to oppose the Spirit of God in this way is to be in danger of committing an eternal sin (Matt. 12:31–32).

Few Workers

9:35 Then Jesus went throughout all the towns and villages, teaching in their synagogues, preaching the good news of the kingdom, and healing every kind of disease and sickness.

Christ's purpose was to reach the whole population of Israel with the gospel, and so he would not be confined to one geographic location. He travelled as an itinerant preacher, preaching the gospel and teaching the word of God in every synagogue throughout the entire region. As he went he healed every kind of sickness and disease as part of his ministry.

9:36 When he saw the crowds, he had compassion on them because they were bewildered and helpless, like sheep without a shepherd.

As huge crowds turned out to meet him and be healed of their sicknesses, Christ the good shepherd had compassion on them, for without him they were without a shepherd (a guide to tend, bless and care for them). Our greatest motivation in ministry and evangelism is not the fact that people are going to hell, but the desire we have for them to know our wonderful blessed Saviour—and this is a desire we shares with Jesus.

9:37 Then he said to his disciples, "The harvest is plentiful, but the workers are few. Therefore ask the Lord of the harvest to send out workers into his harvest."

God has a great work to do. His harvest is the gathering of men to himself from every tribe and nation—people coming to know and worship God through his son Jesus Christ. This work cannot be done by a small group of individuals. There is a world to be reached. Pray that the lord of the harvest, which is God, will send or thrust out labourers into his harvest. Sometimes God needs to *thrust* us out, or we would never go. The work of preaching and teaching the gospel of Christ is a labour—the word means toil—it is hard and often discouraging work.

If a teacher turns up unprepared for a Sunday school class, and doesn't know what they will teach the children, or what activity they will do, then they ought not to be surprised if there is not a result. When Paul says, "do the work of an evangelist" (2 Tim. 4:5), he reveals that God requires hard work. Of a pastor's teaching the word he employs the phrase "the hard working ox should not be muzzled as it treads out the corn" (1 Tim. 5:17–18). Let us not be afraid of such hard work for the master. I have heard some people suggest that hard working ministers are relying on their own efforts rather than on God; but the truth is rather that the harder a man works, the greater his revelation of Christ (see Paul's claim to work "harder than they all" in 1 Cor. 15:10). There is no room for the lazy in the kingdom of God.

Discussion Questions for Chapter 9

1. vv. 1–8. Why do you think the forgiveness of sins is more important than healing?

2. vv. 9–13. In what way does the call of Matthew and his friends illustrate Jesus' mission?

3. vv. 14–17. For what reasons do you think a believer in Christ might fast?

4. vv. 18–26. What conclusions can you make about Jesus from the story of the raising of Jairus' daughter from death, and how might these offer comfort to bereaved families today?

5. vv. 35–37. What kind of workers do you think Jesus wants to send into his harvest field? (Read especially v. 36).

You will find suggested answers to these questions on pages 306–323.

Matthew Chapter 10

Empowered to Preach, Teach and Heal

10:1 Jesus called his twelve disciples and gave them authority over unclean spirits so they could cast them out and heal every kind of disease and sickness.

The time had now come for Jesus to send out the disciples on their own, so he called them together and imparted to them power over evil spirits and power to heal every kind of sickness.

10:2–4 Now these are the names of the twelve apostles: first, Simon (called Peter), and Andrew his brother; James son of Zebedee and John his brother; Philip and Bartholomew; Thomas and Matthew the tax collector; James the son of Alphaeus, and Thaddaeus; Simon the Zealot and Judas Iscariot, who betrayed him.

In these verses Matthew lists the names of the twelve disciples (from now on designated apostles) to whom Jesus gave this power. He emphasizes that Judas Iscariot who betrayed Jesus was given the same power and sent forth with the others. As far as we know Judas did the same miracles as the other disciples.

10:5–6 Jesus sent out these twelve, instructing them as follows: "Do not go to Gentile regions and do not enter any Samaritan town. Go instead to the lost sheep of the house of Israel.

The disciples were not to go anywhere that they choose to; rather, Jesus specifically tells to go only to the Jews, the lost sheep of God. They were not to enter Samaria or any Gentile regions.

10:7 As you go, preach this message: 'The kingdom of heaven is near!'

Jesus gave them the message which they were to preach: the good news that the kingdom of heaven is near and the way of salvation is coming. The message is the same today for every believer to proclaim: Jesus Christ is the Saviour of the world.

10:8 Heal the sick, raise the dead, cleanse lepers, cast out demons. Freely you received, freely give.

As they gave the message, signs and wonders would follow. They were to heal the sick, raise the dead to life, heal lepers and drive out demons. As the disciples had received this power freely from the Lord Jesus Christ so they were to freely give it to others. The Contemporary English Version says, "You received without paying, now give without being paid".

10:9–10 Do not take gold, silver, or copper in your belts, no bag for the journey, or an extra tunic, or sandals or staff, for the worker deserves his provisions.

Jesus did not tell them to go and pack their suitcases and make certain they had enough money to provide for food and lodgings. Rather, they were to go straight away with only the clothes they were wearing. He does add, however, that workers deserve their food (1 Cor. 9:7–11), meaning they should accept hospitality.

10:11 Whenever you enter a town or village, find out who is worthy there and stay with them until you leave.

When they entered a town they were to seek out someone who was worthy enough to have them as their guests and stay with them until they were ready to move on.

10:12 As you enter the house, give it greetings.

As they entered a home they were to give their blessing upon it: "peace to this house" (Luke 10:5 NKJV™).

10:13 And if the house is worthy, let your peace come on it, but if it is not worthy, let your peace return to you.

If that house was indeed worthy, accepting the apostles and their message, then the blessing would remain upon it. If it did not turn out to be worthy then the disciples were to take back the blessing of peace.

10:14 And if anyone will not welcome you or listen to your message, shake the dust off your feet as you leave that house or that town.

If anyone would not receive them or their message they were to leave that home or town and shake the dust off their feet. To the Jews the dust of heathen countries was unclean. Paul and Barnabas did this to the town of Antioch in Pisidia (Acts 13:51).

10:15 I tell you the truth, it will be more bearable for the region of Sodom and Gomorrah on the day of judgment than for that town!

Jesus declared that in the Day of Judgment it will be more endurable for the wicked cities of Sodom and Gomorrah than for any town which although given the opportunity to hear the word of God, had refused to receive it.

Opposition and Persecution

10:16 "I am sending you out like sheep surrounded by wolves, so be wise as serpents and innocent as doves.

Jesus warned them that he was not sending them into pleasant places for they would be like sheep surrounded by people as hard hearted and merciless as wolves. So they were to be as shrewd as serpents and as innocent (or harmless) as doves.

10:17 Beware of people, because they will hand you over to councils and flog you in their synagogues.

They were to beware of people who would take them to court and have them publicly beaten.

10:18 And you will be brought before governors and kings because of me, as a witness to them and the Gentiles.

They would be dragged before governors and kings for Christ's sake in order for them to witness before the Gentiles that Jesus Christ is Lord; just as some time later Paul was brought before Gallio, Felix, Festus and Agrippa (Acts 26:1, 28). Jesus' words indeed apply to all believers facing persecution.

10:19 Whenever they hand you over for trial, do not worry about how to speak or what to say, for what you should say will be given to you at that time.

When they were brought to trial they were not to worry about what they should say or how they should say it. In that very hour they would be given the right words to say.

10:20 For it is not you speaking, but the Spirit of your Father speaking through you.

It would not be them speaking but the Holy Spirit that would be speaking through them.

10:21 "Brother will hand over brother to death, and a father his child. Children will rise against parents and have them put to death.

Jesus warns that throughout the church age, brothers and sisters will betray one another and parents will betray their own children; in addition, children will disown their parents and have them put to death. This has happened many times in Christian history.

10:22 And you will be hated by everyone because of my name. But the one who endures to the end will be saved.

Like the apostles, so we must not expect to be loved by the world, for as Christ's disciples we will be hated by everyone because we are his. Those who endure and remain faithful in the face of persecution will be saved.

10:23 Whenever they persecute you in one place, flee to another. I tell you the truth, you will not finish going through all the towns of Israel before the Son of Man comes.

When the disciples were persecuted in one town for their faith they were to flee to another. Jesus suggests that the disciples would never have time to flee to every town in Israel before his return, and there has been a good deal of debate concerning what Jesus meant by this. Some commentators say that he meant before his death and resurrection; others that he was referring to the destruction of Jerusalem and others take it as a reference to the second coming. It is unlikely to mean the time he comes again, for this period is far too long.

10:24–25 "A disciple is not greater than his teacher, nor a slave greater than his master. It is enough for the disciple to become like his teacher, and the slave like his master. If they have called the head of the house "Beelzebub," how much more will they defame the members of his household!

A disciple is not better than his teacher and a slave is not above his master, so Christ's disciples cannot be better or higher than him. As his disciples we should become like him—he came to serve so his followers should serve others (John 13:13–16). If they called Jesus Beelzebub they are going to call his disciples even worse (Matt. 12:24).

Do not Fear

10:26 "Do not be afraid of them, for nothing is hidden that will not be revealed, and nothing is secret that will not be made known.

We are not to be afraid of those who oppose, persecute and threaten us for nothing is hidden from God; in due time their evil deeds against us will be made uncovered and consequently punished (Jer. 1:8; 1 Pet. 3:14).

10:27 What I say to you in the dark, tell in the light, and what is whispered in your ear, proclaim from the housetops.

The Lord Jesus Christ encouraged his disciples to broadcast the things that he has taught them; to proclaim it in the daytime and shout it from the housetops. We too should not keep the good news about Jesus to ourselves—tell the whole wide world!

10:28 Do not be afraid of those who kill the body but cannot kill the soul. Instead, fear the one who is able to destroy both soul and body in hell.

We should not be afraid of people, for at the end of the day they can only kill the body and not the soul. Instead, we are to have a healthy fear of God, for he alone is able to destroy both body and soul in hell.

10:29. Aren't two sparrows sold for a penny? Yet not one of them falls to the ground apart from your Father's will.

The Lord gives the assurance that God the Father not only cares for the sparrows that are sold two for a penny but he knows them fully and even present with them when they die.

10:30–31 Even all the hairs on your head are numbered. So do not be afraid; you are more valuable than many sparrows.

You may not know how many hairs you have on your head but God the Father numbers them all! So do not be afraid, since you are of more value than a large flock of sparrows, God will care for you too.

10:32–33 "Whoever, then, acknowledges me before people, I will acknowledge before my Father in heaven. But whoever denies me before people, I will deny him also before my Father in heaven.

If you want to avoid persecution then deny your relationship with the Lord Jesus Christ—simple. However, if you confess before the people that Jesus Christ is your Lord and Saviour then he will acknowledge you as his own before his Father in heaven, whilst whoever denies or disowns Jesus Christ before people will be denied and disowned by him before God.

Not Peace but Conflict

10:34 "Do not think that I have come to bring peace to the earth. I have not come to bring peace but a sword.

Jesus warned his disciples that he had not come into the world to bring an end to war and contention, whether between individuals or nations. The "peace on earth" proclaimed by the angel at the birth of Christ referred to the reconciliation of sinners with God which Jesus' death would make possible (Col. 1:21–22). There will be those who will continually oppose the teaching and the person of the Lord Jesus Christ; therefore there will be no peace but only conflict whenever the word of God (which is the sword of the Spirit) is proclaimed (Eph. 6:17; Heb. 4:12).

10:35–36 For I have come to set a man against his father, a daughter against her mother, and a daughter-in-law against her mother-in-law, and a man's enemies will be the members of his household.

The gospel message will even bring division among families; a son will turn against his father, a daughter against her mother, and vice-versa. The enemies of believers will come from within their own families.

10:37 "Whoever loves father or mother more than me is not worthy of me, and whoever loves son or daughter more than me is not worthy of me.

If a Christian has a greater love for his or her parents or children, and put these relations before Christ, then they do not deserve to have him (Mark 3:32–34; Mark 10:28–30).

10:38 And whoever does not take up his cross and follow me is not worthy of me.

Whoever does not deny himself (die to self-will) and embrace the will of God whatever it may cost does not deserve to belong to Christ.

10:39 Whoever finds his life will lose it, and whoever loses his life because of me will find it.

Whoever holds on to his own life will lose out but whoever lets go of his own life, by completely surrendering it to Jesus, will have abundant life (John 10:10; Gal. 2:20).

Rewards

10:40 "Whoever receives you receives me, and whoever receives me receives the one who sent me.

If anyone welcomes a follower of Jesus Christ it is the same as welcoming Jesus himself and whoever welcomes Jesus welcomes God the Father who sent him.

10:41 Whoever receives a prophet in the name of a prophet will receive a prophet's reward. Whoever receives a righteous person in the name of a righteous person will receive a righteous person's reward.

The person who receives a prophet of the Lord as such will receive the same reward as a prophet. Anyone who receives a righteous person because of their righteousness will have the same reward as a righteous person.

10:42 And whoever gives only a cup of cold water to one of these little ones in the name of a disciple, I tell you the truth, he will never lose his reward."

Whoever gives a cup of cold water to the least of the disciples of Jesus Christ, because he is a disciple, is promised that he in turn will never lose his own reward.

Discussion Questions for Chapter 10

1. vv. 1–42. In what ways did Jesus prepare his disciples as he sent them out on a mission?

2. vv. 16–35. What promises does Jesus make to those who are persecuted for the gospel?

3. vv. 34–39. How does Jesus' claim that a believer's enemies will come from his own family apply to your life?

4. vv. 1–42. What does it mean to be fully committed to Jesus?

5. vv. 40–42. Why do you think God would reward the giving of a cup of cold water?

You will find suggested answers to these questions on pages 306–323.

Matthew Chapter 11

John the Baptist's Question

11:1 When Jesus had finished instructing his twelve disciples, he went on from there to teach and preach in their towns.

Although Christ had sent his apostles out to preach, he did not refrain from going to preach himself. In the local church situation, there would be little point in the Lord sending new workers to us if the result were that existing workers ceased their work!

11:2 Now when John heard in prison about the deeds Christ had done, he sent his disciples to ask a question:

John the Baptist had been arrested quite near to the commencement of Jesus' ministry, and so perhaps had seen and heard only little of Christ's work before his imprisonment. John's disciples often visited him in prison, and brought him news of what Jesus was doing. In the darkness of his cell, facing a violent death, John did not so much waver in his faith (see verse 7) as in his courage, but the effects can be similar.

11:3 "Are you the one who is to come, or should we look for another?"

John needed reassurance concerning his own life and ministry. He had been sent to prepare the way of the Lord (John 1:23) and had publicly testified that Jesus was the Christ, the Son of God (John 1:34). Now the glorious times when multitudes gathered for baptism had gone, being replaced by trouble and suffering.

All involved in Christian ministry for any length of time will experience a dark night of the soul similar to that which John experienced. Doubts and questions arise concerning our life and ministry; we may feel that nothing has been accomplished, and that our life has lacked any real significance. The answer of Jesus to John's disciples is sufficient to inspire us, too, with renewed faith and courage to persevere (1 Cor. 16:13).

11:4–6 Jesus answered them, "Go tell John what you hear and see: The blind see, the lame walk, lepers are cleansed, the deaf hear, the dead are raised, and the poor have good news proclaimed to them. Blessed is anyone who takes no offense at me."

At first reading it may not appear that Christ gave John any specific word relevant to his life and ministry. But in fact Christ reveals to John that his ministry had been fulfilled. The object of his service had been realised. His life and ministry were actually, from God's viewpoint, a complete success. John had been sent to prepare the way for the ministry of Jesus, and that ministry had now commenced; and this is the fact that the disciples of John were told to report to him. John had declared Christ to be the Son of God, and through his mighty works, God was now giving witness to that same fact. The poor flocked to hear the gospel. John's life and ministry were not for nothing, but rather they were nothing by themselves. John needed to see his ministry as being part of the wider and greater work of Christ on earth.

This is the meaning behind Jesus words: "blessed is he who is not offended in me." John would be blessed if he considered the work of Christ to be of supreme importance; more important than his own personal success. Only when our lives are completely taken up with Christ and lived for him will they find their true meaning (Matt. 10:39).

The apostle Paul suffered a similar dark night of the soul, but was reassured concerning the significance of his service for Christ, and said: (Acts 20:24) "but none of these things move me, neither count I my life dear unto myself, so that I might finish my course with joy, and the ministry, which I have received of the Lord Jesus, to testify the gospel of the grace of God."

11:7 While they were going away, Jesus began to speak to the crowd about John: "What did you go out into the wilderness to see? A reed shaken by the wind?

It was not to John or his disciples but to the general public that Jesus gave this testimony approving John's life and ministry. He affirms that John was not a man who was easily shaken in his faith or dedication to God by opposition or the threat of death which hung over him.

11:8 What did you go out to see? A man dressed in fancy clothes? Look, those who wear fancy clothes are in the homes of kings!

John's clothes were of camel's hair, and he lived in the wilderness, living on locusts and wild honey in a manner similar to Elijah. He had been no stranger to hardship and difficulty for the sake of Christ all his life. He was no fop at the king's court, but a seasoned warrior of Jesus Christ.

11:9–10 What did you go out to see? A prophet? Yes, I tell you, and more than a prophet. This is the one about whom it is written: 'Look, I am sending my messenger ahead of you, who will prepare your way before you.'

Jesus affirms John's calling to be more than a prophet. As the messenger of the Lord, he prepared the people to receive God's only begotten Son. No prophet before him had received such an honour.

11:11 "I tell you the truth, among those born of women, no one has arisen greater than John the Baptist. Yet the one who is least in the kingdom of heaven is greater than he is.

Because of the honour placed on him, John should be considered as the most exalted of mortal men. Indeed, even being allowed to carry Jesus' sandals would have made him highly honoured, although he considered himself unworthy to do so (Matt. 3:11). Yet every born again believer has an even greater privilege. We are not merely preparing the way for the Lord, but have him dwelling within us, and are his representatives in the world, witnessing for him and ministering to the church which is his body.

11:12 From the days of John the Baptist until now the kingdom of heaven has suffered violence, and forceful people lay hold of it.

From the time John came to announce the coming of Christ, to the moment of Christ spoke these words, the kingdom of heaven had been proclaimed so that men and women might press their way into it. It "suffers violence" in that one does not need any further personal invitation to enter. Since the invitation is to all, it is for those who truly wish to enter to press in with all their might, seeking the blessings of forgiveness and salvation, as being the most important blessing they can have.

11:13–15 For all the prophets and the law prophesied until John appeared. And if you are willing to accept it, he is Elijah, who is to come. The one who has ears had better listen!

Christ announces that the end of the old covenant was with Malachi. John's appearance heralded the bringing in of a new covenant by Christ; and as had been predicted by Malachi, a prophet would come in the spirit and power of Elijah to herald the appearance of the Lord (Mal. 4:5). Those with hearts willing to listen and to be instructed by Christ would understand that this prophecy had been fulfilled in the ministry of John the Baptist.

11:16–17 "To what should I compare this generation? They are like children sitting in the marketplaces who call out to one another, 'We played the flute for you, yet you did not dance; we wailed in mourning, yet you did not weep.'

There was simply no pleasing these people! They had hardened their hearts and refused to listen. Jesus compares them to a group of sulky and awkward children who did not want to play with the others in their games.

11:18–19 For John came neither eating nor drinking, and they say, 'He has a demon!' The Son of Man came eating and drinking, and they say, 'Look at him, a glutton and a drunk, a friend of tax collectors and sinners!' But wisdom is vindicated by her deeds."

John came in the manner of Old Testament prophets, and was separated to God like someone under the vow of a Nazarite—yet he was accused of being mad or demon possessed. When Jesus came in an entirely different manner they rejected him also, accusing him of being over indulgent, and associating with sinners. They simply would not listen to God's word, no matter how it was presented to them.

In our modern day there is a temptation to think that because men and women have not responded to the gospel when it has been presented in a certain way, that they might accept it when presented it in a different way. Some are actually shying away from preaching, for they think that the gospel will be found more palatable if it is rapped or presented in some other "more accessible" format. Whilst there is nothing wrong with presenting the gospel in a host of new ways, the sad fact remains that if the gospel is not responded to, it will make no difference how we present it. Nothing will alter this by our living differently, dressing differently, or outreaching differently. It is the *gospel* people are rejecting, not the manner of the preacher or the method of presentation. Choose whatever method of presentation you like; Jesus' words reveal that the eternal result will be the same.

Woe to the Unrepentant Towns

11:20 Then Jesus began to criticize openly the cities in which he had done many of his miracles, because they did not repent.

The rejection of the gospel would bring certain fearful consequences (Heb. 2:3). Even though Christ had preached and confirmed his word with miraculous signs in many local cities, they had not repented. They had failed to respond and receive the gospel. The word "criticize" used in the NET Bible (above) is slightly misleading. Jesus is pronouncing judgment on these towns, as can be seen from the following verses.

11:21 "Woe to you, Chorazin! Woe to you, Bethsaida! If the miracles done in you had been done in Tyre and Sidon, they would have repented long ago in sackcloth and ashes.

The un-repentance of the Jewish towns of Chorazin and Bethsaida was inexcusable in view of the many miracles which had been done there. If they had been done in the foreign cities of Tyre and Sidon, Jesus says that the inhabitants of those cities would have repented immediately and deeply. The Jews had been privileged to know the law of God, and even more privileged to see and hear Christ in person, but still they did not respond; hence their judgment will be according to their greater privilege. Those who receive more light, yet reject it, will be held to account to a greater extent than those who had less light.

11:22 But I tell you, it will be more bearable for Tyre and Sidon on the day of judgment than for you!

Although judgment would still fall on the unrepentant in those foreign cities, their guilt would not be as great, and so their punishment would be more bearable. This is one of only a few verses which seem to advance the idea that there will be varying degrees of punishment meted out upon unbelievers.

11:23–24 And you, Capernaum, will you be exalted to heaven? No, you will be thrown down to Hades! For if the miracles done among you had been done in Sodom, it would have continued to this day. But I tell you, it will be more bearable for the region of Sodom on the Day of Judgment than for you!"

In a similar manner, Capernaum had been exalted to heaven by the measure of the revelation they had been given of Christ through his teachings and miracles. The whole city had come to Jesus, and he had healed all the sick in that town (Matt. 8:16). Yet even this was insufficient to break the hardened hearts of the people and bring them to repentance. In God's sight, this sin was more serious than that of Sodom and Gomorrah, who, if they had received such revelation, would have repented and been spared the fire which consumed them. Whatever else these verses teach us, they teach us that the most serious sin of all is the rejection of Jesus Christ, for it is the rejection of Christ that results in unbelievers going to hell (John 3:36).

11:25–26 At that time Jesus said, "I praise you, Father, Lord of heaven and earth, because you have hidden these things from the wise and intelligent, and revealed them to little children. Yes, Father, for this was your gracious will.

According to Luke (Luke 10:17–21), Jesus made this statement sometime after the sending out and return of both his 12 apostles and his 70 (or 72) evangelists, who reported to him concerning their preaching and the miracles they had seen. They had gone forth in simple faith, trusting Jesus as a child trusts his mother or father.

It is not through human wisdom or intelligence that God reveals himself to humankind, but through the revelation of faith (1 Cor. 1:26–27). It is the will of God our Father that it should be so, for he would leave none out of his gracious plan of salvation. Men and women who refuse to accept God's wisdom in favour of their own are excluding themselves from receiving God's grace.

11:27 All things have been handed over to me by my Father. No one knows the Son except the Father, and no one knows the Father except the Son and anyone to whom the Son decides to reveal him.

All the authority of God, especially with regard to responsibility for the salvation of mankind, had been handed over to Jesus Christ. By virtue of his eternal generation, all things that are God's are also his, and the Father and son are mutually dependent. It takes a divine being to know a divine being fully, hence Christ announces that only the Son knows the Father and only the Father knows the Son. Yet, following on from the revelation spoken of in verse 25, we see that God the Father is at this time pleased to reveal his Son to people. In Jesus Christ we may know God now and will know him in fuller measure hereafter. It is only by divine revelation that anyone can come to know God.

11:28 Come to me, all you who are weary and burdened, and I will give you rest.

Although some rejected God's purpose for themselves, the way remained wide open for them. With this invitation, Jesus reveals that the way to come to God is through him. "Come to me" is his invitation to all who are weary of life and burdened with sin and the trouble it brings. The rest Christ offers is the rest of the family home. The person at war with God has no rest, but when reconciled he enjoys peace and acceptance as one of God's family (Rom. 5:1). The guilty person has no rest for his conscience; he is living under a heavy burden of sin. When we come to Christ we find that he has lifted our heavy load from us through forgiveness and cleansing; bringing us the peace which a cleansed conscience brings (Heb. 9:14). The person without God has no rest when facing death, but by coming to Christ we receive the hope of everlasting life in heaven.

11:29–30 Take my yoke on you and learn from me, because I am gentle and humble in heart, and you will find rest for your souls. For my yoke is easy to bear, and my load is not hard to carry."

In addition to the rest given when we initially come to Christ, there is a daily rest of following Christ. One might refer to this as the deepening peace which spiritual maturity brings. The yoke was placed over two oxen so that they could share the load and pull the plough together. Usually a younger ox would be yoked to an older, well behaved ox, from which he would learn to copy. This is the picture Christ gives here: as we learn from him and walk in his ways, we shall find the path of peace and blessing. Some young oxen smart at the yoke, and it is difficult for them to submit to it. But when they do learn to submit, they become quiet and obedient, having been broken in.

Our meek and gentle Jesus has such great patience with us as we learn to carry the cross-yoke. Dying to our own self-will and living for God's will may be a crucifying experience, but we are supported in our struggles by our Saviour, and we find his strength sufficient, making the cross easy to bear. He who has born our grief and carried our sorrows is carrying the heavier end for us.

Discussion Questions for Chapter 11

1. v.11. Why did Jesus describe John the Baptist as the greatest of all prophets?

2. vv. 14–16. What signs accompanied Jesus' ministry?

3. vv. 16–19. Why were the people like children in a market?

4. vv. 20–24. Why did Christ denounce many of the cities in which he had performed miracles?

5. v. 28. What kind of rest does Jesus offer the weary?

You will find suggested answers to these questions on pages 306–323.

Matthew Chapter 12

Lord of the Sabbath

12:1 At that time Jesus went through the grain fields on a Sabbath. His disciples were hungry, and they began to pick heads of wheat and eat them.

The disciples of Jesus were hungry so as they were going through a grain field they naturally began to pick the heads of grain and eat them. The law of God gave them the right to do this (Deut. 23:25).

12:2 But when the Pharisees saw this they said to him, "Look, your disciples are doing what is against the law to do on the Sabbath."

The Pharisees, who were ever eager to catch Jesus out, criticised his disciples' behaviour, being quick to point out to him that they were breaking the law (Exodus 20:10).

12:3–4 He said to them, "Haven't you read what David did when he and his companions were hungry – how he entered the house of God and they ate the sacred bread, which was against the law for him or his companions to eat, but only for the priests?

Jesus is never caught off guard and had an answer ready for them. King David, when he and his companions were hungry and there was nothing else to eat, received the holy bread which the priest had taken from the place of worship after putting out fresh bread (1 Sam. 21:6). This was despite the law only allowing the Levites to eat this bread (Lev. 24:7–9).

12:5 Or have you not read in the law that the priests in the temple desecrate the Sabbath and yet are not guilty?

In order to carry out their God given tasks on the Sabbath the priests were allowed to work (e.g. Num. 28:8–9).

12:6 I tell you that something greater than the temple is here.

It was God who had given the ordinances and laws concerning the worship in the temple and the Sabbath day. Jesus tells the Pharisees that there was someone greater and more important than the temple amongst them (2 Chron. 6:18). In fact it was God manifest in the flesh who stood before them (John 1:14; 1 Tim. 3:16).

12:7 If you had known what this means: 'I want mercy and not sacrifice,' you would not have condemned the innocent.

The Pharisees had got it all wrong. They were so taken up with the rituals of worship that they had forgotten the nature and character of God. Instead of offering sacrifices, God wanted them to have mercy and compassion. If they had this then they would not be so quick to condemn those who were innocent (Hosea 6:6).

12:8 For the Son of Man is lord of the Sabbath."

Jesus Christ who is both God and man is therefore lord of the Sabbath (Phil. 2:6; Titus 2:13).

Doing Good on the Sabbath

12:9–10 Then Jesus left that place and entered their synagogue. A man was there who had a withered hand. And they asked Jesus, "Is it lawful to heal on the Sabbath?" so that they could accuse him.

Leaving the corn field Jesus went to their synagogue. In the synagogue was a man whose hand had wasted away, with no muscle or sinew left. Luke informs us that it was his right hand (Luke 6:6). Again the Scribes and Pharisees were seeking to make an accusation against Jesus so they ask if the law allowed someone to heal on the Sabbath day.

12:11 He said to them, "Would not any one of you, if he had one sheep that fell into a pit on the Sabbath, take hold of it and lift it out?

Jesus replied by asking if there was anybody among them who would not rescue their sheep who had fallen into a pit on the Sabbath day. Would they leave it there to suffer until the next day or would they pull it out on the Sabbath? Under the law a Jew had to go to the aid of any of his neighbours' animals that were in trouble, even on the Sabbath day (Deut. 22:4).

12:12–13 How much more valuable is a person than a sheep! So it is lawful to do good on the Sabbath." Then he said to the man, "Stretch out your hand." He stretched it out and it was restored, as healthy as the other.

Jesus makes the point that since people are worth more than animals it is lawful to do good works on the Sabbath. Then turning to the man he tells him to do that which was impossible for him: to stretch out his hand. The man believed Jesus and did so; and his hand was restored just like the other one.

12:14 But the Pharisees went out and plotted against him, as to how they could assassinate him.

The Pharisees proved how right Jesus' words had been about them (v. 7). They could not care less about the man being healed, but began to make plans to kill Jesus.

12:15 Now when Jesus learned of this, he went away from there. Great crowds followed him, and he healed them all.

When Jesus heard of this he left that place and the crowds followed him. It was still the Sabbath day and Jesus continued to heal the people; and they were only too willing to let him, even if it was the Sabbath!

126

The Servant of God

12:16–17 But he sternly warned them not to make him known. This fulfilled what was spoken by Isaiah the prophet:

Jesus warned those whom he healed not to go back to his enemies and tell them what he had done. This was in fulfilment of the words spoken of him by Isaiah the prophet.

12:18 "Here is my servant whom I have chosen, the one I love, in whom I take great delight. I will put my Spirit on him, and he will proclaim justice to the nations

As well as being the Son of God, Jesus Christ is also the servant of God, the chosen one in whom he "is well pleased" (Matt. 3:17). God sent the Holy Spirit on him as he was baptised by John in the River Jordan (Mark 1:10). He shall make known to the nations the truth concerning sin, judgement and the way of salvation.

12:19 He will not quarrel or cry out, nor will anyone hear his voice in the streets.

He will not contend with those who oppose him or call out in the streets.

12:20-21 He will not break a bruised reed or extinguish a smouldering wick, until he brings justice to victory. And in his name the Gentiles will hope."

Jesus will not add to the miseries of those who are battered and bruised from the troubles and difficulties of life (as the Pharisees did with their heavy burden of laws and regulations). Those who have come to the end of their strength and cannot go on any further will not be snuffed out like a candle. Jesus will bring them justice, peace and deliverance through his victorious death on the cross and by his resurrection from the dead (1 Cor. 15:57; 1 John 5:4). His name shall be the hope of all peoples (Rom. 10:13).

A Divided House Cannot Stand

12:22 Then they brought to him a demon-possessed man who was blind and mute. Jesus healed him so that he could speak and see.

They brought to Jesus a man who was possessed by a demon who had made him blind and dumb. Jesus set him free and completely healed him.

12:23 All the crowds were amazed and said, "Could this one be the Son of David?"

The crowds were absolutely amazed by this and asked one another "is this the Son of David, the Messiah?" (Matt. 1:1)

12:24 But when the Pharisees heard this they said, "He does not cast out demons except by the power of Beelzebub, the ruler of demons!"

When the Pharisees heard what he had done they made this most ridiculous and blasphemous statement! They accused Jesus of casting out the demon by the power of the devil—this was blasphemy. It was ludicrous to think that Satan would cast out one of his own demons.

Note: Beelzebub was the title of a heathen deity, to whom the Jews ascribed the sovereignty of the evil spirits; Satan, the prince of the devils (Smith's Bible Dictionary).

12:25 Now when Jesus realized what they were thinking, he said to them, "Every kingdom divided against itself is destroyed, and no town or house divided against itself will stand.

Jesus, knowing what they were thinking, makes a logical statement. If a country is divided by civil war it will end up in ruin. If townspeople or a family fight among themselves then they will break apart.

12:26 So if Satan casts out Satan, he is divided against himself. How then will his kingdom stand?

In the same way, if Satan is fighting against himself then he will bring about his own destruction.

12:27 And if I cast out demons by Beelzebub, by whom do your sons cast them out? For this reason they will be your judges.

If Jesus used the power of Satan to cast out demons then by whose power did the followers of the Pharisees cast them out? So their own followers would be the ones that would condemn them. Apparently—simply going by on the evidence of this statement—some kind of exorcism was not unknown among the Jews.

12:28 But if I cast out demons by the Spirit of God, then the kingdom of God has already overtaken you.

If Jesus was driving out demons by the power of God's Spirit then this served to prove that the kingdom of God had already come (Acts 10:38).

12:29 How else can someone enter a strong man's house and steal his property, unless he first ties up the strong man? Then he can thoroughly plunder the house.

Here is another argument that Jesus gave to prove that he could not be casting out demons by Satan's power. No one can enter a strong man's house unless he first overpowers him and ties him up, and then he can take whatever he wants. It is only by a greater power than Satan that Jesus Christ can overcome the devil and his works; and that is the power of God (Col. 2:15; Heb. 2:14; Rev. 20:10).

12:30 Whoever is not with me is against me, and whoever does not gather with me scatters.

Anyone who is not on Christ's side is opposed to him and anyone who is not working with him to gather in a harvest of souls is sending them to hell. Satan continually opposes Jesus Christ and ever works to takes souls into the lake of fire with him.

Outside the Reach of Forgiveness

12:31 For this reason I tell you, people will be forgiven for every sin and blasphemy, but the blasphemy against the Spirit will not be forgiven.

Here is one of the most difficult teachings in all of scripture. The Pharisees had deliberately and maliciously ascribed the work of Christ to the evil one. Jesus warns them that this is indicative of their unrepentant and obdurate hearts. The works Christ performed were not his own, but were wrought by the Holy Spirit. To compare the Holy Spirit to the devil, or to call the Holy Spirit the devil is such a blasphemy that will never be forgiven. This may well be because the state to which a man must come before he does this is such, that his heart is hardened beyond all remedy. In this sense, many commentators refer to the blasphemy of the Holy Spirit as the rejection of Christ.

It is my opinion that the scribes and Pharisees knew what they were doing. They were ascribing the works of the Holy Spirit to the evil one in order to put people off following Christ. To oppose the Spirit of God in this way is to put oneself outside of the reach of God's salvation and forgiveness, for it is the Holy Spirit who brings us through conviction to repentance and faith in Christ (John 16:8).

12:32 Whoever speaks a word against the Son of Man will be forgiven. But whoever speaks against the Holy Spirit will not be forgiven, either in this age or in the age to come.

Jesus clearly explains his own teaching concerning the blasphemy against the Holy Spirit. He defines it as speaking against the Holy Spirit. Only the hardened in heart would do this.

The Bible exhorts Christians to "test the sprits" especially when it comes to supernatural manifestations (1 John 4:1). We must test prophecy, which is a supernatural utterance, because even when a person is genuinely filled and inspired by the Spirit, their gift is only a partial revelation and so will not be perfect (1 Cor. 13:9); it must be judged in the light of God's word (1 Cor. 14:29). So, if we were to make an error in our judgment; if we said this is of God or not, but we were mistaken; that is not what Jesus means by blaspheming the Holy Spirit; for although blasphemy involves the mouth, it also involves the whole personality being opposed to God as Jesus goes on to show. We may sadly deduce from Jesus words that there are some people that will never be saved, like those Pharisees who, even in the face of the influence and gracious power of the Holy Spirit, continued to harden and reject him and even speak evil of him.

As a pastor I have sometimes met believers who are worried about whether or not they have blasphemed the Holy Spirit. My reply is simply this: if you are concerned about it, then you certainly have not done so. For a person who is as hardened as these Pharisees would not care about being forgiven, but would curse Christ all the way down to hell.

The Tree and its Fruit

12:33 "Make a tree good and its fruit will be good, or make a tree bad and its fruit will be bad, for a tree is known by its fruit.

If a tree is healthy, it will produce good fruit. But if it is diseased, the fruit will also be diseased. The nature of the tree is discerned by the fruit it produces. The Pharisees, though outwardly religious, had revealed the true state of their hearts by their words of opposition to Christ and the work of the Holy Spirit.

12:34 Offspring of vipers! How are you able to say anything good, since you are evil? For the mouth speaks from what fills the heart.

It is because of the corruption in the human heart, which the scripture declares to be absolute, (e.g. Rom. 7:18) that the Pharisees were unable to speak of what was good. Jesus describes them as a brood of snakes, in other words children of the devil (Rev. 12:9), those whose nature was perverse and sinful. We are by nature alienated from God, and children of wrath (Eph. 2:3), and our mouths are simply organs through which we express the sinfulness of our souls. A man may claim to speak and teach for God, but unless his heart has first been cleansed by the new birth—unless he has received a new nature—he cannot teach correctly about God, for he cannot speak the truth which he does not know (John 3:3).

12:35 The good person brings good things out of his good treasury, and the evil person brings evil things out of his evil treasury.

Since only God is good (Mark 10:18), only those who share the divine nature (1 Peter 1:3) may be called good people. They are born again of his Spirit and he resides in them. It is out of this good treasure that they are able to speak the pure words of truth. If a man is not born of the Spirit then he does not have the new nature of Christ within him, but remains in the nature of sin. He is so utterly corrupt that he can neither do nor say anything that is pleasing to God (Rom. 8:7–8).

12:36 I tell you that on the Day of Judgment, people will give an account for every worthless word they speak.

All of us are accountable to God for what we say, do and even think. God has kept a record of every word we utter, even casual comments, and will hold us to account for them on the Day of Judgment

(Rev. 20:12). The only hope any sinner has of escape from this judgment is through the Lord Jesus Christ.

12:37 For by your words you will be justified, and by your words you will be condemned."

The Pharisees sealed their own condemnation by their words which were hostile to Christ.

The means of God's justification is also through speech. For if we believe in our hearts that God has raised Jesus from the dead, and confess with your mouth that Jesus is Lord, we will be saved (Rom. 10:9). Jesus said, "If any man confess me before men, I will confess him before the angels of God" (Luke 12:8); for "it is with the mouth that confession is made unto salvation" (Rom. 10:10).

A Generation without Excuse

12:38–39 Then some of the experts in the law along with some Pharisees answered him, "Teacher, we want to see a sign from you." But he answered them, "An evil and adulterous generation asks for a sign, but no sign will be given to it except the sign of the prophet Jonah.

After all the miracles he had just performed, which they had openly criticised and rejected, the petulant Pharisees demanded a sign, rejecting Christ's authority to say these words. It is as if they are saying "we won't listen to you unless you do a sign". That is why he describes them as evil and unfaithful to God (adulterous).

The only sign that would be offered to the Pharisees is the same sign that is offered to everyone in the world: the resurrection of Christ, which Jesus expounds from the life of Jonah.

12:40 For just as Jonah was in the belly of the huge fish for three days and three nights, so the Son of Man will be in the heart of the earth for three days and three nights.

Just as Jonah spent three days and three nights in the whale's belly, so the Lord Jesus would be in the heart of the earth for three days and three nights. His body of course, would be in the grave but his soul was in the "heart of the earth", or paradise (Luke 23:43), where he descended to announce his victory to those faithful who were waiting for his coming there (Eph. 4:9).

12:41 The people of Nineveh will stand up at the judgment with this generation and condemn it, because they repented when Jonah preached to them -- and now, something greater than Jonah is here!

Jesus uses the ministry of Jonah to reveal to the Pharisees their condemnation. The people of Nineveh repented when they heard Jonah's preaching, but the Pharisees did not repent even when they heard the preaching of one far greater than Jonah. At the Day of Judgment, the repentance of the one group will condemn the unrepentance of the other, for it shows that although both groups were given the opportunity to repent, one accepted and one rejected. It is our rejection of Christ which condemns us (John 3:36).

12:42 The queen of the South will rise up at the judgment with this generation and condemn it, because she came from the ends of the earth to hear the wisdom of Solomon -- and now, something greater than Solomon is here!

Similarly, the Queen of Sheba will arise from the dead at the Day of Judgement, and her response to Solomon's wisdom will condemn those who failed to respond to the wisdom of Christ. This queen came a long distance to hear the wisdom of Solomon, but even his wisdom could not compare with that of Christ, who is wisdom personified (1 Cor. 1:24).

12:43 "When an unclean spirit goes out of a person, it passes through waterless places looking for rest but does not find it.

It was Jesus' casting out devils which began this confrontation with the Pharisees (12:22–24). So Jesus teaches them that when a devil is cast out, he is in limbo. He wants rest, a place to inhabit, but is unable to find one. To him, being without a body is like being in a desert (waterless places).

12:44–45 Then it says, 'I will return to the home I left.' When it returns, it finds the house empty, swept clean, and put in order. Then it goes and brings with it seven other spirits more evil than itself, and they go in and live there, so the last state of that person is worse than the first. It will be that way for this evil generation as well!"

Because the demon wants to inhabit a body, he will seek someone who is open and vulnerable to possession. But not finding any, he returns to the person from whom he had been cast out. Finding him clean and put right, yet *empty* (that is the key word), he re-enters the person.

Jesus cast out many evil spirits by his word, but unless the delivered person later accepted him as Lord and allowed him to take up residence within their souls and bodies, they remained empty and vulnerable to renewed possession. They would revert to what they were before. In fact, it would be worse, for the evil spirit takes seven other spirits with him to possess such a person, so that in the end they are in a worse state than before.

This is what would happen to the people who had been so blessed by Christ's ministry but who rejected him as Saviour and Lord. It can also be observed in the life of the backslider. To harden your heart to Jesus Christ and turn away from him is to open the door to all kinds of evil influence and to the oppression of the devil.

Jesus' Mother and Brothers

12:46–50 While Jesus was still speaking to the crowds, his mother and brothers came and stood outside, asking to speak to him. Someone told him, "Look, your mother and your brothers are standing outside wanting to speak to you." To the one who had said this, Jesus replied, "Who is my mother and who are my brothers?" And pointing toward his disciples he said, "Here are my mother and my brothers! For whoever does the will of my Father in heaven is my brother and sister and mother."

Christ recognised that he had a spiritual relationship with his followers, and indicated that this was far greater than the natural tie which binds families together (2 Cor. 5:16). Family ties are important, and the Christian is commanded to love and honour his or her parents; parents are to provide for their children and so on.

But Jesus Christ is the Son of God, an eternal and spiritual being, who brings us into an eternal and spiritual relationship with God. We become sons of God through faith in Jesus Christ (Gal. 3:26). There is no gender in the kingdom (Gal. 3:28), which is why at one and the same time we can be his brother and sister and mother. We are all these things. In other words we have a family relationship with Jesus greater than any that has previously been known on earth. This relationship has been brought about by new birth, and is revealed through the love and obedience shown by his followers; those who do "the will of [his] father in heaven" (John 14:15).

It is worthy of mention that Jesus gives no special position to Mary as his mother, but rather gives all believers an equal status to Mary in this heavenly kingdom. Indeed, at this point in the gospel, Mary is left out altogether, for she has not yet come to the full understanding of faith which we see she has in Acts: and even then her status is of someone who is with the eleven and "together with the women" (Acts 1:14).

Discussion Questions for Chapter 12

1. vv. 1–8. Explain why Jesus is the lord of the Sabbath.

2. vv. 18–21. In Matthew, Jesus' ministry is mainly to Israel. How does the prophecy of Isaiah point forward to a wider ministry?

3. vv. 22–30. Explain why Satan cannot cast out Satan.

4. vv. 38–45. In what way did the people of Nineveh condemn the people of Jesus' time?

5. vv. 46–50. How does someone become part of Jesus' family?

You will find suggested answers to these questions on pages 306–323.

Matthew Chapter 13

Sowing the Word of God

13:1–2 On that day after Jesus went out of the house, he sat by the lake. And such a large crowd gathered around him that he got into a boat to sit while the whole crowd stood on the shore.

On the same day that Jesus had been preaching and working miracles he left the house and went to sit by the lake of Galilee. A great multitude of people gathered together so he got into Simon Peter's boat (Luke 5:3) while the crowd stood on the shore.

The Parable of the Sower

13:3 He told them many things in parables, saying: "Listen! A sower went out to sow.

He began to tell them many truths concerning the kingdom of heaven using parables. The common definition of a parable is an earthly story with a heavenly meaning. It would be more correct however to say that it is using an everyday activity or item to illustrate a spiritual truth. Jesus begins with the parable of the sower. He makes it clear that he wants the full attention of his listeners as he uses the imperative "listen". Before anything can be accomplished the sower has to put his hand to plough and then go out to the field to sow the seed.

13:4 And as he sowed, some seeds fell along the path, and the birds came and devoured them.

The method of sowing was to scatter the seed by hand over the ground. Using this method it was inevitable that some seed would fall where it would not find sufficient soil to grow. The good thing about it was that every inch would be covered with seed. Some of the seed fell on the hard path and became food for the birds.

13:5–6 Other seeds fell on rocky ground where they did not have much soil. They sprang up quickly because the soil was not deep. But when the sun came up, they were scorched, and because they did not have sufficient root, they withered.

Other seeds fell on rocky ground where there was hardly any soil. These began to sprout but because the soil was very thin they could not take root; so when the sun came up they were scorched and died.

13:7 Other seeds fell among the thorns, and they grew up and choked them.

Other seed fell among thorns and grew up together with them until the weeds became too strong and suffocated them.

13:8 But other seeds fell on good soil and produced grain, some a hundred times as much, some sixty, and some thirty.

As the sower was planting his seed in a field that he had already prepared then it follows that most of the seed should have fallen on fertile soil. The result was that some plants produced an abundant crop; some a hundred times as much.

13:9 The one who has ears had better listen!"

Anyone who hears this parable had better pay attention.

An Explanation why Jesus Speaks in Parables
13:10 Then the disciples came to him and said, "Why do you speak to them in parables?"

As soon as they had opportunity, the disciples came to Jesus to ask why he spoke to the people in parables.

13:11 He replied, "You have been given the opportunity to know the secrets of the kingdom of heaven, but they have not.

He replied that he had chosen them so that he could make known to them those things concerning the kingdom of heaven which are hidden from other people.

13:12 For whoever has will be given more, and will have an abundance. But whoever does not have, even what he has will be taken from him.

To those who respond to the spiritual truths they hear, more will be given so that they will have an abundant knowledge of these things. Those who will not listen to Christ cannot receive knowledge of spiritual truth, and so the little they have will be taken away from them. A progressive hardening of heart against the truth is implied.

13:13 For this reason I speak to them in parables: Although they see they do not see, and although they hear they do not hear nor do they understand.

The reason why Jesus spoke to the people in parables was because although they saw him and his miracles, and heard him speak the things of God, they could only come to understand these things through faith in him. Without faith, they could neither see nor hear the truth.

13:14 And concerning them the prophecy of Isaiah is fulfilled that says: You will listen carefully yet will never understand, you will look closely yet will never comprehend.

Jesus' use of parables was in fulfilment of the prophecy of Isaiah, that although the people would listen carefully to what the Christ said, and see the mighty things that he did, they would not understand or recognise what these things meant.

13:15 For the heart of this people has become dull; they are hard of hearing, and they have shut their eyes, so that they would not see with their eyes and hear with their ears and understand with their hearts and turn, and I would heal them.'

This is because their hearts had become hardened to God and therefore they could not hear his word. They had shut their eyes to the truth and put their hands over their ears so that they could not hear. They did not want to understand and believe in their hearts and turn to the Lord; if they did he would forgive their sins (Mark 4:12).

13:16 "But your eyes are blessed because they see, and your ears because they hear.

Blessed are the disciples whose eyes and ears had been opened to see and hear the spiritual truths Christ taught and believe them.

13:17 For I tell you the truth, many prophets and righteous people longed to see what you see but did not see it, and to hear what you hear but did not hear it.

There were many prophets and righteous people who longed to see and hear what the disciples saw and heard; but they did not, even though they prophesied concerning these things (1 Pet. 1:10–12; Heb. 11:39–40).

The Meaning of the Parable

13:18 "So listen to the parable of the sower:

Jesus next explained the meaning of the parable of the sower to his disciples.

13:19 When anyone hears the word about the kingdom and does not understand it, the evil one comes and snatches what was sown in his heart; this is the seed sown along the path.

The seed is the word of God and the sower is, in the first instance, the Lord Jesus Christ; and is later followed by those whom he has commissioned (Mark 16:15). The seed that falls on the hard path are those who hear the word but have no understanding; so the word goes no further than their ears. Like the bird that comes and snatches the seed away so the devil comes and takes the word away from their hearts.

13:20–21 The seed sown on rocky ground is the person who hears the word and immediately receives it with joy. But he has no root in himself and does not endure; when trouble or persecution comes because of the word, immediately he falls away.

The seed that falls on rocky ground represents those emotional hearers who receive the word with great joy and they seem to flourish for a while; but since they have not taken the word deep into their hearts, when trouble comes and they are persecuted for Christ's sake they fall away and follow him no more.

13:22 The seed sown among thorns is the person who hears the word, but worldly cares and the seductiveness of wealth choke the word, so it produces nothing.

The seed that falls among thorns represent the worldly hearers. They receive the word of God but are so tied up with the world that they never become separate from it. They continue to walk in the ways of the world and desire to fill themselves with it until the word of God is crowded out and there is no room for spiritual fruit to grow in them (1 John 2:15, Rom. 12:2).

13:23 But as for the seed sown on good soil, this is the person who hears the word and understands. He bears fruit, yielding a hundred, sixty, or thirty times what was sown."

The seed that falls on good ground stands for those with a prepared and receptive heart. Such people receive the word in the very depths of their soul where it abides and matures. They grow in the grace and knowledge of the Lord and the fruit of the Spirit abounds in them. This parable is generally applied to the sowing of the gospel message and to the unsaved but it is equally applicable to believers and how deeply they respond to the word of God. Jesus required the attention of his hearers, in verse three he said "listen" and having heard the explanation of the parable we are now responsible for how receive and respond to it.

The True and False Growing Together

13:24 He presented them with another parable: "The kingdom of heaven is like a person who sowed good seed in his field.

Jesus told a second parable concerning the kingdom of heaven which has a similar setting. A man once more went out to sow good seed in his field. Once again the seed is the Word of God and the sower is the Lord Jesus Christ.

13:25 But while everyone was sleeping, an enemy came and sowed weeds among the wheat and went away.

During the night when everyone was asleep his enemy came and sowed weeds among his wheat and stole away. This enemy is the devil whose greatest delight is to sow seeds of evil. Notice this was done in the dark when no one was on guard. This is how the devil always works, false prophets slipping into the church unnoticed (Gal. 2:4; 2 Tim. 4:3–5; 2 Pet. 2:1).

13:26 When the plants sprouted and bore grain, then the weeds also appeared.

These weed seeds grew up amongst the good seed. The weeds stand for false prophets and bogus believers within the church.

13:27 So the slaves of the owner came and said to him, 'Sir, didn't you sow good seed in your field? Then where did the weeds come from?'

When the servants of the owner saw the weeds growing among the wheat they asked him if he was sure that he had only sown good seed in his field. If so, then where did all the weeds come from? God is the owner of the field and he can only sow good seed (James 1:17).

13:28 He said, 'An enemy has done this.' So the slaves replied, 'Do you want us to go and gather them?'

The owner knew who had done this work and informs his servants that it was an enemy. So they ask him if he wanted them to pull up and burn the weeds, but there was no need. Jesus Christ is not deceived by anyone; he knows those who are his.

13:29 But he said, 'No, since in gathering the weeds you may uproot the wheat with them.

The owner tells his servants to leave the weeds where they are in case they disturb and pull up the wheat with them. Jesus Christ's greatest concern is for the care of his own, those whom he has redeemed, and he will not suffer anything to be done that will cause them harm in their faith.

13:30 Let both grow together until the harvest. At harvest time I will tell the reapers, "First collect the weeds and tie them in bundles to be burned, but then gather the wheat into my barn."

The true and false are to grow up together until the harvest is ready to be gathered in. Then the weeds are to be collected tied in bundles and thrown in the fire to be burned. After this the wheat can be safely gathered in (Rev. 14:15–16). The "harvest" is the end of the age; the Day of Judgement when the devil, his demons and those who worship him shall be cast into the lake of fire (Rev. 19:20; 2 Pet. 2:9; 2 Pet. 3:7).

The Parable of the Mustard Seed

13:31–32 He gave them another parable: "The kingdom of heaven is like a mustard seed that a man took and sowed in his field. It is the smallest of all the seeds, but when it has grown it is the greatest garden plant and becomes a tree, so that the wild birds come and nest in its branches."

The growth of the mustard seed is an amazing phenomenon of nature. The smallest of all the garden seeds, it grows into a tree, so that the birds may rest in its branches. In the same way, the kingdom of heaven appears to be small, in as much as it is invisible to the eye, yet as it grows and develops each individual life into the likeness of Christ, until his life can be clearly seen. In fact, for "kingdom of heaven", we could substitute "Christ", and realize that his presence, though invisible to the eye, is made tangible by its effects on the life of anyone in whom the life of Christ is allowed to grow.

13:33 He told them another parable: "The kingdom of heaven is like yeast that a woman took and mixed with three measures of flour until all the dough had risen."

Just as a woman would add yeast to dough, so that it permeates the whole bread, so the life of Christ can fill and saturate the whole life, so that the likeness of Christ is formed within the soul. This truth, applied to the individual, may also be applied to the church as a whole.

Is Christ lord of your whole life? He is certain to graciously move on all believers until we yield our whole lives to him, just like yeast is meant to fill the whole bread.

13:34 Jesus spoke all these things in parables to the crowds; he did not speak to them without a parable.

Perhaps it was because of the profundity of his teaching concerning spiritual matters that Christ was compelled to use parables to teach the people. Without the parables, the people could not understand.

It is of note that in the epistles the teachings of Christ are expounded in clear, straightforward terms; no longer veiled by parables.

13:35 This fulfilled what was spoken by the prophet: "I will open my mouth in parables, I will announce what has been hidden from the foundation of the world."

This practice of Jesus confirmed him again to be the chosen one, the Messiah, because it was in fulfilment of the scripture. Truths which had been hidden since the foundation of the world were now made known through him (Eph. 3:8–9). Christ is the fulfilment of all God's plans and purposes for humankind.

Explanation of the Parable of the Weeds

13:36 Then he left the crowds and went into the house. And his disciples came to him saying, "Explain to us the parable of the weeds in the field."

The source of all wisdom and knowledge is Christ (Col. 2:3). If we would know the meaning of his word, we could do no better than to ask him directly, as his disciples did. On this occasion the disciples specifically wanted to know the meaning of the parable of the weeds. It is always good to inquire and seek God in prayer for understanding of his word. You will notice from Jesus' reply the simplicity of meaning which he attaches to his own parable. This should warn us never to look for elaborate hidden meanings in the parables of Christ—meanings which Christ never meant them to convey.

13:37–38 He answered, "The one who sowed the good seed is the Son of Man. The weeds are the people of the evil one,

Christ is the only one who produces *good seed;* those who are saved by his grace and made children of God. The field is the world and the good seed are the children of the kingdom. Believers are chosen out of the world to become part of God's spiritual and eternal kingdom. Those who refuse to accept and believe the gospel are those who, blinded by the devil, refuse to accept Christ as their Saviour. Those who reject Christ are described as the children of the devil, for they listen to him and, albeit unwittingly, do his will (John 8:44).

13:39–43 and the enemy who sows them is the devil. The harvest is the end of the age, and the reapers are angels. As the weeds are collected and burned with fire, so it will be at the end of the age. The Son of Man will send his angels, and they will gather from his kingdom everything that causes sin as well as all lawbreakers. They will throw them into the fiery furnace, where there will be weeping and gnashing of teeth. Then the righteous will shine like the sun in the kingdom of their Father. The one who has ears had better listen!

At the end of the world, those who have constituted themselves to be the devil's children and enemies of God by rejecting Jesus Christ will be seized by the angels and cast into the fiery furnace of everlasting punishment, "Where there will be weeping and gnashing of teeth." That is, their punishment will never cease; they will not be annihilated, but consciously tormented forever in hell.

After the final Judgment comes a new heaven and a new earth, wherein only righteousness dwells; sin, and those who practiced lawlessness having been removed.

The Parable of the Treasure in a Field

13:44–46 "The kingdom of heaven is like a treasure, hidden in a field, that a person found and hid. Then because of joy he went and sold all that he had and bought that field. Again, the kingdom of heaven is like a merchant searching for fine pearls. Again, the kingdom of heaven is like a merchant searching for fine pearls. When he found a pearl of great value, he went out and sold everything he had and bought it.

These two famous parables have two possible meanings. Both convey the truth, but from different aspects. Firstly, the merchant and the person finding treasure can be likened to Christ, who came into this world, not to find pearls, but souls of men. He considered the church to be such a prize worth gaining that he emptied himself of all his privileges, and humbled himself to the death of the cross, giving all he had to purchase the church. Because of joy—it was for the joy set before him that Christ endured the cross, despising the shame, and sat down at the right hand of God (Heb. 12:2). Despising the shame means he thought nothing of it in comparison to the joy of gaining souls—bringing many sons to glory.

It is of note, that if the field here is the world, then Christ has *potentially* paid the price to redeem all men; in other words he has died for the sin of the world. Even so, only when people accept what he did for them does the *potential* become authentic in their experience.

On the other hand, one might think of the merchant as any man or woman who realizes the great worth of the treasures contained in the gospel—forgiveness, redemption and salvation—and is willing to part with all things and follow Christ in order to gain such blessings. It is better to lose all and to gain Christ (Phil. 3:8) than to gain all and, without Christ, lose one's own soul (Matt. 16:26).

The Parable of the Fishing Net

13:47–50 Again, the kingdom of heaven is like a net that was cast into the sea that caught all kinds of fish. When it was full, they pulled it ashore, sat down, and put the good fish into containers and threw the bad away. It will be this way at the end of the age. Angels will come and separate the evil from the righteous and throw them into the fiery furnace, where there will be weeping and gnashing of teeth.

This parable is almost a repeat of the parable of the weeds in the field. The gospel is proclaimed to all people; yet only those who believe and receive Christ will obtain eternal life. These are the *good fish*. Those who reject Christ as Saviour are the *bad fish* that are thrown into the lake of fire. The fact that it is the angels who do the separation is significant because it shows that the final judgment takes place outside of the sphere of this world. It will be at the end of time, when earth and heaven have passed away, that this judgment will take place. One might imagine the angels as heaven's police officers, ensuring with inevitable justice that none will get away or escape (Heb. 2:3).

13:51–52 Have you understood all these things?" They replied, "Yes." Then he said to them, "Therefore every expert in the law who has been trained for the kingdom of heaven is like the owner of a house who brings out of his treasure what is new and old."

The disciples, simple though they were, as a result of Jesus' teaching and explanation, understood these parables perfectly.

Jesus declared that if people understand the word of God in the Old Testament, and in the new, then they would be able to draw lessons about God's truth from each. The lessons of the Old Testament still stand: the lessons of the new have not replaced them, but revealed them much more fully.

13:53–58 Now when Jesus finished these parables, he moved on from there. Then he came to his hometown and began to teach the people in their synagogue. They were astonished and said, "Where did this man get such wisdom and miraculous powers? Isn't this the carpenter's son? Isn't his mother named Mary? And aren't his brothers James, Joseph, Simon, and Judas? And aren't all his sisters here with us? Where did he get all this?" And so they took offense at him. But Jesus said to them, "A prophet is not without honor except in his hometown and in his own house." And he did not do many miracles there because of their unbelief.

The crowds on the other hand, although deeply challenged (astonished) by his words, refused to submit to Jesus' authority, choosing instead to focus on the lowly origins from which he came. Jesus recognised this, and was unable to perform many great works among them as a consequence of their unbelief.

Discussion Questions for Chapter 13

1. vv. 10–17. Why do you think Jesus taught in parables?

2. vv. 3–23. In the parable of the sower, describe the significance of each type of soil.

3. vv. 10–17. Why did the people fail to understand the parables?

4. vv. 24–32; 36–43. What do the seeds of the evil one represent?

5. vv. 47–50. Contrast the good and bad fish in Jesus parable. Who do they represent?

You will find suggested answers to these questions on pages 306–323.

Matthew Chapter 14

Recap of John the Baptist's Death

14:1–2 At that time Herod the tetrarch heard reports about Jesus, and he said to his servants, "This is John the Baptist. He has been raised from the dead! And because of this, miraculous powers are at work in him."

This Herod Antipas was the son of Herod the Great who had been king at the time of the birth of Jesus. When he heard about all the miracles that Jesus was doing his reason, guided by a guilty conscience, could only conclude that John the Baptist, whom he had beheaded, was raised from the dead.

14:3–4 For Herod had arrested John, bound him, and put him in prison on account of Herodias, his brother Philip's wife, because John had repeatedly told him, "It is not lawful for you to have her."

Herod had divorced his first wife and married his brother Phillip's wife Herodias. Since she was daughter of Aristobulus, another son of Herod the Great, Herodias was in fact a niece to them both. John the Baptist had repeatedly told Herod that it was against the Law of God for him to marry her (Lev. 18:16) and so Herod, being angry, had John imprisoned.

14:5 Although Herod wanted to kill John, he feared the crowd because they accepted John as a prophet.

Herod would not have hesitated to kill John but he feared the people who believed John to be a prophet of God.

14:6–7 But on Herod's birthday, the daughter of Herodias danced before them and pleased Herod, so much that he promised with an oath to give her whatever she asked.

However, the daughter of Herodias danced before Herod at his birthday party and she pleased him to such an intoxicating extent that he promised on oath to give her whatever she asked of him.

14:8 Instructed by her mother, she said, "Give me the head of John the Baptist here on a platter."

Matthew and Mark both tell us that she immediately went to her mother for advice about what she should ask for (Mark 6:24). This would suggest that the whole thing was planned by Herodias before the party began. Herodias hated John and was determined that he should die, so told her daughter to ask for the head of John the Baptist on a plate.

14:9 Although it grieved the king, because of his oath and the dinner guests he commanded it to be given.

Although Herod had wanted John killed in the first place, he now regretted his promise; yet because he had made it before all his guests and did not want to lose face he commanded it to be done.

14:10–11 So he sent and had John beheaded in the prison. His head was brought on a platter and given to the girl, and she brought it to her mother.

This was immediately done in the prison and John's head was brought and given to the girl, who in turn gave it to her mother.

14:12 Then John's disciples came and took the body and buried it and went and told Jesus.

John's disciples would have sought permission from Herod to come and take his body away. Having buried it, they went to inform Jesus.

14:13 Now when Jesus heard this he went away from there privately in a boat to an isolated place. But when the crowd heard about it, they followed him on foot from the towns.

In hearing about the death of his cousin, Jesus went by boat across the Sea of Galilee to a remote area, not through fear, but in order to have time to himself. But the crowd heard where he had gone and followed him by foot around the shore of the sea.

Feeding More Than 5000

14:14 As he got out he saw the large crowd, and he had compassion on them and healed their sick.

As he got out of the boat, Jesus met with the large crowd and moved with compassion towards them he healed all those who were sick.

14:15 When evening arrived, his disciples came to him saying, "This is an isolated place and the hour is already late. Send the crowds away so that they can go into the villages and buy food for themselves."

When evening arrived his disciples came to Jesus, calling attention to the fact that they were in an isolated place and it was already late. As they had come without food, they asked Jesus to send the people away so that they could go to the nearby villages to find food for themselves.

14:16–17 But he replied, "They don't need to go. You give them something to eat." They said to him, "We have here only five loaves and two fish."

Jesus astounded his disciples by telling them that there was no need for the people to go away; instead, they should give the people something to eat. This seemed all the more incredible when it was discovered that they only had five loaves of bread and two fish between them.

14:18–19 "Bring them here to me," he replied. Then he instructed the crowds to sit down on the grass. He took the five loaves and two fish, and looking up to heaven he gave thanks and broke the loaves. He gave them to the disciples, who in turn gave them to the crowds.

Jesus asked his disciples to bring him the loaves and fish and then instructed the people to sit down on the grass. Jesus took the food in his hands, looked up to heaven and gave thanks, blessing the food. He then gave the food to his disciples who began to distribute it to the people.

14:20 They all ate and were satisfied, and they picked up the broken pieces left over, twelve baskets full.

They all ate as much as they wanted and the disciples gathered the fragments left over—enough to fill twelve baskets (one for each disciple).

14:21 Not counting women and children, there were about five thousand men who ate.

Without counting the women and children around five thousand men had been fed by these five loaves and two fish and there was still plenty left over for the disciples.

Peter's Faith Tested

14:22 Immediately Jesus made the disciples get into the boat and go ahead of him to the other side, while he dispersed the crowds.

As soon as the fragments were gathered up Jesus made his disciples get into the boat and go before him to the other side of the lake while he sent the crowds away.

14:23 And after he sent the crowds away, he went up the mountain by himself to pray. When evening came, he was there alone.

We remember that in verse 13 Jesus had intended to go to a quiet place by himself but that the crowds had followed him. Now, having sent them and his disciples away, he goes up to the mountain alone to pray; and while he was there darkness fell.

14:24 Meanwhile the boat, already far from land, was taking a beating from the waves because the wind was against it.

While Jesus was on the mountain the disciples (in the boat) had gone a long way from land and were in difficulty as the wind became very strong and the waves very high.

14:25 As the night was ending, Jesus came to them walking on the sea.

Somewhere between the hours of three and six in the early morning (in nautical terms, the fourth watch), Jesus came to the disciples walking on the water. Remember that this was not a calm sea.

14:26 When the disciples saw him walking on the water they were terrified and said, "It's a ghost!" and cried out with fear.

When the disciples saw him walking on the water towards them they were terrified, believing him to be a ghost, and cried out with fear.

14:27 But immediately Jesus spoke to them: "Have courage! It is I. Do not be afraid."

When Jesus heard their cry he called out to tell them not to be afraid. "Be of good courage" he said, for he was with them; just as he is always with us in times of difficulty.

14:28 Peter said to him, "Lord, if it is you, order me to come to you on the water."

Peter, always the impetuous one, called out to Jesus: "Lord if it is really you command me to come to you walking on the water".

14:29 So he said, "Come." Peter got out of the boat, walked on the water, and came toward Jesus.

Jesus bids Peter to come to him; so getting out of the boat Peter began to walk on the water towards Jesus.

14:30 But when he saw the strong wind he became afraid. And starting to sink, he cried out, "Lord, save me!"

The wind was still blowing powerfully and the waves were still high, causing Peter to take his eyes off Jesus and look at his surroundings. As he took his eyes off Jesus his faith began to sink, and so did he, into the water. He immediately called on the Lord to save him. The lesson about keeping our eyes on Jesus was not lost on the early Christians (Heb. 12:2; Titus 2:13).

14:31 Immediately Jesus reached out his hand and caught him, saying to him, "You of little faith, why did you doubt?"

At the same time Jesus reached out his hand and caught hold of Peter, chiding his little faith and asking why he doubted (James 1:6). We might find this remarkable, considering that Peter had for a time walked on water, that Jesus regarded his faith as small.

14:32 When they went up into the boat, the wind ceased.

The moment that Jesus and Peter got into the boat the wind ceased.

14:33 Then those who were in the boat worshiped him, saying, "Truly you are the Son of God."

When the disciples saw that the wind immediately ceased the moment Jesus entered the boat they worshiped him, acknowledging him as the Son of God.

A Touch from Jesus

14:34 After they had crossed over, they came to land at Gennesaret.

Having crossed the Sea of Galilee they came safely to the region of Gennesaret.

14:35–36 When the people there recognized him, they sent word into all the surrounding area, and they brought all their sick to him. They begged him if they could only touch the edge of his cloak, and all who touched it were healed.

When the people there recognized that it was Jesus they sent word of his arrival right throughout the area, and all the people brought their sick to him. All who touched him (even those who barely managed to touch his clothes) were immediately healed.

Discussion Questions for Chapter 14

1. vv. 1–5. Why did Herod want to kill John the Baptist?

2. vv. 1–5. What, for a time, stopped Herod carrying out his wish to kill John?

3. vv. 12–13 & 22–23. What might we infer from these verses about Jesus' reaction to John's death?

4. vv. 14–21. What do you think was significant about Christ's challenge to his disciples "*you* give them something to eat"?

5. vv. 22–33. How do you think it was possible for Peter to walk on the water as Jesus did?

You will find suggested answers to these questions on pages 306–323.

Matthew Chapter 15

What Defiles a Man?

15:1–2 Then Pharisees and experts in the law came from Jerusalem to Jesus and said, "Why do your disciples disobey the tradition of the elders? For they don't wash their hands when they eat."

It was neither out of concern for their own spiritual condition, nor for that of the people, but in order to oppose Jesus that the Pharisees came all the way from Jerusalem to Galilee. Their question was designed to discredit Jesus and to stir the people against him, as they accused him of failing to instruct his disciples to obey the various religious regulations which they themselves had laid down; on this occasion, that of ceremonial hand-washing.

15:3 He answered them, "And why do you disobey the commandment of God because of your tradition?

Firstly, Jesus confronts the question of man-made regulations, and only later deals with the matter of ceremonial washing. Any tradition which has at its heart obeying the commandments of God is good, but the Pharisees had substituted religious tradition for the commandments of God.

15:4 For God said, 'Honor your father and mother' and 'Whoever insults his father or mother must be put to death.'

Jesus reminded them of the commandment to honor and respect parents. The word *honor*, as Jesus teaching goes on to clarify, involves the idea of financial help and practical support.

15:5–6 But you say, 'If someone tells his father or mother, "Whatever help you would have received from me is given to God," he does not need to honor his father.' You have nullified the word of God on account of your tradition.

By their teaching, the Pharisees had led people to devote to God, by gifts and offerings, money which was supposed to be used to help elderly parents. The act of giving to God may have seemed very commendable, but not when it involved the breaking of his laws. God did not want any gifts of time or money to be given to him on this basis.

15:7–9 Hypocrites! Isaiah prophesied correctly about you when he said, 'This people honors me with their lips, but their heart is far from me, and they worship me in vain, teaching as doctrines the commandments of men.' "

This substitution of the doctrines of men for the word of God revealed just how far the Pharisees' hearts had strayed from God. They praised God with their mouths, but they failed to obey his commandments. They were hypocrites, play actors, showing men that they were righteous, when in fact they were not willing to humble themselves before God.

15:10–11 Then he called the crowd to him and said, "Listen and understand. What defiles a person is not what goes into the mouth; it is what comes out of the mouth that defiles a person."

Jesus now returns to the question of ceremonial washing, and his answer in fact deals with every external religious practice. Later, he explained his comments more fully to his disciples. Nothing that enters a person's mouth can cause him to be unclean in the presence of God. What we eat does not bring us to God, what we do not eat does not bring us to God. Washing our hands before we eat may well be good for the prevention of disease, but it has no impact whatever on our relationship with God. It is what comes from within the heart, and is revealed through his mouth, that affects our relationship to God.

False Teachers

15:12–14 Then the disciples came to him and said, "Do you know that when the Pharisees heard this saying they were offended?" And he replied, "Every plant that my heavenly Father did not plant will be uprooted. Leave them! They are blind guides. If someone who is blind leads another who is blind, both will fall into a pit."

Jesus' disciples saw that the Pharisees were offended by his censure of their artificial religion. But Jesus is neither sorry nor apologetic. "Every plant which my heavenly father did not plant will be uprooted"; if the Pharisees would repent and turn to God in faith, then they would be born again, and become plants of his planting. But since they are not, they are like the weeds Jesus spoke of in his earlier parable, which are to be burned (Matt. 13:40–42).

In saying this Jesus completely rejects all forms of false religion as having no association with God. Those who are wilfully blind cannot be persuaded, which is why Jesus says "leave them". If Christ's words offend them, what good can our words accomplish? They are blind guides, for although they teach others the way of God, they are ignorant of that way themselves, and so can only teach error. The result of not following Christ is to fall into the pit of everlasting destruction which awaits all unbelievers (John 3:36).

15:15–16 But Peter said to him, "Explain this parable to us." Jesus said, "Even after all this, are you still so foolish?

The fact that Peter requires an explanation of Christ's teaching is disappointing to Jesus. The word foolish can be translated dull, unable to perceive and take in spiritual truth, when he should have done so. Didn't they understand by now? Peter mistakenly thought that this straight forward teaching was a parable.

15:17 Don't you understand that whatever goes into the mouth enters the stomach and then passes out into the sewer?

Whatever food we eat is digested in the body, the nutrients used and the waste expelled. The food we eat has absolutely no impact on our spiritual lives.

15:18–19 But the things that come out of the mouth come from the heart, and these things defile a person. For out of the heart come evil ideas, murder, adultery, sexual immorality, theft, false testimony, slander.

But what is revealed by a man's words to be in his heart are those sinful things which defile the man, and make him unclean, a sinner in the sight of God.

These are the evil imagination of the heart, the hatred which leads to murder, the lust which leads to sexual immorality and adultery, the greed which leads to theft, the crookedness which leads to telling lies and the envy and spite which lead to slander.

15:20 These are the things that defile a person; it is not eating with unwashed hands that defiles a person."

These are the things which defile the life, not whether or not we have washed our hands, or taken part in any other religious observance, including those ordinances enjoined by the Lord himself. For if our hearts are not right with God, even the observance of the outward signs of baptism or receiving communion will be of no benefit to us.

An Object Lesson in Faith

15:21–22 After going out from there, Jesus went to the region of Tyre and Sidon. A Canaanite woman from that area came and cried out, "Have mercy on me, Lord, Son of David! My daughter is horribly demon-possessed!"

In foreign parts, a foreign woman came to ask Jesus to perform a miracle by casting a demon out of her daughter. She recognized his power and ability to do such miracles, and that he had been invested with this authority by God himself, for she called him Lord and Son of David (Christ).

15:23 But he did not answer her a word. Then his disciples came and begged him, "Send her away, because she keeps on crying out after us."

In order to teach an object lesson in faith, Jesus initially does not reply. Notice how the woman is not at all deterred, but continues to call out after him in the same way. The disciples become uncomfortable. If you're ignoring her Lord, best send her away. Tell her to stop.

15:24–25 So he answered, "I was sent only to the lost sheep of the house of Israel." But she came and bowed down before him and said, "Lord, help me!"

But Jesus had no intention of deterring the woman's faith. He explains to her that his present mission was for Jews only, not Gentiles. But this did not deter the woman either, and being confident of Jesus' ability and willingness, she persisted with her request.

15:26 "It is not right to take the children's bread and throw it to the dogs," he said.

One might have thought this final rebuff would be sufficient to stop anyone from persisting. If what was given to the children of Israel was for them alone, it should not be given to foreigners, who were like dogs.

15:27 "Yes, Lord," she replied, "but even the dogs eat the crumbs that fall from their masters' table."

The woman wins the victory, for her faith will not be deterred by such arguments. What if she were not a Jew, but a dog, even dogs take a share in what is being given to the family. There is bound to be something in this for me, she decides.

15:28 Then Jesus answered her, "Woman, your faith is great! Let what you want be done for you." And her daughter was healed from that hour.

Jesus had achieved his goal of producing in this woman a faith which would not be deterred. She shows us how to get something from Jesus. Jesus gladly granted her request, and the demon immediately left her daughter permanently. Later, Christ's mission was extended as he sent his disciples to the entire world, to every people group. If this woman got what she wanted when the time was not right, how much easier it should be now that the time is right to get what we need from Jesus. Yet to receive we must follow the same example of faith.

An Object Lesson in Unbelief

15:29–31 When he left there, Jesus went along the Sea of Galilee. Then he went up a mountain, where he sat down. Then large crowds came to him bringing with them the lame, blind, crippled, mute, and many others. They laid them at his feet, and he healed them. As a result, the crowd was amazed when they saw the mute speaking, the crippled healthy, the lame walking, and the blind seeing, and they praised the God of Israel.

Jesus, as his custom was, went up the mountain in order to sit and teach the crowds of people the word of God. Yet as they thronged to him for healing he did not disappoint them, for they were all healed of various diseases. The crowd were astonished to see the results of miraculous healing, and gave glory to God.

15:32 Then Jesus called the disciples and said, "I have compassion on the crowd, because they have already been here with me three days and they have nothing to eat. I don't want to send them away hungry since they may faint on the way."

It was not long since the feeding of the five thousand. Jesus had miraculously healed everyone present; yet notice how he again tests his disciples' faith. Once more Jesus wants to feed the multitudes, since they had remained to hear his word and had no food left. Christ was concerned lest they fainted on the way home. We should always keep in mind that Christ is concerned for our physical condition, and adopts a very common sense approach to keeping our bodies healthy. The people needed to eat.

15:33–39 The disciples said to him, "Where can we get enough bread in this desolate place to satisfy so great a crowd?" Jesus said to them, "How many loaves do you have?" They replied, "Seven — and a few small fish." After instructing the crowd to sit down on the ground, he took the seven loaves and the fish, and after giving thanks, he broke them and began giving them to the disciples, who then gave them to the crowds. They all ate and were satisfied, and they picked up the broken pieces left over, seven baskets full. Not counting children and women, there were four thousand men who ate. After sending away the crowd, he got into the boat and went to the region of Magadan.

But the disciples still had not got the point. Although they had already witnessed the feeding of the five thousand, they failed to trust Jesus for the present need, and began looking at their own resources, concluding that it was impossible. Their unbelief, of course, did not hinder the Lord Jesus Christ from doing what he had determined to do—a repeat of his earlier miracle; only this time with seven baskets left over. And as before, Jesus dismissed the crowd before leaving by boat for Magdala.

Discussion Questions for Chapter 15

1. vv. 1–20. Why are external religious observances not as important as a person's spiritual condition?

2. vv. 4–6. Why did Jesus say it was wrong to devote certain gifts to God?

3. vv. 12–14. By saying "leave them" Jesus apparently instructs his disciples not to debate with false teachers. Why was this?

4. vv. 21–28. What can we learn about faith from Jesus' encounter with the Syro-Phoenecian woman?

5. vv. 29–39. Why do you think the disciples failed to get the point of the feeding of the 5,000?

You will find suggested answers to these questions on pages 306–323.

Matthew Chapter 16

Sign Seeking

16:1 Now when the Pharisees and Sadducees came to test Jesus, they asked him to show them a sign from heaven.

The Pharisees and Sadducees were so opposed to the Lord Jesus Christ that they continually baited him even though they were not really interested in hearing his response. There are those today who will seek to waste our time in the same way. Not content with all the miracles that he had done—which they obviously did not think came from heaven—they had the audacity to ask him for another sign!

16:2–3 He said, "When evening comes you say, 'It will be fair weather, because the sky is red,' and in the morning, 'It will be stormy today, because the sky is red and darkening.' You know how to judge correctly the appearance of the sky, but you cannot evaluate the signs of the times.

We are all familiar with the kind of answer that Jesus gave and have most probably used similar expressions ourselves. The Pharisees knew how to read the signs in the sky concerning the weather. In the United Kingdom we say, "Red sky at night shepherds' delight, red sky in the morning shepherds' warning". But they had so blinded themselves with unbelief that they could not see the fulfilment of the signs predicted in the Old Testament that were happening before their eyes.

16:4 A wicked and adulterous generation asks for a sign, but no sign will be given to it except the sign of Jonah." Then he left them and went away.

Jesus tells them that only those that have evil designs and are unfaithful to God ask for signs. The only sign they would receive is that which was given through the prophet Jonah (Matt. 12:40; Jonah 1:17); that Jesus would die and rise again.

A Lack of Understanding

16:5 When the disciples went to the other side, they forgot to take bread.

As they went on their way in the boat to Magdala the disciples suddenly realised that they had forgotten to bring any food with them.

16:6 "Watch out," Jesus said to them, "beware of the yeast of the Pharisees and Sadducees."

While they were talking about this, Jesus warned them to beware of the yeast of the Pharisees and Sadducees.

16:7 So they began to discuss this among themselves, saying, "It is because we brought no bread."

Because their minds were so full of feeding their stomachs they misunderstood him and thought that he said this because they had forgotten to bring any food.

16:8 When Jesus learned of this, he said, "You who have such little faith! Why are you arguing among yourselves about having no bread?

Jesus knew what they were discussing among themselves and rebuked them for their incredibly small faith; arguing about having no bread and most probably blaming each other for forgetting it.

16:9–10 Do you still not understand? Don't you remember the five loaves for the five thousand, and how many baskets you took up? Or the seven loaves for the four thousand and how many baskets you took up?

What was so incredible was that they had witnessed the miracle of the feeding of the five thousand and four thousand and yet they could not believe that, if necessary, they could be fed again in the same way. Had they not collected twelve and seven baskets of leftovers?

16:11 How could you not understand that I was not speaking to you about bread? But beware of the yeast of the Pharisees and Sadducees!"

How could they fail to understand that he was not talking about bread to eat but warning them about the corrupt teachings of the Pharisees and Sadducees?

16:12 Then they understood that he had not told them to be on guard against the yeast in bread, but against the teaching of the Pharisees and Sadducees.

At last the penny dropped, and the truth dawned that he was warning them against the deceptive teaching of the religious leaders.

Who Do You Say Jesus Is?

16:13 When Jesus came to the area of Caesarea Philippi, he asked his disciples, "Who do people say that the Son of Man is?"

As they came into the region of Caesarea Philippi Jesus asked his disciples who the people believed him to be.

16:14 They answered, "Some say John the Baptist, others Elijah, and others Jeremiah or one of the prophets."

They told him that some believed that he was John the Baptist, others that he was the prophet Elijah or Jeremiah, still others that he must be one of the other prophets of the past.

16:15 He said to them, "But who do you say that I am?"

Jesus did not ask this for his own benefit but that he may bring them to answer this leading question. They had been with him some time now, had heard his teachings and seen the mighty things he had done so he asks, "Who do you say I am"

16:16 Simon Peter answered, "You are the Christ, the Son of the living God."

It was Simon Peter who was the first to speak up and confess that Jesus was the Christ (Messiah), the Son of the living God.

16:17 And Jesus answered him, "You are blessed, Simon son of Jonah, because flesh and blood did not reveal this to you, but my Father in heaven!

Peter did not receive this revelation by his own ability or from any man but directly from God the Father.

16:18 And I tell you that you are Peter, and on this rock I will build my church, and the gates of Hades will not overpower it.

This verse is often misunderstood and in some Christian circles purposely so. A careful study of the words that Jesus used shows clearly that he did not say that his church would be built upon Peter. The name that Jesus gave to Simon is *petros* meaning a small rock and indeed Peter proved to be a steadfast rock in the early church. The word that Jesus used, however, when he said he would build his church is *petra*, a large rock. Jesus Christ is the rock (1 Cor. 10:4). Peter called Jesus the "living stone" and the "chief corner stone" (1 Peter 2:4–6). Paul speaks of Jesus Christ as the foundation that the church is built on (1 Cor. 3:11; Rom. 9:33). It is because Christ builds his church that the gates of hell shall not overpower it.

16:19 I will give you the keys of the kingdom of heaven. Whatever you bind on earth will have been bound in heaven, and whatever you release on earth will have been released in heaven."

The keys of the kingdom of heaven were to be employed by preaching the gospel in the name of the Lord Jesus Christ; that is, with the authority and power that is invested in him. In his name not only Peter but all who are Christ's can bind things on earth and they shall be bound in heaven and whatever is loosed on earth will be loosed in heaven. In other words the gospel is proclaimed with heavenly authority.

16:20 Then he instructed his disciples not to tell anyone that he was the Christ.

Having said this, Jesus instructed his disciples not to tell anyone at that time that he was the Christ.

God's Thoughts are not Our Thoughts

16:21 From that time on Jesus began to show his disciples that he must go to Jerusalem and suffer many things at the hands of the elders, chief priests, and experts in the law, and be killed, and on the third day be raised.

From this time on Jesus began clearly to show his disciples that his destiny was to go up to Jerusalem and suffer many terrible things at the hands of the religious leaders. He would be killed and on the third day raised from the dead.

16:22 So Peter took him aside and began to rebuke him: "God forbid, Lord! This must not happen to you!"

This statement was beyond Peter's comprehension. "God forbid" means that Peter believed that such things must not be allowed to happen to Jesus! Peter did not know that it was God's plan and purpose that his only begotten Son should die for the sins of the whole world, and that it was for this reason he came into the world (John 12:27).

16:23 But he turned and said to Peter, "Get behind me, Satan! You are a stumbling block to me, because you are not setting your mind on God's interests, but on man's."

Jesus knew that the devil was using Peter to oppose and hinder God's plan. So he rebuked Satan and tells Peter that he is seeing things only from a human point of view and not God's.

The Cost of Discipleship

16:24 Then Jesus said to his disciples, "If anyone wants to become my follower, he must deny himself, take up his cross, and follow me.

Then Jesus said to all his disciples that if anyone wanted to follow him, he must not please himself but deny himself and every day take up his cross, submitting to God's will and being prepared to sacrifice by following the footsteps of Jesus.

16:25 For whoever wants to save his life will lose it, but whoever loses his life for my sake will find it.

Whoever wants to save his own life—that is, live only for himself—will find that he will lose his life. But whoever is prepared to give his life for the sake of Jesus Christ will know abundant and eternal life (1 Cor. 15:30–31; Rom. 8:36–37).

16:26 For what does it benefit a person if he gains the whole world but forfeits his life? Or what can a person give in exchange for his life?

What benefit is it to a person if he or she should have all this world's goods and approval but lose his or her own soul and be destroyed?

16:27–28 For the Son of Man will come with his angels in the glory of his Father, and then he will reward each person according to what he has done. I tell you the truth, there are some standing here who will not experience death before they see the Son of Man coming in his kingdom."

Jesus Christ is going to come again with his angels in all the splendour and glory of his Father. When he comes he will reward all those who have done his will. Moreover, the kingdom of God itself, the good news of salvation, is to be proclaimed to all people before his return; it is that proclamation which those listening to Jesus would live to see and take part in.

Discussion Questions for Chapter 16

1. vv. 1–4. Why do you think the Pharisees were wrong to ask for a sign from Jesus?

2. vv. 5–12. In what way was the teaching of the Pharisees like yeast?

3. vv. 13–20. What might the peoples' opinions about Jesus' identity reveal to us about his perceived character?

4. vv. 13–20. What are the keys of the kingdom?

5. vv. 21–28. Why did Peter find himself rebuked?

You will find suggested answers to these questions on pages 306–323.

Matthew Chapter 17

The Transfiguration of Jesus

17:1 Six days later Jesus took with him Peter, James, and John the brother of James, and led them privately up a high mountain.

Six days after Peter had taken Jesus aside and remonstrated with him for saying that he would suffer and die at Jerusalem, Jesus took Peter, James and John up a high mountain to be alone.

17:2 And he was transfigured before them. His face shone like the sun, and his clothes became white as light.

While they were there Jesus was transfigured before their eyes. The word used in the original is *metamorphoo* from which we derive the English word metamorphosis, meaning to change form. Christ's body remained the same shape and substance—it was still flesh—but at the same time his Divinity as "God in the flesh" was manifested in its glorious form; shining out of his face like the noonday sun and even through the clothes that he wore.

17:3 Then Moses and Elijah also appeared before them, talking with him.

As the disciples stood there in awesome wonder, Moses and Elijah came and talked with Jesus. The Bible clearly tells us that Moses had died (Deut. 34:5), whereas Elijah was taken up into heaven in a chariot of fire (2 Kings 2:11). Nevertheless, they appeared in bodies that were recognizable to the disciples; the dead in Christ are not vapours or ghosts but have a form. The rich man who was in Hades recognized Abraham and Lazarus in Paradise (Luke 16:23). There has been much surmising as to what Moses and Elijah were saying to Jesus; the main consensus being that they spoke concerning his forthcoming death on the cross.

17:4 So Peter said to Jesus, "Lord, it is good for us to be here. If you want, I will make three shelters – one for you, one for Moses, and one for Elijah.

Peter, completely overwhelmed by what he saw and realizing that he, James and John were privileged to be there, wanted to make three booths (shelters); one for each of the glorified forms. This type of shelter would only be temporary, usually made of tree branches. Obviously Peter was not expecting Moses and Elijah to remain.

17:5 While he was still speaking, a bright cloud overshadowed them, and a voice from the cloud said, "This is my one dear Son, in whom I take great delight. Listen to him!"

Even while he was speaking a bright cloud of light enveloped them and the voice of God spoke from it declaring that Jesus was his "dearly beloved Son" in whom he took great delight. If Moses and Elijah represent the law and the prophets, the voice of God was indicating Christ's superiority to these, and hence the superiority of the new covenant—and its mediator—over the old.

17:6–8 When the disciples heard this, they were overwhelmed with fear and threw themselves down with their faces to the ground. But Jesus came and touched them. "Get up," he said. "Do not be afraid." When they looked up, all they saw was Jesus alone.

On hearing this voice the disciples were overwhelmed with fear and threw themselves down with their faces to the ground. Jesus came over and touched them to dispel their fears and told them to get up. When they lifted up their heads it was only Jesus that they saw; Moses and Elijah had gone.

17:9 As they were coming down from the mountain, Jesus commanded them, "Do not tell anyone about the vision until the Son of Man is raised from the dead."

As they were coming down the mountain, Jesus told them that they were not to tell anyone about the vision until after his resurrection. John refers to it at the beginning of his gospel (John 1:14), and Peter in 2 Peter 1:16–18.

17:10 The disciples asked him, "Why then do the experts in the law say that Elijah must come first?"

In the light of what they saw the disciples could not understand why the experts in the scriptures said that Elijah had to come before the Messiah.

17:11–13 He answered, "Elijah does indeed come first and will restore all things. And I tell you that Elijah has already come. Yet they did not recognize him, but did to him whatever they wanted. In the same way, the Son of Man will suffer at their hands." Then the disciples understood that he was speaking to them about John the Baptist.

Jesus affirmed that the experts were quite correct in what they said. Elijah does come before the Messiah to prepare the way before him. But Elijah had already come and was not recognized, nor treated appropriately. In the same way the Son of Man was about to suffer much at their hands.

It was at this time that the disciples realized that Jesus was speaking to them about John the Baptist.

Faith, Prayer and Fasting Brings Deliverance

17:14–15 When they came to the crowd, a man came to him, knelt before him, and said, "Lord, have mercy on my son, because he has seizures and suffers terribly, for he often falls into the fire and into the water.

When they came down from the mountain they were confronted by a man who knelt before Jesus. He cried on the Lord to have pity on his son who suffered terribly from epilepsy and often fell into fire and water.

17:16 I brought him to your disciples, but they were not able to heal him."

This man had originally brought his son to the disciples who remained at the foot of the mountain, but they could not heal him.

17:17 Jesus answered, "You unbelieving and perverse generation! How much longer must I be with you? How much longer must I endure you? Bring him here to me."

It was not to his disciples that Jesus addressed his remarks but to the unbelieving Jews who had twisted the word of God to suit themselves. Barnes says that the word perverse means "that which is twisted or turned from the proper direction; and is often used of the eyes, when one or both are turned from their natural position." Jesus asked how long must he put up with their faithlessness, and then asks the father to bring his son to him.

17:18 Then Jesus rebuked the demon and it came out of him, and the boy was healed from that moment.

In the case of this boy the supposed epilepsy was actually caused by a demon and Jesus commanded it to come out of him; it immediately did and the boy was healed. We must make it clear that not all epilepsy was thought to be caused by demon possession in those days—and nor should it be today.

17:19 Then the disciples came to Jesus privately and said, "Why couldn't we cast it out?"

Afterwards the disciples came to Jesus and asked why it was that they could not cast the demon out. Jesus had previously sent his disciples out on their own and given them power over unclean spirits (Matt. 10:1).

17:20 He told them, "It was because of your little faith. I tell you the truth, if you have faith the size of a mustard seed, you will say to this mountain, 'Move from here to there,' and it will move; nothing will be impossible for you."

On this occasion Jesus told them that they did not have enough faith to cast the spirit out. In fact their faith must have been extremely small, for Jesus said that if they had faith that was only the size of a mustard seed they could "move mountains", meaning that nothing they were called upon to do in Christ's service would be impossible for them.

17:21 However, this kind does not go out except by prayer and fasting."

However the kind of demon that had possessed this boy could not be cast out by faith alone; in this case faith needed to be accompanied by prayer and fasting.

Jesus Foretells His Betrayal, Death and Resurrection

17:22–23 When they gathered together in Galilee, Jesus told them, "The Son of Man is going to be betrayed into the hands of men. They will kill him, and on the third day he will be raised." And they became greatly distressed.

When they came together in Galilee, Jesus told them that he would be betrayed and delivered into the hands of his enemies who would kill him but on the third day he would be raised from the dead. On hearing this, the disciples became deeply grieved.

Paying Taxes

17:24 After they arrived in Capernaum, the collectors of the temple tax came to Peter and said, "Your teacher pays the double drachma tax, doesn't he?"

On arriving in Capernaum those who collected the temple tax came and asked Peter if Jesus paid the half shekel tax (Exodus 30:13–14).

17:25 He said, "Yes." When Peter came into the house, Jesus spoke to him first, "What do you think, Simon? From whom do earthly kings collect tolls or taxes – from their sons or from foreigners?"

Peter answered in the affirmative and went into his house. Before he could say anything Jesus asked from whom did he think the kings of the earth collected taxes from—their own sons or from outsiders?

17:26–27 After he said, "From foreigners," Jesus said to him, "Then the sons are free. But so that we don't offend them, go to the lake and throw out a hook. Take the first fish that comes up, and when you open its mouth, you will find a four drachma coin. Take that and give it to them for me and you.

Peter answered that they collected it from foreigners. Jesus said that if this was so then the sons were free. Strictly speaking, God was not going to tax his own son. Moreover, Jesus may have seen this particular tax as having questionable status; perhaps not directly equivalent of that instituted by Moses. Nevertheless, so as not to cause an offense which might hinder the officials from hearing and responding to the gospel, Jesus miraculously provided for and paid this tax.

Discussion Questions for Chapter 17

1. vv. 1–13. Describe what you think was happening as Jesus was transfigured.

2. vv. 1–13. What might be the significance of Moses and Elijah appearing to talk with Jesus?

3. vv. 14–21. Why do you think prayer and fasting was necessary to deliver the demon possessed boy?

4. vv. 24–27. What should be the Christian's attitude to paying taxes?

5. vv. 24–27. In what way should our honest living have an impact on unbelievers?

You will find suggested answers to these questions on pages 306–323.

Matthew Chapter 18

The Least shall be Greatest

18:1 At that time the disciples came to Jesus saying, "Who is the greatest in the kingdom of heaven?"

At the same time that Jesus had been telling his disciples that he would be betrayed and killed, the disciples came to ask him a question. Mark tell us that the disciples had been arguing about who would be the greatest in the kingdom of heaven (Mark 9:33). So they came to Jesus to ask him who would be greatest.

18:2–3 He called a child, had him stand among them, and said, "I tell you the truth, unless you turn around and become like little children, you will never enter the kingdom of heaven!

To their amazement he called a little child to come to him and stood him in the midst of them; telling them solemnly that unless they were prepared to change and become like young children (having the simplicity and humility of a child, thinking themselves of no importance) they would never even enter the kingdom of heaven (Rom. 12:3, 16; Gal. 6:3).

18:4 Whoever then humbles himself like this little child is the greatest in the kingdom of heaven.

It is those who humble themselves like a child who will be the greatest in the kingdom of heaven.

18:5 And whoever welcomes a child like this in my name welcomes me.

Whoever accepts and receives a child in the Lord's name and for his sake is reckoned as having received Jesus Christ and also his Father who sent him into the world to save sinners (John 13:20).

18:6 "But if anyone causes one of these little ones who believe in me to sin, it would be better for him to have a huge millstone hung around his neck and to be drowned in the open sea.

Having made clear that it is those who are considered least who are the greatest, Jesus gives a warning to anyone who should cause the least of his disciples to fall into sin. Such a person would be better off being thrown into the deepest sea with a huge millstone tied around their neck.

Causing Offense

18:7 Woe to the world because of stumbling blocks! It is necessary that stumbling blocks come, but woe to the person through whom they come.

Great sorrow is in the world because of the offenses of sin and the temptation to sin. Temptations are inevitable but pity the person who does the tempting!

18:8 If your hand or your foot causes you to sin, cut it off and throw it away. It is better for you to enter life crippled or lame than to have two hands or two feet and be thrown into eternal fire.

We must point out here that Jesus is not advocating that a hand or foot should be cut off or an eye plucked out literally. The disciples must have clearly understood this, for they neither practised nor preached mutilation.

So what did Jesus mean? To "offend" in the KJV or sin (above) does not mean to upset or annoy but to be a stumbling block and to cause someone else to sin.

"Cut it off" means to mortify or account as dead, unable to perform a deed. In Romans 6:6 Paul puts it this way "our old self was nailed to the cross with him (Christ) in order that our body which is the instrument of sin, might be made ineffective, and inactive for evil, that we may no longer be the slaves of sin." (Amp. N.T.) How are we able to do this when there are so many temptations that we find very hard to resist? Paul gives us the answer to this "walk in the Spirit, and you shall not fulfil the lusts of the flesh" (Gal. 5:16). So we do not cut off parts of our body but when we are tempted to use them to sin; instead we are to consider them as unable to do such things because they crucified with Christ.

Although it may appear that by taking such action we lose out in this life, in fact we gain for we are able to live the life that Christ has given us in abundant measure: "for me to live is Christ, and to die is gain" (Phil. 1:21).

"Hell" here is Gehenna. There is only one alternative to eternal life and that is the second death where those who have not received Jesus Christ as their Saviour shall go by their own choice; choosing to live a life of sin rather than the life of Christ.

The words "eternal torment" clarify that the second death will not mean annihilation, for the penalty of sin will go on forever (Rev. 14:11).

"If your hand". With the hand we take, hold onto, and do things; Jesus is talking about the times when we are tempted to steal, touch or hold on to things we should not, or do things that we should not. "If your foot". With our feet we go places. If we are tempted to go to places that we should not (Psalm 1:1) then we must take action to stop going to these places.

18:9 And if your eye causes you to sin, tear it out and throw it away. It is better for you to enter into life with one eye than to have two eyes and be thrown into fiery hell.

"If your eye". Jesus said "the light of the body is the eye" (Matt. 6:22) with the eye we see and obtain understanding. What we see enters our minds and our hearts more readily than by any other means. If we are tempted to read or look at things that are unwholesome then we must turn away from them (1 John 2:16). It is better to go throughout life without these things than to be thrown into hell.

18:10 "See that you do not disdain one of these little ones. For I tell you that their angels in heaven always see the face of my Father in heaven.

Referring again to those "little ones", that is, babes in Christ who have a simple faith, Jesus says that they are not be looked down on, disdained or lightly esteemed. In heaven their angels always have access to the presence of God (Heb. 1:14).

Lost and Found

18:11 For the Son of Man has come to save that which was lost.

The sole purpose in Jesus Christ coming from heaven to earth and taking upon himself a body of flesh was that through his death he might save those who are lost in sin.

18:12 What do you think? If someone owns a hundred sheep and one of them goes astray, will he not leave the ninety-nine on the mountains and go look for the one that went astray?

If a farmer owns a hundred sheep but one of them wanders off, what will he do? Will he turn his back on it and leave it to pay the penalty for its folly? No, he leaves the ninety nine on the hills and goes looking for the one that is lost.

18:13 And if he finds it, I tell you the truth, he will rejoice more over it than over the ninety-nine that did not go astray.

His efforts are rewarded for he finds his lost sheep and he brings it back home, rejoicing more over it that the others who had not gone astray.

18:14 In the same way, your Father in heaven is not willing that one of these little ones be lost.

Just as the farmer deals with his sheep, so God deals with all who have gone astray (Isaiah 53:6). He is not willing that any should perish but that all should repent and be saved (2 Peter 3:9). He has a love and concern for every individual person and does everything that is possible to bring sinners to Himself (John 3:16).

Putting Things Right

18:15 "Moreover if your brother sins against you, go and tell him his fault between you and him alone. If he hears you, you have gained your brother.

If a brother or sister in the Lord wrongs you or offends you then do not let neglect to do anything about it; for this may cause bitterness to grow in your heart. Do not spread it abroad but go to your brother or sister on your own and put the matter right. If he or she puts it right with you then you have won that person back.

18:16 But if he does not listen, take one or two others with you, so that at the testimony of two or three witnesses every matter may be established.

However, if he or she refuses to listen then take one or two other Christians with you and try again. This is in accordance with the word of God for by the testimony of two or three witnesses shall a matter be proved (Deut. 19:15).

18:17 If he refuses to listen to them, tell it to the church. If he refuses to listen to the church, treat him like a Gentile or a tax collector.

If he or she still refuses to listen then the matter must be brought before the church. If they will not heed the church then they are to be treated like pagans—unbelieving sinners.

Unity

18:18 "I tell you the truth, whatever you bind on earth will have been bound in heaven, and whatever you release on earth will have been released in heaven.

Jesus here repeats what he had said in Matthew 16:19 that all who are Christ's can bind things on earth and it shall happen because they have been bound in heaven and whatever is loosed on earth will be loosed in heaven. In other words, what we ask in prayer from God who is in heaven shall be accomplished through our prayers upon earth.

18:19 Again, I tell you the truth, if two of you on earth agree about whatever you ask, my Father in heaven will do it for you.

He further adds that if two of his followers agree together to ask something of the Father in heaven then it will be done on earth.

18:20 For where two or three are assembled in my name, I am there among them."

Jesus gave this certain promise that wherever two or three come together in his name he would be there with them.

Always Forgive

18:21 Then Peter came to him and said, "Lord, how many times must I forgive my brother who sins against me? As many as seven times?"

Peter, having listened to all the Lord had said about offending and doing wrong against a brother or sister, asks the Lord how many times he should be prepared to forgive someone who has sinned against him. Is there a limit to this, say seven times?

18:22 Jesus said to him, "Not seven times, I tell you, but seventy-seven times!

I wonder if Peter was surprised to hear the answer Jesus gave him. Perhaps he thought to himself "well I could forgive seven times but that's as far as I'm prepared to go". In fact Jesus tells him that there is no limit to the number of times that we should forgive. Although he says 490 times, let us not be like the little boy who was determined to write down in a notebook every time his older brother did something unkind. He intended to forgive him only 490 times and not a single time more!

18:23 "For this reason, the kingdom of heaven is like a king who wanted to settle accounts with his slaves.

Jesus then proceeds to liken the kingdom of heaven to a king who wanted to bring his accounts up to date to discover who owed him money.

18:24 As he began settling his accounts, a man who owed ten thousand talents was brought to him.

As he commenced this work, a man was brought before him who owed an exceedingly large amount of money.

18:25 Because he was not able to repay it, the lord ordered him to be sold, along with his wife, children, and whatever he possessed, and repayment to be made.

We are not told what he had done with all this money but the point is that he owed it and could not pay it back. In order to regain his losses the king ordered him, his wife and children to be sold as slaves together with all of his possessions.

18:26 Then the slave threw himself to the ground before him, saying, 'Be patient with me, and I will repay you everything.'

This man threw himself on the ground and begged the king to be patient with him and he would repay everything he owed.

18:27 The lord had compassion on that slave and released him, and forgave him the debt.

The master had compassion on his servant and gave him back his freedom, cancelling the debt. We all owe a debt to God that we cannot repay, for all have sinned and come short of the glory of God (Rom. 3:23) and the soul that sins shall die (Ezek. 18:4). But Jesus Christ paid that debt for us upon the cross (1 Peter 1:18–19) and has set us free (John 8:36).

18:28 After he went out, that same slave found one of his fellow slaves who owed him one hundred silver coins. So he grabbed him by the throat and started to choke him, saying, 'Pay back what you owe me!'

However, this man did not go out and do for others as his master had done for him. He went to a fellow servant who owed him a comparatively small amount and demanded by force that he should repay straight away.

18:29–30 Then his fellow slave threw himself down and begged him, 'Be patient with me, and I will repay you.' But he refused. Instead, he went out and threw him in prison until he repaid the debt.

In the same way that the first man had thrown himself on the mercy of the king, so his fellow servant begged him for time to repay; but he refused and threw him into prison.

18:31 When his fellow slaves saw what had happened, they were very upset and went and told their lord everything that had taken place.

When some of the other servants saw this they were very grieved and went to the king and told him about it.

18:32–33 Then his lord called the first slave and said to him, 'Evil slave! I forgave you all that debt because you begged me! Should you not have shown mercy to your fellow slave, just as I showed it to you?'

The king summoned the man to be brought before him and justly called him a wicked servant; for having been set free with his debt cancelled he should have followed the example of his master and shown mercy to his fellow servant who was in exactly the same position as he had been (Matt. 10:8).

18:34 And in anger his lord turned him over to the prison guards to torture him until he repaid all he owed.

The king was so angry that he handed the man over to the jailers who tortured him until he had repaid all that he owed—which of course, he could not; there was no escape from the torment.

18:35 So also my heavenly Father will do to you, if each of you does not forgive your brother from your heart."

In the same way, those who refuse to forgive others are closing their hearts to God's forgiveness; adopting such a position can only lead to eternal punishment.

Discussion Questions for Chapter 18

1. vv. 1–6. Why do you think the least shall be called great in the kingdom of heaven?

2. vv. 7–10. Why is Jesus' warning so serious to those who cause believers to turn from him?

3. vv. 7–10. How are we to understand Jesus' statements about cutting off hands and feet?

4. vv. 15–17. How is Christ's teaching about putting things right with other Christians related to his teaching in vv. 1–14?

5. vv. 21–35. Why should a believer forgive someone who wrongs him/her?

You will find suggested answers to these questions on pages 306–323.

Matthew Chapter 19

Marriage and Divorce

19:1 Now when Jesus finished these sayings, he left Galilee and went to the region of Judea beyond the Jordan River.

After he had taught his disciples about forgiveness, Jesus again left Galilee and crossed the River Jordan into Judea.

19:2 Large crowds followed him, and he healed them there.

News of Jesus' ministry, and particularly of his healing ministry, had spread rapidly until almost everywhere he went large crowds gathered to him. They came for healing and he healed them all.

19:3 Then some Pharisees came to him in order to test him. They asked, "Is it lawful to divorce a wife for any cause?"

Some of the religious rulers who belonged to the strict sect of Pharisees also came to Jesus, but they sought neither healing nor blessing. They wanted to catch him in his words so that they might discredit his ministry among the people. Their question was about a point of Jewish law, given by Moses. Did the Law of Moses permit divorce, and if so under what circumstances?"

19:4–6 He answered, "Have you not read that from the beginning the Creator made them male and female, and said, 'For this reason a man will leave his father and mother and will be united with his wife, and the two will become one flesh'? So they are no longer two, but one flesh. Therefore what God has joined together, let no one separate."

Jesus replied with reference to God's original act of creation. Marriage was ordained of God from the beginning, for God saw that it was not good for man to be alone. So he made man a helper comparable to him, and she was his wife. In this way marriage was ordained for mutual fellowship. It was ordained by the wisdom of God that when a man reached the age when he wished to leave father and mother, that he should marry a wife, and be united sexually with her. In this way marriage was ordained for the procreation of children, and as a pure way of fulfilling the sexual desires which come as the natural result of the creator "making them male and female". Having been joined together, they would no more be two but one flesh. Since it is God who has joined man and woman together as one, no man has the authority (for it would necessarily have to be greater than God's) to separate them. Man cannot undo a union formed by his creator.

19:7 They said to him, "Why then did Moses command us to give a certificate of dismissal and to divorce her?"

Still wishing to test Jesus, the Pharisees demanded to know why it was, if God opposed divorce, that Moses gave instructions relating to legal divorce and permitted the issuing of divorce certificates.

19:8 Jesus said to them, "Moses permitted you to divorce your wives because of your hard hearts, but from the beginning it was not this way.

Jesus explained how Moses realised that some marital situations were untenable, and so since the hearts of men were hardened to any other solution, he permitted separation as the lesser of two evils. Such a law might at least provide a measure of restraint against the tide of fornication and adultery. But this action was permitted rather than desired, and Jesus makes clear that it was certainly not God's will from the beginning. Rather, it was to curtail the spread of sin and immorality that this law was introduced.

19:9 Now I say to you that whoever divorces his wife, except for immorality, and marries another commits adultery."

Here is a greater authority than Moses. What Christ says applies to all throughout the Christian dispensation. Whoever divorces his wife except for immorality commits adultery in the sight of God, no matter what the law of the land or the policy of the church may be. Hence Jesus permits divorce only when one partner has been unfaithful (i.e. has committed adultery).

What about the issue of re-marriage after divorce? Jesus makes clear in Matthew 5:32 that the divorced woman is not to remarry, since this is to be considered as adultery. It would be fair, then to suppose that such is also the case for the divorced man. Paul made clear that he believed that separation should not be seen as the precursor to remarriage (1 Cor. 7:11). This teaching has serious consequences for modern practise. For if a divorcee remarrying whilst their first spouse still lives is to be considered adultery, then in such a case any minister of the gospel who conducts the marriage service might be seen as condoning adultery, undermining the sacredness of marriage and being a partaker in other people's sins.

There is a great variety of positions within the Christian church regarding this difficult subject, most of them based on what ought to be considered as exceptions to Jesus' teaching. It is worth considering, however, why the Lord (who knows every situation that can possibly arise) failed to mention such exceptions.

19:10 The disciples said to him, "If this is the case of a husband with a wife, it is better not to marry!"

The disciples, many of whom were married men, thought that if the situation between a husband and a wife was so bad that they were actively seeking a divorce, then it would have been better for them never to have married in the first place! Divorce is as bad as it gets; God refers to it as an act of violence, tearing apart rather than healing and reconciling (Mal. 2:16).

19:11–12 He said to them, "Not everyone can accept this statement, except those to whom it has been given. For there are some eunuchs who were that way from birth, and some who were made eunuchs by others, and some who became eunuchs for the sake of the kingdom of heaven. The one who is able to accept this should accept it."

Jesus realized that men and women marry because of the real needs which they have as the result of creation. Specifically, most men and women need the satisfaction of a sexual relationship, and that relationship has been provided for by God within marriage (Heb. 13:4). However, Jesus (who knows all) knew also that some people were able to live perfectly happily without a sexual partner.

Some of these were born that way (eunuchs from birth), and are happy to remain single all their lives. Jesus is saying that this is the right course if it is the natural course for them. Something in their make-up makes it less necessary for them to have a sexual partner. Others, says Jesus, were made eunuchs by men, that is (understand that Jesus said this in the days of slaves) they have been castrated, and so no longer have any sexual desires at all.

Others have heard the call of God in such a way that they are completely abandoned to him, and have made up their minds not to get married, for the sake of giving their time fully to the work of God. They are gifted with enough self-control to channel their energies into the work of God. Paul expands on this theme in 1 Corinthians 7, where he makes plain that the man or woman who is able to refrain from marriage is gifted by God in this respect, and should use this gift well, for it is better to remain unmarried. But for those who feel a sexual desire, it is better to marry than to burn with lust, resulting in immorality. As a result of the fall, marriage will never be perfect, but it is still an estate ordained by God, and is regarded as a means of avoiding immorality.

Little Children

19:13 Then little children were brought to him for him to lay his hands on them and pray. But the disciples scolded those who brought them.

The result of the marriage union will be children. Every caring parent wants the best for their child, and what could be better than to seek the lord of glory that he might bless our children? Mothers and fathers brought their children to Jesus for this reason. But the over-wrought disciples rebuked them, for they thought their master was too busy for children; implying that they thought children less important than adults.

19:14–15 But Jesus said, "Let the little children come to me and do not try to stop them, for the kingdom of heaven belongs to such as these. And he placed his hands on them and went on his way.

Here is one of the few places in the New Testament where Jesus is angered. To him, each child was a precious human being with a living soul, loved by God every bit as much as his father or mother. What is more, every child is capable of receiving spiritual blessing, and many were already old enough to receive spiritual instruction; in particular, the kind of instruction which comes by participation. If they could not learn much from Jesus' preaching, yet they could learn much from his love and his welcome. By refusing to welcome them, the disciples were in danger of misrepresenting God to the children. The kingdom of heaven belongs to such as these—that is, each one could potentially be saved and receive God's eternal blessings.

Modern surveys suggest that most people who become Christians do so before their sixteenth birthday. Children's ministry is not a second rate ministry, it is on the cutting edge. A church without an active children's ministry is a lopsided church, is out of touch with the heart of God for children, and will be extinct within a generation. Jesus' heart always reached out to children; may we do the same.

What Must I do to Gain Eternal Life?

19:16 Now someone came up to him and said, "Teacher, what good thing must I do to gain eternal life?"

The scripture offers two ways in which we might obtain eternal life. The first was by the keeping of the law and commandments of God, and the other is by faith in Jesus Christ who fulfilled the law for us. Because of sin, every man and woman has already failed to be right with God through keeping the law. We have all sinned and come short of the glory of God. That is why "by the deeds of the law, no flesh shall be justified" (Rom 3:20).

Jesus wanted to help this young man realise that he was a sinner. Notice how Jesus says that there is only one good, which is God, implying that "there is no man good, no not one" (Rom. 3:12). The commandments which the young man had kept in letter he had broken in spirit, even as to be angry with one's brother without cause is to commit murder (Matt. 5:22). If he had kept many of the commandments, yet to break one law is to be a rebel against the law-giver (James 2:10).

19:17–20 He said to him, "Why do you ask me about what is good? There is only one who is good. But if you want to enter into life, keep the commandments. Which ones?" he asked. Jesus replied, "Do not murder, do not commit adultery, do not steal, do not give false testimony, honor your father and mother, and love your neighbour as yourself. The young man said to him, "I have wholeheartedly obeyed all these laws. What do I still lack?"

Jesus firstly mentions only those commands which relate to the young man's relationship with other people, and the man insists that with regard to his duty to humanity he has been upright and wholehearted in his law keeping. Yet there was something lacking, he had "fallen short" of the glory of God.

19:21–22 Jesus said to him, "If you wish to be perfect, go sell your possessions and give the money to the poor, and you will have treasure in heaven. Then come, follow me." But when the young man heard this he went away sorrowful, for he was very rich.

Jesus now turns his attention to the man's relationship with God; in this test, he fails utterly. The law demanded that a man love God with all his heart, mind, soul, and strength (Deut. 6:5). Jesus himself had said that it is impossible to serve God and money (Luke 16:13). Yet when the young man is challenged to put his relationship with God before his money, he fails to do so; a failure which reveals that he did not love the Lord his God with all his heart.

19:23–24 Then Jesus said to his disciples, "I tell you the truth, it will be hard for a rich person to enter the kingdom of heaven! Again I say, it is easier for a camel to go through the eye of a needle than for a rich person to enter into the kingdom of God."

With sorrow in his heart, Jesus tells his disciples that a rich man is not easily parted from his love of money. It is not wrong to have money or worldly possessions, but if holding on to those possessions keeps a person from the kingdom of heaven, then they are deadly possessions indeed, for they will damn that person's soul. No wonder James writes: "your gold and silver have rusted and their rust will be a witness against you. It will consume your flesh like fire. It is in the last days that you have hoarded treasure" (James 5:3).

The only way for the rich to enter the kingdom of God is for them to forego, or denounce, their riches. Jesus asks us to part with all for his name sake, and sometimes this will literally mean the loss of all worldly possessions. It may not literally mean that in each case, but every person must be wiling for it to come to that. As Christians, we realise that we have more enduring treasures in heaven (Heb. 10:34).

19:25–26 The disciples were greatly astonished when they heard this and said, "Then who can be saved?" Jesus looked at them and replied, "This is impossible for mere humans, but for God all things are possible."

Of course, it is impossible for a camel to enter the eye of a needle. It is also impossible for a person to enter the kingdom of God, without a miracle. But it is God who provides the miracle, and in the hearts of those who are willing to hear and obey the gospel, whether they are rich or poor, he will perform this miracle of salvation. For all things are possible with God. The rich come to see their riches as worthless, and the poor see their poverty as nothing, in the light of Christ's great riches.

Rewards for Those who Leave all to Follow Christ

19:27 Then Peter said to him, "Look, we have left everything to follow you! What then will there be for us?"

Peter realised that his commitment to follow the Lord Jesus Christ had meant him forsaking all. If the rich who failed to follow Christ were not blessed, what of the poor who did follow Christ? "What's in it for me?" is a paraphrase of Peter's question.

19:28–30 Jesus said to them, "I tell you the truth: In the age when all things are renewed, when the Son of Man sits on his glorious throne, you who have followed me will also sit on twelve thrones, judging the twelve tribes of Israel. And whoever has left houses or brothers or sisters or father or mother or children or fields for my sake will receive a hundred times as much and will inherit eternal life. But many who are first will be last, and the last first.

Christ promises eternal blessings to everyone who forsakes everything to follow him. We are never the losers with God. Whether we are great (first) or small (least), we possess greater things than this world could ever provide. In this case, Jesus tells Peter that he and the other apostles will obtain a position of rank and authority, the honour of being seen as his esteemed servants. This will be when "the Son of Man sits on his glorious throne", which is after the resurrection of the saints. Then honour shall be given to all those who truly follow Christ.

Yet even in this life, by entering in and partaking of the kingdom of God, we receive great riches through our relationships with others who are also in the kingdom. They will be to us brothers, sisters, fathers and mothers, and their homes and hospitality shall be at our disposal. Peter later found that the needs of the missionary were met by the people whom he laboured among, or those who financially supported his work (as we see from 1 Cor. 9:4–7).

Discussion Questions for Chapter 19

1. vv. 1–12. Summarise Jesus' teaching on marriage and divorce.

2. vv. 13–15. Why were children so important to Jesus?

3. vv. 16–26. Why was the rich young ruler sad when Jesus challenged his commitment?

4. vv. 16–26. How can a rich person be saved?

5. vv. 27–30. What rewards will believers have for leaving everything to follow Christ?

You will find suggested answers to these questions on pages 306–323.

Matthew Chapter 20

God Deals Justly

20:1 "For the kingdom of heaven is like a landowner who went out early in the morning to hire workers for his vineyard.

This parable follows on from Peter's statement in the previous chapter: "Look, we have left everything to follow you! What then will there be for us?" Jesus uses the illustration of a landowner who goes out early in the morning to find workers to work in his vineyard.

20:2 And after agreeing with the workers for the standard wage, he sent them into his vineyard.

He agreed to pay those he had hired the standard wage for those days which was a Roman penny—the denarius.

20:3–4 When it was about nine o'clock in the morning, he went out again and saw others standing around in the marketplace without work. He said to them, 'You go into the vineyard too, and I will give you whatever is right.'

At about nine o'clock he went to the marketplace and saw other men standing about doing nothing. He engaged them to go and work in his vineyard also and told them he would pay them a fair wage at the end of the day.

20:5 So they went. When he went out again about noon and three o'clock that afternoon, he did the same thing.

So they went to the work. The landowner went out again to the marketplace at twelve o'clock and three o'clock and employed those who were hanging around and agreed to pay the same wage as the others.

20:6 And about five o'clock that afternoon he went out and found others standing around, and said to them, 'Why are you standing here all day without work?'

At five o'clock in the afternoon he found other men standing around and asked them why they were not working.

20:7 They said to him, 'Because no one hired us.' He said to them, 'You go and work in the vineyard too.'

They replied that no one had hired them so he also told them to go and work in his vineyard. The point being made is the different times of day that these men were employed.

20:8 When it was evening the owner of the vineyard said to his manager, 'Call the workers and give the pay starting with the last hired until the first.'

At the end of the day the owner of the vineyard told his manager to call the workers to him that he might pay them, starting with the men who were hired last.

20:9–10 When those hired about five o'clock came, each received a full day's pay. And when those hired first came, they thought they would receive more. But each one also received the standard wage.

He paid those who had worked the least hours a full day's pay. The workers who had worked all day from early morning thought that they would be paid more. But each one received the standard wage.

20:11–12 When they received it, they began to complain against the landowner, saying, 'These last fellows worked one hour, and you have made them equal to us who bore the hardship and burning heat of the day.'

When they saw that they had received the same amount as those who had only worked for an hour they complained to the owner. It was not fair that those who had only worked a very short time should receive equal pay with those who had worked hard in the burning hot sun all day.

20:13 And the landowner replied to one of them, 'Friend, I am not treating you unfairly. Didn't you agree with me to work for the standard wage?

Although this might seem unjust, the owner insists that he was acting fairly. They had agreed to work for the standard wage and that is what he paid them.

20:14–15 Take what is yours and go. I want to give to this last man the same as I gave to you. Am I not permitted to do what I want with what belongs to me? Or are you envious because I am generous?'

Without further argument he told them to take their money and go. As the owner of the vineyard, he could chose to pay his workers whatever he wanted; it was no business of theirs. If he wanted to be generous why should they be jealous?

20:16 So the last will be first, and the first last." For many are called, but few chosen."

The whole purpose of Jesus telling his disciples this parable may be understood from this concluding verse. The first to be called into the kingdom of heaven will have no advantage over those who enter in later. All are equal in the sight of God (Deut. 10:17; Eph. 6:9). "Many are called..."—there are many who hear the call of the gospel message but there are few in proportion that obey and are saved. It is Jesus Christ who will give out the rewards at his coming and no one can complain at what they may receive for God is a just God (Rev. 22:12).

Jesus Foretells His Death for the Third Time

20:17–18 As Jesus was going up to Jerusalem, he took the twelve aside privately and said to them on the way, "Look, we are going up to Jerusalem, and the Son of Man will be handed over to the chief priests and the experts in the law. They will condemn him to death,

On their way to Jerusalem, Jesus took the twelve disciples aside and told them once again the reason why they were going up to the city at that time. Those who were conspiring against him would hand him over to the chief priests and scribes and they would condemn him to death.

20:19 and will turn him over to the Gentiles to be mocked and flogged severely and crucified. Yet on the third day, he will be raised."

They in their turn would hand him over to the Romans to be ridiculed, flogged and then crucified. But on the third day he would be triumphantly raised to life.

To Minister and not be Ministered To

20:20–21 Then the mother of the sons of Zebedee came to him with her sons, and kneeling down she asked him for a favour. He said to her, "What do you want?" She replied, "Permit these two sons of mine to sit, one at your right hand and one at your left, in your kingdom."

The mother of James and John, the sons of Zebedee, came to Jesus with them; kneeling in worship before him she asked a favour for her sons. She asked that one of her sons should sit on his right hand and the other on his left in his kingdom. In Matthew 19:28 Jesus had promised his twelve disciples that they would sit on thrones judging the twelve tribes of Israel. Perhaps it was in response to this that James and John sought to obtain a greater position than that of the other disciples.

20:22 But Jesus answered and said, "You do not know what you ask. Are you able to drink the cup that I am about to drink, and be baptized with the baptism that I am baptized with?" They said to him, "We are able." (NKJV™)

Jesus tells them that they have no idea what they asking for and challenges them: are they able to drink the cup that he is about to drink (Matt. 26:39)? The cup that he drank was for our sins, the sins of the whole world (2 Cor. 5:21), yet they replied (without realizing what he meant) that they were. Were they able to be baptized with the baptism that he is baptized with? This baptism refers to his sufferings and death upon the cross. "Yes" was their bold reply!

20:23 He told them, "You will drink my cup, but to sit at my right and at my left is not mine to give. Rather, it is for those for whom it has been prepared by my Father."

Jesus foretells that they would indeed drink of his cup—they would join in his sufferings—but to sit on his right hand and at his left was not his to give but would be given to whosoever God the Father had chosen.

20:24 Now when the other ten heard this, they were angry with the two brothers.

When the other disciples heard what James and John had been up to they were not very pleased, and became angry with the two brothers.

20:25 But Jesus called them and said, "You know that the rulers of the Gentiles lord it over them, and those in high positions use their authority over them.

So Jesus called the twelve disciples to him and reminded them of the fact that they saw every day among the Romans who ruled over them. The rulers in Gentile nations rule with a rod of iron and dominate their people, and those who are given positions of authority do the same.

20:26–27 It must not be this way among you! Instead whoever wants to be great among you must be your servant, and whoever wants to be first among you must be your slave –

This must not been so among Christ's followers; it has to be the complete opposite. Whoever is given authority within Christ's church must serve Christ's people. Whoever wants to have first place must be a servant.

20:28 just as the Son of Man did not come to be served but to serve, and to give his life as a ransom for many."

Jesus Christ himself was the prime example of this. He had all authority and power yet he did not come to be served but to minister, work and care for others. Ultimately he gave his life as a ransom to redeem many souls.

Two Blind Men

20:29–30 As they were leaving Jericho, a large crowd followed them. Two blind men were sitting by the road. When they heard that Jesus was passing by, they shouted, "Have mercy on us, Lord, Son of David!"

As they were leaving Jericho to continue their journey to Jerusalem a large crowd followed them. Two men who were sitting by the roadside begging heard that Jesus was coming that way, so they began shouting out for him to have mercy on them. They acknowledged that he was Lord, who had supreme authority; the promised Son of David, the Messiah.

20:31–34 The crowd scolded them to get them to be quiet. But they shouted even more loudly, "Lord, have mercy on us, Son of David!" Jesus stopped, called them, and said, "What do you want me to do for you?" They said to him, "Lord, let our eyes be opened." Moved with compassion, Jesus touched their eyes. Immediately they received their sight and followed him.

The crowds yelled at them to be quiet but they shouted all the louder. On hearing them, Jesus stopped and called out, asking what it was they wanted from him.

They had no doubt that Jesus was able to give them their sight. As they asked in simple faith to receive their sight, Jesus was moved with pity and love. He touched their eyes and healed them. The grateful men followed Jesus along the road.

Discussion Questions for Chapter 20

1. vv. 1–16. What appeared to be unfair about the actions of the landowner? How did he explain his behaviour?

2. vv. 20–28. What do you think was wrong with James' and John's request?

3. vv. 20–28. According to Jesus reply, what seem to be the conditions of entering his kingdom?

4. vv. 20–28. Rather than seeking greatness according to the world's standards, what were the disciples to do?

5. vv. 29–34. Can you suggest a reason why Matthew inserted the story of the two blind men at this particular point in the narrative?

You will find suggested answers to these questions on pages 306–323.

Matthew Chapter 21

Entry to Jerusalem

21:1 Now when they approached Jerusalem and came to Bethpage, at the Mount of Olives, Jesus sent two disciples,

Jesus was about to enter Jerusalem to celebrate Passover for the last time. Drawing near to the city he arrived at a village called Bethpage which is on the slopes of the Mount of Olives.

21:2 Telling them, "Go to the village ahead of you. Right away you will find a donkey tied there, and a colt with her. Untie them and bring them to me.

He sent two of his disciples (we are not told their names here) into the village to obtain transport. God had foreordained that the Christ should enter Jerusalem sitting on a donkey and her colt. No one else was party to the arrangements. The colt and donkey were in their appointed place. The disciples, under the authority of the Lord Jesus Christ, were to untie them and bring them to him.

21:3 If anyone says anything to you, you are to say, 'The Lord needs them,' and he will send them at once."

No one could actually resist this authority of the Lord, but if any one did challenge the disciples they were to reply with the words Jesus gave them. If the creator chose to commandeer his creation for his own purposes who was to stop him?

Later, at his arrest, his enemies would find that even they were in his hands (John 18:6); but here at Bethpage we see Christ exerting his absolute sovereignty and yet remaining gentle and humble.

21:4–5 This took place to fulfil what was spoken by the prophet: Tell the people of Zion, 'Look, your king is coming to you, unassuming and seated on a donkey, and on a colt, the foal of a donkey.' "

This event had been predicted by the prophet Zechariah, that Christ would show both his authority and his gentleness by riding into Zion (Jerusalem) on a donkey's foal. Warriors rode into battle on mighty horses, but our king is the king of peace and not a king of war.

21:6 So the disciples went and did as Jesus had instructed them.

Obedience to Jesus Christ always requires faith, and the disciples carried out their instructions without doubting.

21:7 They brought the donkey and the colt and placed their cloaks on them, and he sat on them.

As a mark of respect, the disciples first put their own outer coats on the donkey as both cushion and saddle before Christ rode on it.

21:8 A very large crowd spread their cloaks on the road. Others cut branches from the trees and spread them on the road.

The same respect due to a king was shown by the great crowd of followers who had accompanied Christ from Galilee and the surrounding area. They lay their cloaks on the road, or if they had no cloaks they strewed the road with palm branches to make a carpet for the king to ride on. In modern terms we would say they "rolled out the red carpet" for the king.

21:9 The crowds that went ahead of him and those following kept shouting, "Hosanna to the Son of David! Blessed is the one who comes in the name of the Lord! Hosanna in the highest!"

Inspired by the Spirit of God, the disciples began shouting their praises to the Lord as he entered Jerusalem. They recognised him as the

Christ, the Son of David. They knew him to be the one sent by God, who would bring God's salvation (hosanna means "Lord save us", or salvation). They knew him to be king of the highest glory.

21:10–11 As he entered Jerusalem the whole city was thrown into an uproar, saying, "Who is this?" And the crowds were saying, "This is the prophet Jesus, from Nazareth in Galilee."

These verses shed light on a problem connected with this passage. Many preachers have said that the same crowds who shouted "Hosanna" on Palm Sunday shouted "crucify him" less than a week later. Noting could be further from the truth. The crowds which accompanied him from Galilee shouted "Hosanna" as he entered Jerusalem. The crowds already in Jerusalem met him with hostility: "who is this?" was their discourteous question. It was this Jerusalem crowd that later shouted for his blood early one morning, as the followers from Galilee were mostly camped without the city.

Cleansing the Temple

21:12 Then Jesus entered the temple area and drove out all those who were selling and buying in the temple courts, and turned over the tables of the money changers and the chairs of those selling doves.

The New Testament writers record that Jesus had visited the temple several times before this event (e.g. Luke 2:41–42). Indeed, it is quite likely that in accordance with the law, Jesus had visited the temple every year since he came of age. No doubt the buying and selling had not only started that year, which suggests that this was no sudden act of anger or passion. Christ had long planned this show of authority, and the right time had now come. He had come to rid false religion from the land and bring in the true. Disrespect for God, especially in a place of worship, is hateful to Christ in every age and generation. Modern Christians ought always to remember this.

21:13 And he said to them, "It is written, 'My house will be called a house of prayer,' but you are turning it into a den of robbers!"

Contrary to what some commentators have implied, Christ was not angry that the poor were being cheated. Note his words, as they disclose the reason for his anger. The holy place where God was to be worshipped, the house of God and the house of prayer, was being treated with irreverence. The matter of cheating the people (den of robbers) was a serious one, but entirely secondary to the honour and glory of his father.

What is your attitude when you come to the house of God? Do you come to meet with God in worship? Do you treat his presence with the awe it deserves? Or do you treat being in God's presence or in God's house as something no different to sitting in your room chatting to your friends?

21:14 The blind and lame came to him in the temple courts, and he healed them.

It is always the will of God that men and women should find healing in his house and in his presence. No special occasion was needed, just the presence of Jesus. In our churches, he is present, for "where two or three are gathered in my name, I am there in the midst of them" (Matt. 18:20).

21:15 But when the chief priests and the experts in the law saw the wonderful things he did and heard the children crying out in the temple courts, "Hosanna to the Son of David," they became indignant

The indignation of the chief priests came from their unbelief. Had they known and accepted who Christ was, they would not have been irritated by his healing ministry or by the fact that he received praise as God in God's temple. For a person to be angry with God reveals the true nature of their hearts, that they are enemies of God through wicked works (Col. 1:21).

21:16 and said to him, "Do you hear what they are saying?" Jesus said to them, "Yes. Have you never read, 'Out of the mouths of children and nursing infants you have prepared praise for yourself'?"

The Pharisees were so opposed to Christ that they begrudged him the praises of the children. Unbelief results in envy and jealousy. Yet Christ saw their praise as the fulfilment of scripture. The witness of the children was the greatest of the day, for who had taught them to say such things? Not their parents. It was unplanned, yet they sang spontaneously by divine inspiration. It is as if Jesus is telling the Pharisees, "listen to the children, for they will tell you the truth about me."

21:17 And leaving them, he went out of the city to Bethany and spent the night there.

It is significant that although Christ had ridden triumphantly into the city, he was so unwelcome there that he was given no place to stay. He resorted on foot to a little house almost two miles away where he was welcome, quite probably the home of Lazarus, Martha and Mary. Even Christ found the home of love to be the preferred place of lodging, rather than the palaces of the mighty (Prov. 15:17).

The Fig Tree

21:18 Now early in the morning, as he returned to the city, he was hungry.

Early next morning, Jesus returned on foot to the city of Jerusalem. We have no reason to doubt that he had been offered breakfast by his hosts at Bethany, but nevertheless he was hungry.

21:19 After noticing a fig tree by the road he went to it, but found nothing on it except leaves. He said to it, "Never again will there be fruit from you!" And the fig tree withered at once.

God had provided fruit trees as food for people (Gen. 2:9). We are not sure if before mankind fell into sin, the trees in Eden bore fruit every month, as they do (typically) in heaven (Rev. 22:2). Yet the fig tree was not in season, and so was not fulfilling the purpose God had for it. The creator himself was unable to find food on it. By inference, the people of Jerusalem were not fulfilling God's will, and whereas the master should have found the fruit of love and obedience, he found the bitterness of rejection. What happened to the fig tree would be a picture of what would happen to Jerusalem as a result of their rejection.

21:20 When the disciples saw it they were amazed, saying, "How did the fig tree wither so quickly?"

The withering of the fig tree was noticed immediately, and its complete death was referred to by Peter later that day. They had seen Christ heal immediately, perhaps their amazement stemmed from the fact that they had never before seen Christ's word acting in judgment.

21:21 Jesus answered them, "I tell you the truth, if you have faith and do not doubt, not only will you do what was done to the fig tree, but even if you say to this mountain, 'Be lifted up and thrown into the sea,' it will happen.

Here Jesus uses the withered fig tree as an object lesson of faith for his disciples. What he had done, they would do, if they had faith in God. Indeed, by faith in God nothing is impossible. Surely God does not wish us to tell mountains to fall into the sea, but *should he call upon us to do so*, we will be enabled even for that by his word of command.

21:22 And whatever you ask in prayer, if you believe, you will receive."

When we pray, we must bear in mind the mighty power of God, and believe that we will receive; else what is the point of prayer? If we believe that God hears and has answered us, we shall receive from him the answer.

By Whose Authority?

21:23 Now after Jesus entered the temple courts, the chief priests and elders of the people came up to him as he was teaching and said, "By what authority are you doing these things, and who gave you this authority?"

Jesus returned to Jerusalem after staying the night in Bethany. He again entered the temple and began teaching the people about the kingdom of God. The chief priests and scribes were joined by the elders, the heads of the tribes and clans of the Jewish nation. They wanted to know by whose authority he had the previous day driven out the buyers and sellers from the temple. But more than this they questioned his authority to teach the people about the things of God. After all he was not a qualified man. He did not have letters after his name! Who had given him this authority? In asking this they were in fact acknowledging that he spoke as one having authority (Luke 4:36; Mark 1:22).

21:24 Jesus answered them, "I will also ask you one question. If you answer me then I will also tell you by what authority I do these things.

Jesus replied that if they would give him an answer to his question then he would tell them by whose authority he was doing these things.

21:25 Where did John's baptism come from? From heaven or from people?" They discussed this among themselves, saying, "If we say, 'From heaven,' he will say, 'Then why did you not believe him?'

213

Did John's authority to baptise come from heaven or did it come from men? They put their heads together and discussed this question amongst themselves. They knew that if they said John's authority was from heaven then Jesus would ask them why they did not repent and believe his teaching.

21:26 But if we say, 'From people,' we fear the crowd, for they all consider John to be a prophet."

On the other hand, they were too afraid of what the people would do to them if they said that John's authority was of men, because the people believed John to be a prophet.

21:27 So they answered Jesus, "We don't know." Then he said to them, "Neither will I tell you by what authority I am doing these things.

So they played safe and answered Jesus that they did not know from whom John had received his authority. They did not meet the Lord's condition and so he did not tell them who had given him his authority.

Surrendering to Divine Authority

21:28 "What do you think? A man had two sons. He went to the first and said, 'Son, go and work in the vineyard today.'

Jesus went on to tell them a parable about a man who had two sons. He went to the elder son and asked him to go and work in the vineyard.

21:29 The boy answered, 'I will not.' But later he had a change of heart and went.

Without hesitation this son said that he would not go, but later on repented and went.

214

21:30 The father went to the other son and said the same thing. This boy answered, 'I will, sir,' but did not go.

The father was not put off by his elder son's refusal, and so went to his younger son who politely said that he would go, but he did not go.

21:31 Which of the two did his father's will?" They said, "The first." Jesus said to them, "I tell you the truth, tax collectors and prostitutes will go ahead of you into the kingdom of God!

Jesus asked the chief priests and elders which of the two sons did the will of their father. That was an easy question it was obviously the elder son. The parable was intended to bring home to these religious leaders that they were like the second son who said he would go and work in the vineyard but did not. They were making pretence of serving God but were not surrendering to his will. Jesus told them that those who were thought of as the dregs of society would enter the kingdom of heaven before them.

21:32 For John came to you in the way of righteousness, and you did not believe him. But the tax collectors and prostitutes did believe. Although you saw this, you did not later change your minds and believe him.

John the Baptist came preaching repentance and the right way to live but the religious leaders would not believe him. It was the people whom they considered sinners who gladly heard the message and believed. Although they saw the response from these "sinners", and the change in their lives, they still did not believe John's message.

Rejecting the Son

21:33 "Listen to another parable: There was a landowner who planted a vineyard. He put a fence around it, dug a pit for its winepress, and built a watchtower. Then he leased it to tenant farmers and went on a journey.

If the first parable was to show the religious leaders their rejection of John the Baptist's preaching, the second shows them their rejection of the Son of God, Jesus Christ.

A man who owned land planted a vineyard and enclosed it with a fence. Then he dug a pit to put its winepress in and built a watchtower to guard it. He rented his vineyard out to tenant farmers and went away.

21:34 When the harvest time was near, he sent his slaves to the tenants to collect his portion of the crop.

When the time came to harvest the grapes he sent his servants to the tenants to collect a portion of the crop.

21:35 But the tenants seized his slaves, beat one, killed another, and stoned another.

However the tenants took hold of his servants, beat one, killed another and stoned another.

21:36 Again he sent other slaves, more than the first, and they treated them the same way.

He was not put off by the brutal treatment of his servants so he sent another deputation, greater in number than the first, but they treated these in the same way.

21:37 Finally he sent his son to them, saying, 'They will respect my son.'

Eventually he sent his own only son believing that they would show respect for him.

21:38–39 But when the tenants saw the son, they said to themselves, 'This is the heir. Come, let's kill him and get his inheritance!' So they seized him, threw him out of the vineyard, and killed him.

But when the tenants saw the son they reasoned among themselves that if the heir was killed then the inheritance would become theirs. So they laid hands on him, threw him out of the vineyard and killed him.

21:40 Now when the owner of the vineyard comes, what will he do to those tenants?"

Jesus asked the religious leaders what the owner of the vineyard would do to those tenants when he came back.

21:41 They said to him, "He will utterly destroy those evil men! Then he will lease the vineyard to other tenants who will give him his portion at the harvest."

They rightly answered that he would completely destroy these evil men and rent out his vineyard to other tenants who would give him the portion of the harvest that he asked for.

21:42 Jesus said to them, "Have you never read in the scriptures: The stone the builders rejected has become the cornerstone. This is from the Lord, and it is marvellous in our eyes'?

To bring out the truth of the parable Jesus quotes the scriptures from Psalm 118:22–23. The people of Israel were God's chosen people, his vineyard (Isaiah 5:7), to whom he had entrusted his word; he appointed their religious leaders to take care of his people and teach them his word. They had failed in their duty. God had sent many prophets to call them to repentance but they had brutally treated and killed them. Finally God sent his only begotten Son to them, the Lord Jesus Christ, the cornerstone, but they rejected him, too.

21:43 For this reason I tell you that the kingdom of God will be taken from you and given to a people who will produce its fruit.

It is because of the rejection of Jesus Christ their Messiah that the kingdom of God would be taken from them and given to people from among all nations, many of whom will believe and many will be saved.

21:44 The one who falls on this stone will be broken to pieces, and the one on whom it falls will be crushed."

The stone is the Lord Jesus Christ; whoever hears the gospel of salvation through him and will not accept it will suffer severe consequences. Those on whom judgment falls will perish.

21:45–46 When the chief priests and the Pharisees heard his parables, they realized that he was speaking about them. They wanted to arrest him, but they were afraid of the crowds, because the crowds regarded him as a prophet.

The chief priests and Pharisees knew that Jesus was speaking about them in these parables. Because of this they wanted to kill him; but they were afraid of the people because they thought Jesus was a prophet.

Discussion Questions for Chapter 21

1. vv. 1–7. Why do you think Jesus was able to commandeer someone else's donkey?

2. vv. 12–17. Why was Jesus angered by what he saw in the temple?

3. vv. 18–22. What does the parable of the fig tree illustrate?

4. vv. 28–32. How could Jesus say that he tax collectors and prostitutes were doing the will of God when the Pharisees and other religious leaders were not?

5. vv. 33–46. According to Jesus' teaching about the vineyard, for what were the religious leaders going to be held accountable before God?

You will find suggested answers to these questions on pages 306–323.

Matthew Chapter 22

The Parable of the Wedding Banquet

22:1 Jesus spoke to them again in parables, saying:

Following on directly from chapter 21, Jesus is still speaking in parables; teaching the people in the temple courts in the hearing of the Pharisees and scribes.

22:2 "The kingdom of heaven can be compared to a king who gave a wedding banquet for his son.

In this parable the king represents God and Jesus is his son. The wedding banquet prepared by God stands for the eternal blessings made available to men through Christ, which are received through salvation (Eph. 1:3).

22:3 He sent his slaves to summon those who had been invited to the banquet, but they would not come.

The servants of God were sent to invite those whom he wished to welcome as guests at this banquet. The gospel of salvation is for all men, and God is not willing that any should perish (2 Pet. 3:9). In this parable Jesus makes clear that it was to the Jewish nation that the message of salvation was first sent. Indeed, the words of this verse, "summon those who have been invited", imply that the invitation had already been given through the writings of the prophets, and that the apostles of the New Testament were merely announcing that the time had come for these prophetic writings to be fulfilled (Mark 1:15). Unfortunately, by and large those who heard the heralds refused to respond to the invitation.

We must bear in mind that this gospel was first spoken by the Lord Jesus Christ (Heb. 2:3). It was the invitation of the son himself that the Pharisees refused, though later they also rejected that of the apostles (1 Thess. 2:15). The sin here is of obduracy and disobedience as they refused to listen, obey and come.

22:4–5 Again he sent other slaves, saying, 'Tell those who have been invited, "Look! The feast I have prepared for you is ready. My oxen and fattened cattle have been slaughtered, and everything is ready. Come to the wedding banquet." 'But they were indifferent and went away, one to his farm, another to his business.

God is longsuffering, and so more messengers were sent. Again and again God appeals for lost souls to receive his son. But those portrayed in this verse are indifferent to the things of God. They thought nothing of the fact that God had prepared everything for them. The king in the parable had slaughtered his oxen and fattened cattle and prepared everything, they did not even need to pay for admission; they only had to bring themselves.

God has done everything required for our eternal blessing and salvation through the Lord Jesus Christ, who has died and who is raised again; so that whoever responds to his call and comes to him in faith will be saved. So little did these men esteem the invitation of the king that they considered manual labour more important. In point of fact there is nothing more important than the salvation of our souls and we should give more earnest heed to the things that are spoken and ensure we obey so that our souls might be saved (Heb. 2:1–3).

22:6 The rest seized his slaves, insolently mistreated them, and killed them.

Just as seriously some of those who rejected the invitation abused and murdered the messengers of the king (see Luke 11:49). The rejection of Jesus Christ was serious enough, but even so the murder of his servants will not go unpunished either.

22:7 The king was furious! He sent his soldiers, and they put those murderers to death and set their city on fire.

God's wrath was aroused by the people's rejection of his son and his servants, and he was determined to repay them for their sin. Significantly, Jesus said that he burned their city with fire—which is exactly what happened to Jerusalem when it was raised to the ground by the Romans in AD 70.

22:8–9 Then he said to his slaves, 'The wedding is ready, but the ones who had been invited were not worthy. So go into the main streets and invite everyone you find to the wedding banquet.'

The wedding was so important, and the desire of the king was so great for his son's honour, that the original rejection of the people did not deter the king from continuing to invite others; indeed everyone in the whole country was invited. When Jesus says those who were invited were not worthy he means that they had made themselves unworthy by rejecting the gracious invitation (Acts 13:46); for we notice that those who rejected the message received the same genuine invitation as those who accepted it. It was not God who rejected them. God's concern is that his servants should go everywhere and invite everyone (Mark 16:15; John 3:16).

22:10–12 And those slaves went out into the streets and gathered all they found, both bad and good, and the wedding hall was filled with guests. But when the king came in to see the wedding guests, he saw a man there who was not wearing wedding clothes. And he said to him, 'Friend, how did you get in here without wedding clothes?' But he had nothing to say.

222

The evangelists went out to plead with all people and as a result great crowds gathered in the hall where the wedding was to take place. Yet, as the wedding was about to begin, the king spoke personally to one man who was not wearing wedding clothes. These special clothes were a gift provided by the king for all of his guests. It was a serious affront to a king not to wear his gifts.

The significance of these verses lies in the fact that our salvation is provided for us as a gift of God (Rom. 6:23). Just as the king provided the wedding clothes, so it is God who clothes us with the garments of salvation and arrays us with the robe of righteousness (Isa. 61:10). When we receive Jesus Christ as our Saviour he removes our filthy garments of sin, which he nailed to the cross, and gives us the robe of his own righteousness (Jer. 23:6).

We cannot hope to enter heaven any other way than the one which God has provided. If we want to enter God's wedding banquet than we must first accept his gift. Being in the wedding hall or among the congregation of God's people (joining a church) is not what saves us; receiving the God's gift of eternal life does. You can spend your entire life among Christians, you may have been born into a Christian family, but one day you will have to personally meet with and be examined by God. Are you sure that you have received his gift of righteousness through faith in Christ?

22:13 Then the king said to his attendants, 'Tie him up hand and foot and throw him into the outer darkness, where there will be weeping and gnashing of teeth!'

The end for all those who do not accept the free gift of salvation through faith in Christ is an eternal punishment, in outer darkness where there is endless regret and pain.

22:14 For many are called, but few are chosen."

We should understand this concluding verse of the parable in the context of the whole parable. Many had been called, the invitation went out to all equally, but only those who responded in the affirmative received the wedding garments and so were chosen. Whilst God has sovereignly prepared the salvation banquet, he has not forced any man to attend. God has sovereignly announced the means of salvation, yet man can of his own free will choose to accept or reject what God offers.

Paying Taxes to Caesar

22:15 Then the Pharisees went out and planned together to entrap him with his own words.

The Pharisees knew in their hearts that they were among those who rejected the king's messengers and were plotting the death of his son. They were cut to the heart by Christ's words and hated him for exposing the truth. Those who are enemies of God will always hate those who are truly his servants. They plotted to trap Jesus in something he might say for the sole purpose of handing him over to the power of the Roman Governor (Luke 20:20) that he might be put to death. This was the motive behind the following question.

22:16–17 They sent to him their disciples along with the Herodians, saying, "Teacher, we know that you are truthful, and teach the way of God in accordance with the truth. You do not court anyone's favour because you show no partiality. Tell us then, what do you think? Is it right to pay taxes to Caesar or not?"

The Pharisees united with their enemies the Herodians to trap Christ in his words. They began, as those who hate us often will, with lying and flattery, before asking Christ to answer a controversial question. Is it right to pay taxes to Caesar or not? The Herodians (supporters of Herod) were puppets of Rome and would have supported the tax, whilst the Pharisees were known to be opposed to it, describing the money as idolatrous.

22:18 But Jesus realized their evil intentions and said, "Hypocrites! Why are you testing me?

The lord of glory knows all things and is never fooled by the deception of men. He denounces them as pretenders and confronts them with the truth: that they were trying to trap him.

22:19 Show me the coin used for the tax." So they brought him a denarius.

Jesus nevertheless answers their duplicitous question. He demands to be shown the coin used for the tax, not because he had never seen one, but in order to make his point.

22:20–21 Jesus said to them, "Whose image is this, and whose inscription?" They replied, "Caesar's." He said to them, "Then give to Caesar the things that are Caesar's, and to God the things that are God's."

Again, Christ knew whose image and inscription was on the coin; he wanted to hear it from the mouths of his questioners. If the money was minted by Caesar as a means of exchange and taxation, then they should not refuse to give to him what was his own. Christians are commanded to pay their dues both in terms of taxation and service to the civil authorities (Rom. 13:1–7). Nor should they, like the men in the parable, refuse to give God what is rightly his—the complete obedience of their hearts and lives (Rom. 12:1).

22:22 Now when they heard this they were stunned, and they left him and went away.

The men were stunned, for they had never imagined that Christ could answer their question without incriminating himself, let alone silence them with his wisdom and absolute authority. They decided it was best to beat a hasty retreat.

Marriage and the Resurrection

22:23 The same day Sadducees (who say there is no resurrection) came to him and asked him,

The Sadducees were like the Pharisees, an influential religious group in Jerusalem; but unlike the Pharisees they did not believe in the resurrection or even in angels. Christ had often referred to resurrection, raising a number of people from the dead, most recently Lazarus (John 11). The Sadducees opposed and wished to discredit Christ's teaching by means of an absurd question.

22:24 "Teacher, Moses said, 'If a man dies without having children, his brother must marry the widow and father children for his brother.'

They began by quoting a regulation from the Law of Moses, which was written in order to keep land and property in the family. One can imagine the difficulties involved when a landed man died if his wife remarried and the new husband acquired rights to his land. This might be catastrophic for other dependents, such as elderly parents. Of course, if the dead man had children, they would inherit the land and so the problem would not arise.

22:25 Now there were seven brothers among us. The first one married and died, and since he had no children he left his wife to his brother.

The Sadducees were not concerned about the validity of this point of law, but simply used in an attempt to discredit Christ's teaching about the resurrection. They claimed that one woman was married to seven brothers in the same family, a story which is unlikely to be true. When the woman eventually died, whose wife will she be in the resurrection, since all seven had her? To their minds, this question reveals the absurdity of the idea of resurrection, how could she live again with all of her seven husbands?

22:26–29 The second did the same, and the third, down to the seventh. Last of all, the woman died. In the resurrection, therefore, whose wife of the seven will she be? For they all had married her." Jesus answered them, "You are deceived, because you don't know the scriptures or the power of God.

Jesus answered that the reason they were blinded by such error was their ignorance of the scripture and their lack of any experimental knowledge of God's power. Had they experienced the power which raises a soul from death to life, they would have little trouble believing in the power that will raise dead bodies too (John 5:25–29).

22:30 For in the resurrection they neither marry nor are given in marriage, but are like angels in heaven.

In one short sentence, Christ states what Paul spends several verses explaining in 1 Corinthians 15. When the dead are raised they are raised with immortal, incorruptible bodies, and are no longer subject to the laws with which we are familiar on earth, such as the laws of gender and marriage.

22:31–32 Now as for the resurrection of the dead, have you not read what was spoken to you by God, 'I am the God of Abraham, the God of Isaac, and the God of Jacob'? He is not the God of the dead but of the living!"

Christ illustrates from scripture that God is the God of resurrection, as he refers to Abraham, Isaac and Jacob as *living* when they had been dead for hundreds of years. God is the eternal God and to him all live.

22:33 When the crowds heard this, they were amazed at his teaching.

Although the crowds were amazed by this teaching, you will observe that Matthew does not allude to the Sadducees changing their hardened view as a result of it, although Christ had confounded and silenced them.

The Greatest Commandment

22:34 Now when the Pharisees heard that he had silenced the Sadducees, they assembled together.

Next the Pharisees tried again. This time one of their highly educated experts of the law tested Christ with a question. Which was the greatest law?

22:35–40 And one of them, an expert in religious law, asked him a question to test him: "Teacher, which commandment in the law is the greatest?" Jesus said to him, "'Love the Lord your God with all your heart, with all your soul, and with all your mind.' This is the first and greatest commandment. The second is like it: 'Love your neighbour as yourself.' All the law and the prophets depend on these two commandments."

Jesus was never perplexed by the questions of the religious leaders, no matter how difficult; for he knew all things. Every word which came from Jesus' mouth is perfect knowledge and wisdom, for he is the wisdom of God.

Even as a child aged twelve years old he had astounded these same men with his comprehension of the scriptures and of the reality of God. In two short sentences Jesus expresses the whole law. In the first he speaks of the laws in associated with a person's relationship to God, and in the second laws dealing with relationships between people. Behaving in a way that agrees with the love of God will result in the fulfilment of all these laws (Rom. 13:10). The Pharisees were unable to trap him in his answer.

Whose Son is the Christ?

22:41–46 While the Pharisees were assembled, Jesus asked them a question: "What do you think about the Christ? Whose son is he?" They said, "The Son of David." He said to them, "How then does David by the Spirit call him 'Lord, 'saying, 'The Lord said to my lord, "Sit at my right hand, until I put your enemies under your feet" '? If David then calls him 'Lord,' how can he be his son?" No one was able to answer him a word, and from that day on no one dared to question him any longer.

Now it was Christ's turn ask a question of his opponents. He knew that they considered the Christ to be the Son of David, and that they were opposed to his claim to be the Christ, the Son of God. So he asks: how it can be that in the prophetic writings of the Psalms, David referred to the Christ as Lord? "Lord" means one greater in authority, and David, King of Israel knew only one Lord, and that was the Lord God. David was sat on the throne of Israel but not at the position of honour and power in heaven at the right hand of God. David's lord would be given all power and authority in heaven and earth, with every enemy placed under his feet by God.

Who could such a lord be? Certainly not a lesser than David, who never ascended to the throne of God, and who never once enjoyed the whole world bowing down to him. It is Jesus Christ who has been highly exalted, given the name above every name, and who is ascended to heaven to sit at God's right hand until the time that he takes up his authority and returns to earth to reign. God has made him lord of all men, that at the name of Jesus every knee should bow (Phil. 2:9–11). Such revelation had not yet been given and was certainly unknown to Christ's enemies, although he spoke to them again about it at his trial (Matt. 26:63–64).

Discussion Questions for Chapter 22

1. vv. 1–14. Why was it that many of those who were invited to the wedding banquet failed to attend?

2. vv. 10–14. Why was the man without wedding clothes cast out? What spiritual truth does this illustrate?

3. vv. 15–22. What do you think it means to pay to Caesar what is Caesar's and to God what is God's?

4. vv. 23–33. Why did the Sadducees get it wrong about there being no resurrection?

5. vv.41–46. How did Jesus explain to the Pharisees that Christ was someone greater than David's son?

You will find suggested answers to these questions on pages 306–323.

Matthew Chapter 23

Doers of the Word not Just Teachers

23:1–2 Then Jesus said to the crowds and to his disciples, "The experts in the law and the Pharisees sit on Moses' seat.

Jesus addresses these next ten verses to the crowds and his disciples. He wants them to show respect to the scribes and Pharisees because they are the leaders of Israel and teachers of the Law of Moses.

23:3 Therefore pay attention to what they tell you and do it. But do not do what they do, for they do not practice what they teach.

They are to obey everything they are taught by them from the word of God, but not follow their example; because they do not practice what they teach (Rom. 7:12; Gal. 3:24).

23:4 They tie up heavy loads, hard to carry, and put them on men's shoulders, but they themselves are not willing even to lift a finger to move them.

They impose their own rules and regulations that are heavy burdens and too oppressive to be borne. They will not lift a finger to relieve anyone.

23:5 They do all their deeds to be seen by people, for they make their phylacteries wide and their tassels long.

They are nothing but show-offs. Everything they do publicly is only to attract attention to themselves. They wear extra-large phylacteries (prayer boxes containing scripture verses) on their arms and foreheads (Deut. 6:6–8). All their good deeds are done so that others can see and know them. They attach long fringes on the edges of their robes (Num. 15:38–39).

23:6 They love the place of honour at banquets and the best seats in the synagogues.

They love to have the seats of honour at banquets and to sit in the best seats in the meeting places.

23:7 And elaborate greetings in the marketplaces, and to have people call them 'Rabbi.'

When they are going about the marketplace they delight to hear the people give them respectful greetings and acknowledge them as Rabbi.

23:8 But you are not to be called 'Rabbi,' for you have one Teacher and you are all brothers.

Jesus tells his followers that they should not have anyone call them Rabbi, for there is only one teacher and that is Jesus Christ. They are brothers in Christ.

23:9 And call no one your 'father' on earth, for you have one Father, who is in heaven.

In a religious or priestly sense do not call any man father on earth, for there is only one Father of the soul—God in heaven.

23:10 Nor are you to be called 'teacher,' for you have one teacher, the Christ.

Again Jesus tells his followers not to let anyone call them teacher, for he alone is their teacher.

23:11 The greatest among you will be your servant.

The person who is an elder or leader among them is to serve the others.

23:12 And whoever exalts himself will be humbled, and whoever humbles himself will be exalted.

Those who put themselves above others with haughtiness shall be brought down. Whoever humbles himself in spirit and manner shall be raised to honour.

Religious Hypocrites

23:13 "But woe to you, experts in the law and you Pharisees, hypocrites! You keep locking people out of the kingdom of heaven! For you neither enter nor permit those trying to enter to go in.

Jesus addressed his next remarks to the scribes and Pharisees who were not ignorant of the law and who taught the people its ordinances. Because of their knowledge they would suffer much sorrow. By their hypocrisies (their insincerity in pretending to have qualities or beliefs that they did not really have) they keep shutting the door into the kingdom of heaven in peoples' faces. By opposing Christ's teaching they will not go in themselves and will not allow others to enter in.

23:14 (NKJV™) Woe to you, scribes and Pharisees, hypocrites! For you devour widows' houses, and for a pretence make long prayers. Therefore you will receive greater condemnation.

Great sorrow awaits these teachers of the law for they cheated widows out of their homes whilst pretending to be very holy and offering long prayers to God. Because they disguise their evil behind the mask of pretended righteousness they will receive the greater condemnation.

23:15 "Woe to you, experts in the law and you Pharisees, hypocrites! You cross land and sea to make one convert, and when you get one, you make him twice as much a child of hell as yourselves!

Again great sorrow awaits these people because they go to great lengths to convert one person to Judaism and having ensnared them make twice as bad as themselves. In fact Jesus says they make their converts children of hell like themselves.

23:16 "Woe to you, blind guides, who say, 'Whoever swears by the temple is bound by nothing. But whoever swears by the gold of the temple is bound by the oath.'

For the fourth time Jesus tells them that great sorrow awaits them, for although they are spiritually blind they still try to lead the people into spiritual truths; which they themselves cannot see (or rather do not want to see). They tell the people that if they make an oath by the temple it is meaningless. But if they make an oath by the gold of the temple then it is binding.

23:17–18 Blind fools! Which is greater, the gold or the temple that makes the gold sacred? And, 'Whoever swears by the altar is bound by nothing. But if anyone swears by the gift on it he is bound by the oath. '

As far as spiritual things are concerned they are blind fools who think that the gold of the temple is greater than what the temple represents. It is the God of the temple who sanctifies the gold that adorns it. The Pharisees also taught that if anyone made an oath by the altar it did not signify anything. But if someone made an oath by the sacrificial gift on the altar then they are bound by their oath.

23:19–21 You are blind! For which is greater, the gift or the altar that makes the gift sacred? So whoever swears by the altar swears by it and by everything on it. And whoever swears by the temple swears by it and the one who dwells in it.

Are these hypocrites so blind that they cannot see which is the greater: the altar or the sacrificial gift? Jesus insists that whoever makes an oath by the altar is swearing by everything that is on it, and is bound by their oath. Likewise whoever makes on oath by the temple is swearing by God, by whose dwelling place it is.

23:22 And whoever swears by heaven swears by the throne of God and the one who sits on it.

Again whoever makes an oath in the name of heaven is swearing by the throne of God and by him who sits on it. Note that Jesus is addressing the hypocrisy of the scribes and Pharisees when he speaks about making oaths; he is not advocating that Christians should make an oath (James 5:12).

23:23 "Woe to you, experts in the law and you Pharisees, hypocrites! You give a tenth of mint, dill, and cumin, yet you neglect what is more important in the law – justice, mercy, and faithfulness! You should have done these things without neglecting the others.

These hypocrites made a big show of tithing every little thing—even the herbs they grew. Yet they neglected to do the most important parts of the law, which are to do with justice, love, mercy and faithfulness. These they ought particularly to have done without neglecting any other point of the law.

23:24 Blind guides! You strain out a gnat yet swallow a camel!

Jesus does not spare them at all. Again he says they are spiritually blind guides who, if they had a gnat in their water would strain it out, but they would swallow a camel! In other words, they take great care in keeping the minor parts of the law but the most important parts they neglect. This is in reference to the preceding verse.

23:25 "Woe to you, experts in the law and you Pharisees, hypocrites! You clean the outside of the cup and the dish, but inside they are full of greed and self-indulgence.

The Pharisees were most particular about washing cups, dishes, hands, feet and clothes; all the outward adorning. This was not a matter of cleanliness, but the observance of a religious ritual. Yet inside they were still unclean and full of greed, selfishness and sin (Isaiah 64:6; Rom. 3:10).

23:26 Blind Pharisee! First clean the inside of the cup, so that the outside may become clean too!

Particularly addressing the Pharisees who were full of self-righteousness, Jesus tells them that it is the heart they need to get clean first and then their outward life would become clean too (Jer. 4:14; Ezek. 18:31; Heb. 1:3; Heb. 10:12).

23:27–28 "Woe to you, experts in the law and you Pharisees, hypocrites! You are like whitewashed tombs that look beautiful on the outside but inside are full of the bones of the dead and of everything unclean. In the same way, on the outside you look righteous to people, but inside you are full of hypocrisy and lawlessness.

These scribes and Pharisees were like tombs that had been whitewashed; looking beautiful on the outside but with dead corrupting bodies inside. They are like tombs on the outside in that they look very clean and righteous but in their hearts they are full of hypocrisy and sin (Eph. 2:1).

23:29–30 "Woe to you, experts in the law and you Pharisees, hypocrites! You build tombs for the prophets and decorate the graves of the righteous. And you say, 'If we had lived in the days of our ancestors, we would not have participated with them in shedding the blood of the prophets.'

These hypocrites built elaborately decorated tombs for the prophets and adorned the graves of the righteous. They made the boast that if they had lived in the days of these prophets whom their forefathers had murdered they would not have participated with them.

23:31–32 By saying this you testify against yourselves that you are descendants of those who murdered the prophets. Fill up then the measure of your ancestors!

By this declaration they were condemning themselves, showing that they were the descendants of those who had killed the prophets. Jesus not only meant that they were their natural descendants, they were also their spiritual counterparts; he knew that they were plotting to kill him (Matt. 26:4). So he tells them to go ahead and finish what their ancestors had started.

23:33 You snakes, you offspring of vipers! How will you escape being condemned to hell?

Jesus' final caustic words to them revealed their true nature. They were snakes and sons of vipers (snakes have poison is their mouths). They would be unable to escape the eternal punishment of suffering in hell.

Jesus Foretells the Destruction of Jerusalem

23:34 "For this reason I am sending you prophets and wise men and experts in the law, some of whom you will kill and crucify, and some you will flog in your synagogues and pursue from town to town,

To warn them of the eternal danger they were in, Jesus would send them prophets, wise people and experts in the law of God. Yet despite this God-given opportunity for repentance, the religious leaders would kill and crucify some of these, whilst flogging others and throwing them out of the synagogues; persecuting them from town to town (Acts 5:40; 7:57–58; 9:1–2; 12:2).

23:35 so that on you will come all the righteous blood shed on earth, from the blood of righteous Abel to the blood of Zechariah son of Barachiah, whom you murdered between the temple and the altar.

As a result of their treatment of the prophets this present generation of Jews would be held responsible for the murder of all godly people: from righteous Abel to the blood of Zechariah son of Barachiah who they slew between the temple and the altar. Of this event we have no other record, if 2 Chron. 24:20–21 is (as it appears to be) a reference to a different Zechariah.

23:36 I tell you the truth, this generation will be held responsible for all these things!

It was certain that this came to pass on the people living in Jesus' time, for it was they who finally rejected the Son of God who had come to save them. To use a Biblical picture, the nation's "cup" of sin would become full and provoke judgment. The nation that had killed the prophets would now kill God's son and later reject the witness of the early church.

23:37 "O Jerusalem, Jerusalem, you who kill the prophets and stone those who are sent to you! How often I have longed to gather your children together as a hen gathers her chicks under her wings, but you would have none of it!

It is evident from this beseeching cry of Jesus that he earnestly desired the salvation of the Jews. Those who had killed and stoned the prophets would hand him over to be crucified. In love he reached out to them continuously and yearned for them to come into his outstretched arms that he might protect and comfort them as a mother does for her chicks. But they would have none of it.

23:38–39 Look, your house is left to you desolate! For I tell you, you will not see me from now until you say, 'Blessed is the one who comes in the name of the Lord!'

Here in this verse Jesus foretells the destruction of Jerusalem and the temple in A.D. 70 by the Romans. Yet it also seems to foretell a day (possibly near the end of time) in which the Jewish nation, which at this time had rejected Christ, would repent as one nation to receive and welcome him.

Discussion Questions for Chapter 23

1. vv. 1–3. In what ways were the scribes and Pharisees to be obeyed?

2. vv. 1–12. In what ways were the examples of the scribes and Pharisees not to be followed?

3. vv. 13–33. List the reasons for the woes which Jesus pronounced on the scribes and Pharisees.

4. vv. 34–36. Why did Jesus say that punishment was about to come on the people of Jerusalem?

5. vv. 37–39. From the words Jesus uses about Jerusalem, what do you think were his own feelings about the city and its coming destruction?

You will find suggested answers to these questions on pages 306–323.

Matthew Chapter 24

Signs of the End of the World

24:1 Now as Jesus was going out of the temple courts and walking away, his disciples came to show him the temple buildings.

The disciples of Jesus were absorbed with the things which relate to the material world. They could see the beautiful and expensive buildings which made up the temple, and wanted to share their wonder and admiration with the Lord.

24:2 And he said to them, "Do you see all these things? I tell you the truth, not one stone will be left on another. All will be torn down!"

But Jesus' mind was at all times, and especially at this time, fixed on eternal things. The world held no appeal for him; indeed nothing in the world will remain one day, and that is why we must live for eternity. The temple and the sacrificial system which it represented would be abolished by the bringing in of a new covenant (Heb. 10:9), and so the significance of the temple would cease (John 4:21–24). From that time on, the temple of God would be within and among his people (2 Cor. 6:16). The temple itself would be literally demolished, with every stone torn out individually. This happened when the Romans took Jerusalem in AD 70 under Titus.

24:3 As he was sitting on the Mount of Olives, his disciples came to him privately and said, "Tell us, when will these things happen? And what will be the sign of your coming and of the end of the age?"

As Jesus was sitting on the Mount of Olives, some of his disciples came to him, eager to know more details about these terrible and seemingly apocalyptic events. They linked the destruction of the temple with the end of the world, and they were to some extent right.

The destruction of the temple marked the *beginning* of the end, with Israel scattered all over the world. But that beginning of the end was almost 2,000 years ago, and Jesus wanted to put these events into context for his disciples.

24:4–6 Jesus answered them, "Watch out that no one misleads you. For many will come in my name, saying, 'I am the Christ,' and they will mislead many. You will hear of wars and rumours of wars. Make sure that you are not alarmed, for this must happen, but the end is still to come.

Christ began by urging his disciples not to listen to false Christs or their messengers (false apostles and prophets). Many were to come (and have since come) claiming to be the chosen one of God. Later, John warned of these false messengers (1 John 2:18) but assures us that we have been given the anointing of the Holy Spirit to guard us from their erroneous doctrine (1 John 2:20, 2:27). Paul also warned of the Holy Spirit's witness that a great falling away from truth would occur as the end of time approached (1 Tim. 4:1).

Clearly, the world would not end with the destruction of the temple; there would be far more dreadful and significant events on earth besides that. These events are sometimes referred to as the signs of the times, or the signs of Jesus' coming. With the increase of these things on earth, we become aware that the coming of Christ is drawing nearer.

24:7 For nation will rise up in arms against nation, and kingdom against kingdom. And there will be famines and earthquakes in various places.

Jesus predicted wars affecting whole nations. Also there would be rumours of wars, implying sedition and espionage, as well as civil unrest and acts of terrorism. In addition there would be famines and earthquakes of increasing magnitude in an increasing number of places.

241

As the severity and frequency of these events increase we can be sure that our Lord's coming draws nearer.

24:8 All these things are the beginning of birth pains.

Yet Jesus did not regard these events as taking place at the latter end of time. They would not usher in the end of the world, but rather would occur throughout the church age. Like a pregnant woman going into labour pains before giving birth, so these pains must come before the renewal of all things.

24:9 "Then they will hand you over to be persecuted and will kill you. You will be hated by all the nations because of my name.

Throughout the church age there has been persecution of Christian believers, even to death. This is happening at this present time more than at any other time in history. Jesus predicted that there would be times when, in every nation, believers would be at risk of harm from unbelievers; every nation will hate us. It is always the case that the world hates us, but it is only sometimes that this hatred spills over into violence and murder.

24:10–12 Then many will be led into sin, and they will betray one another and hate one another. And many false prophets will appear and deceive many, and because lawlessness will increase so much, the love of many will grow cold.

Here is one of the most terrible warnings in the Bible, a warning which is repeated several times in the epistles. Because of the increasing evil in the world, many believers will turn from the faith and become apostates. Rather than suffer for Christ's sake (not necessarily to death) they will abandon their faith in him. People have denied Christ for less than death. As a result of their turning from Christ they will, like Judas, betray their Christian brothers too; in some cases to the point of death.

From experience we know that those who leave Jesus Christ, as close as they have been to us before when they knew the Lord, will hate us and be our complete enemies afterward. That is no fault on our part; it is because they are no longer right with God. Throughout the history of the church there have been false prophets who have claimed to speak in the name of God. Some might be classified as being outside the church, such as Joseph Smith who founded the Mormons. Others conceal themselves within the church, seeking to do Satan's work by leading the church into destructive error. Many, says Jesus, will be deceived both within and without the church.

24:13 But the person who endures to the end will be saved.

In the face of false teaching, faithfulness to the Lord Jesus Christ and his truth will be called for, both from individuals and from the church as a whole. The Bible gives us safeguards to protect us from falling away. For example, we are not to forsake the assembling of ourselves together (Heb. 10:25) but to continue in prayer, fellowship and study of the word (Acts 2:42).

24:14 And this gospel of the kingdom will be preached throughout the whole inhabited earth as a testimony to all the nations, and then the end will come.

Whatever else happens on earth in terms of natural disasters and spiritual declension, the gospel of Jesus Christ will still have its way. It will be preached to every creature in the entire world; then, and not before shall the end come. God will give every person a chance to repent and believe on his son Jesus Christ.

We could sum up what Jesus has said so far by saying that evil and sin will grow worse and worse on earth, with men being driven by the power of darkness and Satan, yet his gospel will succeed in saving sinners to the end of time. Whilst these evils are signs that Christ is coming soon, we ought not to presume that he approves of them; when he comes he shall abolish them (Psalm 46:9; Isaiah 2:4).

24:15 "So when you see the abomination of desolation — spoken about by Daniel the prophet — standing in the holy place (let the reader understand),

Christ now turns his attention from the general events of the church age to the events at the very end of time. Many commentators go into great detail about the time of Antiochus Epiphanes and the desecration of the temple, equating Daniels words with this event. It is most significant that our Lord does not do this. He spoke to his disciples about a future day; whereas Epiphanes had died hundreds of years before.

The abomination of desolation is a desecration of God's temple (and his holy name) which shall be so severe as to herald the very end of time and bring down the final judgment of God. Since our Lord is speaking of a time further future than AD 33, and since this event did not precede the destruction of the temple in AD 70, we may readily make several observations: firstly, a new temple will be rebuilt in Jerusalem before this event occurs. At the time of writing (2015) this has yet to happen.

Secondly, the Bible predicts a terrible apostasy at the end of time which involves a certain individual, referred to as "the beast" or "antichrist" sitting in the temple of god and proclaiming that he is God, and demanding worship from all nations of the earth at pain of death (2 Thess. 2:4; Rev. 13:3–8). Furthermore, he shall honour Satan as his God and oblige every person on earth to receive a brand by way of demonstrating allegiance to Satan, or face certain death by starvation or beheading. He will set up a statue of himself in the temple of God, which by satanic power is able to move, speak, and execute those who will not bow to it (Rev. 13:15–17). It therefore seems reasonable to suggest that this man sitting in God's temple claiming to be God could be the abomination of desolation referred to here; indeed, it is difficult to imagine any desecration of God's temple being more serious than this.

24:16–18 then those in Judea must flee to the mountains. The one on the roof must not come down to take anything out of his house, and the one in the field must not turn back to get his cloak.

There will of course be some faithful to God alive on earth at that time. It seems correct to suppose these to be the faithful remnant of Jews who shall face the worst time of persecution in the history of their people, but whom God shall preserve and reconcile to himself. Paul writes of the whole nation of Israel being won to Jesus Christ (Rom. 11:26). Though many shall die rather than worship the beast, it appears that God will include them among the faithful who partake in the first resurrection, for we must not suppose that the rapture closes the age of resurrection (Rev. 20:4). Those Jews who live in Judea are to flee to the mountains with all speed, not stopping so long as to pick up a cloak or take any personal effects. This man, the antichrist, is going to try to round them all up and kill them. But God will provide wings for their escape and protect Israel miraculously (Rev. 12:13–17).

24:19–21 Woe to those who are pregnant and to those who are nursing their babies in those days! Pray that your flight may not be in winter or on a Sabbath. For then there will be great suffering unlike anything that has happened from the beginning of the world until now, or ever will happen.

Once again, these verses make clear that these events predicted by Christ are yet to come. The worst time of persecution and suffering the world (and especially Israel) has ever known would, up until now, be a reference to the Nazi holocaust. But there was no temple at the time of the Nazi holocaust, indicating the possibility of an even worse time yet to come. Clearly, this must be a time of unimaginable evil. It will be especially awful for those women who are pregnant or nursing babies. No doubt many children's lives will be lost. It appears from verse 20 that God is able, in answer to prayer, to delay Satan's purposes, so that the flight from Jerusalem is not in winter (snow, ice and cold might hamper the escape and claim many lives itself), and not on a Sabbath, where pious Jews would not run far enough to be safe.

24:22 And if those days had not been cut short, no one would be saved. But for the sake of the elect those days will be cut short.

So terrible would those days be that if God had not in his mercy limited them, no mortal flesh would survive. But for the sake of those whom he has called of the Jewish nation, the days are shortened (i.e. restricted) to approx. 3 ½ years (Rev. 12:14).

24:23 Then if anyone says to you, 'Look, here is the Christ!' or 'There he is!' do not believe him.

Just as Jesus warned during the church age, so at the end of time especially shall false messiahs appear. But they will only bring false hopes and are not to be followed (Rev. 13:10).

24:24 For false messiahs and false prophets will appear and perform great signs and wonders to deceive, if possible, even the elect.

They will be permitted to perform great signs and wonders by the power of Satan. It is significant that the antichrist will have a false prophet of his own, commanding fire to come out of heaven in the sight of all men (Rev. 13:11–14). The evidence of these supernatural signs will be utterly compelling, but not all that is supernatural is of God.

24:25 Remember, I have told you ahead of time.

Jesus warned his disciples, and his disciples have warned future generations of these events by recording his words. We have been warned.

24:26–27 So then, if someone says to you, 'Look, he is in the wilderness,' do not go out, or 'Look, he is in the inner rooms,' do not believe him. For just like the lightning comes from the east and flashes to the west, so the coming of the Son of Man will be.

Unlike the false messiahs, the real Christ will be seen coming on the clouds of heaven, appearing to the whole world simultaneously and in an instant. Lightning appears at light speed, and lights up the whole heaven. The coming of Christ will be witnessed by the whole cosmos, northern and southern hemispheres, angels and demons, and even those in hell shall not fail to witness this event (Mark 13:26; Rev. 1:7).

24:28–29 Wherever the corpse is, there the vultures will gather. "Immediately after the suffering of those days, the sun will be darkened, and the moon will not give its light; the stars will fall from heaven, and the powers of heaven will be shaken.

At once, at the end of the brief time (approx. 3 ½ years) of unspeakable suffering, the end will come, preceded by several cosmic events. The sun was darkened as Christ hung upon the cross, and will again be darkened at the time of his coming. As the end of the world approaches, the sun will be partially darkened (Rev. 8:12), and later the whole earth will be plunged into darkness (Rev. 16:10).

At the very end of time the sun will no longer be needed, nor the moon (Rev. 21:23). The stars falling from heaven is a reference to their ceasing to exist, vanishing away (2 Pet. 3:10). They shall fall from the sky as ripe figs fall from the tree (Isa. 34:4), but obviously, since stars are massive they will not fall to the earth. They shall be put away like an old garment (Psa. 102:25–26), no longer fit for purpose, together with all the heavenly bodies and powers (such as gravity) which control them .

24:30 Then the sign of the Son of Man will appear in heaven, and all the tribes of the earth will mourn. They will see the Son of Man arriving on the clouds of heaven with power and great glory.

What the sign of the Son of Man is, no one has ever clearly identified. However, it will be a sign of such significance that no one alive of earth shall fail to understand that it is *his* sign and that it portends his immediate revelation. The people of earth will mourn when they see this sign, not in repentance but remorse; not in sorrow for their sin, but in sorrow that they will not escape judgment.

Following this sign (the intervening period of time is not specified, but the words imply almost immediately), they will see Christ coming on the clouds of heaven with great power and glory; the Son of God will be revealed in all his eternal, almighty, and creative power. His glory is great because it is God's glory, and it shall be revealed in its full majesty to all people. Christ is not merely exalted above all else, but *far* above all else (Eph. 1:21). Tragically for humankind, it will be in his role as judge and the avenger of wrongs that he shall appear.

24:31 And he will send his angels with a loud trumpet blast, and they will gather his elect from the four winds, from one end of heaven to the other.

Some take the view that this verse is a reference to an event known as the rapture. The word rapture is not used in scripture, but it has been used to describe that time, before his return to earth, when Jesus will snatch away his own from the world (24:44); resurrected saints will be joined with living saints whose bodies are changed and all shall meet him together in the clouds (1 Thess. 4:13–18). By taking this verse chronologically, some have supposed it to indicate that this rapture of the church does not take place until after Christ's second coming in glory. Yet since other scriptures seemingly contradict this view, we cannot accept its validity. Christ will sound the trumpet to receive his own to himself, and they will be caught up from every corner of the globe to meet with Christ in the clouds. But later they will return to earth with him during the battle of Armageddon (Rev. 19:14).

Two possible explanations present themselves to answer the problem of chronology: either Jesus *is* referring to the rapture of the church, but does not intend these events to be placed in chronological order; or this verse refers not to the rapture but to the gathering of God's faithful Jews alive on earth at this time, who will obtain a place among his people. Taking everything into account I think the former explanation to be more likely.

24:32–33 "Learn this parable from the fig tree: Whenever its branch becomes tender and puts out its leaves, you know that summer is near. So also you, when you see all these things, know that he is near, right at the door.

Just as the changing seasons give evidence of their own approach, so the signs Christ has given are intended to indicate the near approach of his second advent in power and glory.

24:34-35 I tell you the truth, this generation will not pass away until all these things take place. Heaven and earth will pass away, but my words will never pass away.

Jesus gives the assurance that these things will not fail to happen. They cannot be avoided. The present age will not pass away until all these things are accomplished. This is sure, for he has spoken it, and just as man does not live by bread alone, but by every word of God, so the entire existence of the universe is sustained by his powerful and eternal word (Heb. 1:3). God's word cannot fail, for God cannot lie (Tit. 1:2).

24:36 "But as for that day and hour no one knows it — not even the angels in heaven — except the Father alone.

Although we are given to know and understand the signs of the times, yet we are not given to know the exact details and precise timings of these events. In particular, we will not know the time of Christ's coming into the clouds to receive his saints. Such knowledge has not been delegated, either to angels or to people, but is known only to God. Despite what some modern Bible teachers are telling us, God will not give his people any additional prophetic insight at the time of the end; except to say that as these events begin to occur, we shall recognise them for what they really are.

24:37 For just like the days of Noah were, so the coming of the Son of Man will be.

Christ uses the illustration of Noah, since neither Noah nor his contemporaries were specifically told the time of the flood. God had warned them of its coming, and that they should be ready, but life carried on as normal. Most of the people lived without any thought for God; until the day that Noah was taken safely into the ark as God called him in and shut the door.

24:38–39 For in those days before the flood, people were eating and drinking, marrying and giving in marriage, until the day Noah entered the ark. And they knew nothing until the flood came and took them all away. It will be the same at the coming of the Son of Man.

In their unbelief the people were completely ignorant of what was about to happen. They had not believed Noah's warning, and were consequently unprepared. The flood destroyed the whole world of the ungodly (2 Pet. 2:5). This present world, says Peter, is reserved in the same way for fire in the Day of Judgment and perdition of ungodly men (2 Pet. 3:7).

24:40 Then there will be two men in the field; one will be taken and one left.

It does not seem possible to understand these verses as a reference to anything other than the rapture of the church. Jesus' point has been that Noah was taken to a place of safety by God, whilst the ungodly were left outside to face destruction. Believers in Christ will be rescued from the judgment to come by Christ, who will come to meet them in the clouds before judgment falls on earth. Among earth's millions are only two groups of people: unbelievers and Christians. At the time of Christ's calling his people away, one man ploughing a field will be taken, snatched up in the rapture to be with Jesus; the other man, an unbeliever, will be left behind to face the wrath of God.

24:41 There will be two women grinding grain with a mill; one will be taken and one left.

Similarly, two women (one a believer and one an unbeliever) shall be occupied in the same trade, but the rapture will be the event which shall finally and irreparably separate the two.

24:42 "Therefore stay alert, because you do not know on what day your Lord will come.

One of the reasons why God does not make the day and time of Christ's coming known to us is to motivate us to stay alert and watchful. The coming of Christ for his own and our gathering together to him is the blessed hope of all believers, and a powerful incentive for faithfulness; bringing renewed strength to our flagging spirits. It is also a powerful warning to prevent us from backsliding, for we know that we must all give account to God when Christ comes again.

24:43 But understand this: If the owner of the house had known at what time of night the thief was coming, he would have been alert and would not have let his house be broken into.

From this illustration, we see the need to stay alert and watchful in the things of God at all times. Do not allow yourself to fall asleep spiritually, or that day will take you unawares like a thief in the night. This warning is repeated by Paul in 1 Thessalonians 5:1–11. Since we are not in the dark, let us walk in the light as we wait for Christ's coming. We will only be ready for the day of truth to come if we live in the truth day by day.

24:44 Therefore you also must be ready, because the Son of Man will come at an hour when you do not expect him.

Since Christ's coming will be unannounced, we must be ready at all times. This again seems to indicate that Christ is speaking of his parousia, his coming into the air to be united with his own (the rapture), which precedes his return to earth with his saints. I say this because, at his second advent, the armies of earth gather to meet him at his coming, and the sign of the Son of Man is visible in heaven; hence Christ's advent will not be unexpected by the inhabitants of earth. But his coming for his own comes silently and suddenly like a thief in the night, and will snatch his people away before the final time of trouble takes place.

24:45–47 "Who then is the faithful and wise slave, whom the master has put in charge of his household, to give the other slaves their food at the proper time? Blessed is that slave whom the master finds at work when he comes. I tell you the truth, the master will put him in charge of all his possessions.

Luke makes clear that this parable was given in response to Peter's question "Lord are you telling this to us or to all?" Jesus did not want his disciples to be complacent about their spiritual condition.

Those servants who, having been given tasks by their master, are faithfully doing them will have nothing to fear; no matter what time of day their master returns. Indeed, they shall be blessed for their master will richly reward them, giving them stewardship which will entail joint possession of all that he has.

24:48–51 But if that evil slave should say to himself, 'My master is staying away a long time,' and he begins to beat his fellow slaves and to eat and drink with drunkards, then the master of that slave will come on a day when he does not expect him and at an hour he does not foresee, and will cut him in two, and assign him a place with the hypocrites, where there will be weeping and gnashing of teeth.

But, if the servant begins to doubt the master's word (that he will return) and by his conduct begins to demonstrate his unbelief, disobeying his master's commands with abusive and drunken behaviour and joining with those who are his master's enemies (a picture of a backslider) then his master will come without further warning, and since he is living like an unbeliever he will be treated like an unbeliever. His doom shall be unchangeably sealed in hell.

The events of the time of the end are spread out, yet the Bible speaks of them as if they were one event; the reason being that they inevitably follow one another. If a backslider misses the coming of Christ, yet Christ's words will come true upon him, no matter what the time scale might be. He will end up in hell, where there is eternal agony and regret.

Discussion Questions for Chapter 24

1. vv. 1–2. In these verses, why did the beautiful temple seem unimportant to Jesus?

2. vv. 3–14. List some of the signs which Jesus gave to denote the approach of the end of time.

3. vv. 15–25. How would you describe the events Jesus predicted in these verses?

4. vv. 26–36. How did Jesus describe the manner of his coming again?

5. vv. 37–51. In the light of Jesus teaching in these verses, what do you think it means to be a faithful and wise servant of Christ?

You will find suggested answers to these questions on pages 306–323.

Matthew Chapter 25

Proving Professing Christians

25:1 "At that time the kingdom of heaven will be like ten virgins who took their lamps and went out to meet the bridegroom.

The time referred to is the coming of the Lord Jesus Christ for his church. Scripture tells us that the church is like a bride (Rev. 21:2, 9) and Jesus Christ is the bridegroom (Mark 2:19–20). As yet the marriage has not taken place (Rev. 19:7–9), so the church is spoken of as a virgin; and consists of those who have been washed in the blood of the Lamb and made pure and holy by him.

25:2 Five of the virgins were foolish, and five were wise.

The church is divided into two kinds of people. Jesus calls half of them foolish and the other half wise. Who are these people? They are all professing to be Christians and appear to be part of Christ's church.

25:3 When the foolish ones took their lamps, they did not take extra olive oil with them.

The five foolish only had the oil which was in their lamps; they did not take extra oil to refill their lamps. Since they did not know the hour when the bridegroom would come they should have made sure they had extra oil with them. These represent those people who embrace Christianity as a religion and perform religious rituals without embracing its fullness. Paul says they have a form godliness but deny its power or as the New Living Testament puts it "they will act religious, but they will reject the power that could make them godly" (2 Tim. 3:5). They profess to be Christians but have no living experience of Jesus Christ.

25:4 But the wise ones took flasks of olive oil with their lamps.

The wise, however, took containers with them filled with oil ready to refill their lamps. These know Jesus Christ as their personal Lord and Saviour in truth and experience. They endeavour to make certain that they remain ready, whatever hour their Lord comes.

25:5 When the bridegroom was delayed a long time, they all became drowsy and fell asleep.

The bridegroom was delayed for a long time and they all became tired of waiting and fell asleep (1 Thess. 5:6; 2 Peter 3:3–4). The word "delayed" is used in almost every translation but we must not think that the time of the Lord's coming will be delayed from God's point of view. God has appointed the time for this to happen and it will take place at that exact time. From Paul's letters we know that the early church expected the return of the Lord Jesus at any moment, but it has not happened yet. This is what may be considered by human standards as a delay.

25:6 But at midnight there was a shout, 'Look, the bridegroom is here! Come out to meet him.'

At midnight the cry went out that the bridegroom had arrived and the virgins were summoned to come and meet him (1 Cor. 15:52).

25:7 Then all the virgins woke up and trimmed their lamps.

At the shout they all woke up and trimmed their lamps in readiness.

25:8 The foolish ones said to the wise, 'Give us some of your oil, because our lamps are going out.'

Because of the delay the inevitable happened; the oil in the lamps of the foolish ones had run out and they asked the wise to give them some of theirs. These professing Christians were just not ready for the coming of the Lord.

25:9 'No,' they replied. 'There won't be enough for you and for us. Go instead to those who sell oil and buy some for yourselves.'

The wise told them that they only had enough oil to replenish their own lamps; there was not enough for everyone. They would have to go to those who sold oil to get some for themselves. Believers can share by word what they have received from the Lord Jesus Christ; they can tell of their experiences with him, but they cannot impart it to others. No one can live on the experience of another; we have to work out our own salvation (Phil. 2:12).

25:10 But while they had gone to buy it, the bridegroom arrived, and those who were ready went inside with him to the wedding banquet. Then the door was shut.

While they were gone, the bridegroom arrived and those who were ready and prepared went inside with him to the wedding feast. The door was then shut. This reminds us of the time of Noah when he and his family all entered the ark God shut the door (Gen. 7:16); the opportunity of being saved from the flood had past. So will it be when the Lord Jesus Christ comes for his church; the day of grace will end; the door will be closed and the opportunity of salvation will be gone (2 Cor. 6:2).

25:11 Later, the other virgins came too, saying, 'Lord, lord! Let us in!'

A little later, the other five returned and stood outside calling for the Lord to let them in.

25:12 But he replied, 'I tell you the truth, I do not know you!'

He answered them solemnly that he did not know them. Jesus Christ knows only those that are truly his own (John 10:14).

25:13 Therefore stay alert, because you do not know the day or the hour.

In this final verse of the parable the Lord gives the warning that every believer should be watching, waiting and expecting his return; for no one knows the hour that he will come again (1 Thess. 5:2; Rev. 16:15).

Proving Christian Service

25:14 "For it is like a man going on a journey, who summoned his slaves and entrusted his property to them.

The man in this parable represents the Lord Jesus Christ who gives to his followers the truth concerning the kingdom of heaven (John 14:26). He furthermore gave to his church ministry gifts (Eph. 4:11) and various gifts of the Holy Spirit according to his own will (1 Cor. 12:11). Forty days after his resurrection (Acts 1:3) Jesus Christ returned to heaven having entrusted his disciples with the means to proclaim the gospel message (Acts 1:10).

25:15 To one he gave five talents, to another two, and to another one, each according to his ability. Then he went on his journey.

According to 1 Corinthians 12:11 the number of talents (gifts) given to these three men were according to the desire of the Lord, but Jesus says here that they were dispensed according to ability: five, two and one respectively. It is more likely that this is a reference to the way in which different gifts are given to each believer (Rom. 12:6–8).

25:16 The one who had received five talents went off right away and put his money to work and gained five more.

The one who received the most talents (five) immediately put his money to work and doubled it. This was true of the early disciples after Pentecost; they straight away used the gifts given to them to proclaim the gospel message and there were added to them three thousand people (Acts 2:41).

25:17 In the same way, the one who had two gained two more.

The second man did not sit down and complain that he had only been given two talents, but did exactly the same as the one who was given five; doubling his amount.

25:18 But the one who had received one talent went out and dug a hole in the ground and hid his master's money in it.

The man with only one talent perhaps had the greater challenge. Yet he could have done the same as the other two if he had put his talent to use. Instead he did an incredible thing; he went and buried it in the ground (Luke 11:33).

25:19 After a long time, the master of those slaves came and settled his accounts with them.

Just like the master in the parable, the Lord Jesus Christ is coming back and every believer will have to give an account of what they have done with what he entrusted to them (2 Cor. 5:10).

25:20–21 The one who had received the five talents came and brought five more, saying, 'Sir, you entrusted me with five talents. See, I have gained five more. His master answered, 'Well done, good and faithful slave! You have been faithful in a few things. I will put you in charge of many things. Enter into the joy of your master.'

The man given five talents came and brought the other five he had gained, receiving praise from the Lord. It was not for the amount but for his faithfulness that the Lord commended and rewarded him, inviting him to share in his blessedness.

25:22–23 The one with the two talents also came and said, 'Sir, you entrusted two talents to me. See, I have gained two more.' His master answered, 'Well done, good and faithful slave! You have been faithful with a few things. I will put you in charge of many things. Enter into the joy of your master.

The second man came and brought his four talents and presented them to the Lord. He received the same praise as the man who was given the five talents and invited to enter the joy of his Lord.

25:24–27 Then the one who had received the one talent came and said, 'Sir, I knew that you were a hard man, harvesting where you did not sow, and gathering where you did not scatter seed, so I was afraid, and I went and hid your talent in the ground. See, you have what is yours.' But his master answered, 'Evil and lazy slave! So you knew that I harvest where I didn't sow and gather where I didn't scatter? Then you should have deposited my money with the bankers, and on my return I would have received my money back with interest!

Last of all came the man who was given one talent. He professed that he knew the Lord to be a harsh man, harvesting from where he had not sown. Clearly, he did not know the Lord Jesus Christ properly, for he is meek and lowly (Matt. 11:29). He only gathers fruit from his own seed that he has sown. The man professed to be afraid of what the Lord might do to him if lost the talent, but Jesus calls him a lazy, wicked man. If he was really afraid of what the Lord would say and do to him then he should have put the money in a bank where it would have gained interest for his Lord.

25:28 Therefore take the talent from him and give it to the one who has ten.

There was no praise or reward for this man; instead, what had been given to him was taken away and given to the man who brought ten talents back to the Lord.

25:29–30 For the one who has will be given more, and he will have more than enough. But the one who does not have, even what he has will be taken from him. Now throw this useless servant into outer darkness, where there will be weeping and gnashing of teeth.'

To those who are faithful and who use what Christ has given them will be given abundance. But the one who is not faithful and brings nothing to the Lord, even the little he has will be taken away from him. The unfaithful and unprofitable will be cast out into the dark place where "people will cry and grit their teeth in pain." (CEV)

Separating Believers from Unbelievers

25:31–33 When the Son of Man comes in his glory with all of his angels, he will sit on his royal throne. All the nations will be assembled before him, and he will separate people one from another like a shepherd separates the sheep from the goats. He will put the sheep on his right and the goats on his left.

The separating of believers from unbelievers at the last judgment is likened to a shepherd who parts the sheep from the goats. This will take place when Jesus Christ comes with all his angels. Other references to this occasion include 2 Thessalonians 1:7–10 and Revelation 20:11–15.

25:34 Then the king will say to those on his right, 'Come, you who are blessed by my Father, inherit the kingdom prepared for you from the foundation of the world.

He who is the king of kings and lord of lords calls those on his right hand blessed by his Father because they have been redeemed by the blood of the Lamb. They have inherited eternal life and are heirs of the kingdom that has been prepared for them before the world was made (Titus 3:7; James 2:5). These are the sheep.

25:35–40 For I was hungry and you gave me food, I was thirsty and you gave me something to drink, I was a stranger and you invited me in, I was naked and you gave me clothing, I was sick and you took care of me, I was in prison and you visited me.' Then the righteous will answer him, 'Lord, when did we see you hungry and feed you, or thirsty and give you something to drink? When did we see you a stranger and invite you in, or naked and clothe you? When did we see you sick or in prison and visit you?' And the king will answer them, 'I tell you the truth, just as you did it for one of the least of these brothers or sisters of mine, you did it for me.'

Here the Lord makes known that the good works of believers were all done as if to him (Eph. 2:10; Titus 2:14). Whether feeding the hungry, giving a cup of cold water to the thirsty, taking care of the stranger, clothing the naked, nursing the sick or visiting those in prison, Jesus said they had done all these things for him. As far as they were aware they had never even seen him; but the king assures them that every time they ministered to the least of his brothers and sisters in Christ they were ministering to him.

25:41 "Then he will say to those on his left, 'Depart from me, you accursed, into the eternal fire that has been prepared for the devil and his angels!

To those on the left side (the goats, the foolish virgins, the lazy wicked servants), Jesus pronounces the final judgment. They are ordered to depart from him, for they are cursed, for they have sinned against God and not accepted the way of salvation provided for them through his Son. They are cast into the lake of fire prepared for the devil and his angels (Rev. 19:20; Rev. 20:15).

25:42–43 For I was hungry and you gave me nothing to eat, I was thirsty and you gave me nothing to drink. I was a stranger and you did not receive me as a guest, naked and you did not clothe me, sick and in prison and you did not visit me.

Christ reveals their uncompassionate behaviour in refusing to give aid when it was needed (Titus 1:16).

25:44 Then they too will answer, 'Lord, when did we see you hungry or thirsty or a stranger or naked or sick or in prison, and did not give you whatever you needed?'

They ask when it was that they saw him in need and denied him help. The suggestion here is that if they had seen him then they would have met his need.

25:45 Then he will answer them, 'I tell you the truth, just as you did not do it for one of the least of these, you did not do it for me.'

His answer to them was that they had seen him every time they saw those at his right hand, the believers—yet did not lift a finger to help them. This was the same as not doing anything to help him.

25:46 And these will depart into eternal punishment, but the righteous into eternal life."

These unbelievers will go into eternal punishment but the righteous into eternal life.

Discussion Questions for Chapter 25

1. vv. 1–12. Why were the foolish virgins foolish?

2. vv. 1–12. Why were the wise virgins wise?

3. vv. 13–30. Why was the servant with one talent deprived of his talent, when the others were rewarded?

4. vv. 31–45. List the things which Jesus said the righteous had done for him.

5. vv. 31–45. Describe in your own words the difference between the sheep and the goats in this parable.

You will find suggested answers to these questions on pages 306–323.

Matthew Chapter 26

The Crucifixion Near at Hand

26:1–2 When Jesus had finished saying all these things, he told his disciples, "You know that after two days the Passover is coming, and the Son of Man will be handed over to be crucified."

After teaching about his second coming and the final judgment, Jesus turned to his disciples, telling them privately that during the Passover—which was two days away—he would be handed over to the chief priests who would in turn deliver him to the Romans to be crucified.

26:3–4 Then the chief priests and the elders of the people met together in the palace of the high priest, who was named Caiaphas. They planned to arrest Jesus by stealth and kill him.

At that time, the chief priests and elders of the people were gathered together to plot his arrest and death; and although they were unaware of it, this was in fulfilment of God's will and purpose (Acts 2:23; Acts 4:27–28).

26:5 But they said, "Not during the feast, so that there won't be a riot among the people."

The religious rulers prudently decided not to arrest Jesus during the feast, in front of the crowds; for there were so many who followed Jesus that they feared a riot. So they began to look for a way in which to take Christ secretly, which they soon found in the betrayal of Judas Iscariot.

Judas Decides to Betray Jesus

26:6 Now while Jesus was in Bethany at the house of Simon the leper,

For his last nights on earth, Jesus found food and lodging in the home of a man named Simon the leper in Bethany, not far from Jerusalem. Since Simon was at home, no doubt Jesus had cured him of his leprosy. The identity of Simon is uncertain—we do not know, for example, whether he was related to the other friends Jesus had in Bethany: Lazarus, Mary and Martha.

26:7 a woman came to him with an alabaster jar of expensive perfumed oil, and she poured it on his head as he was at the table.

While Jesus was eating the evening meal, a woman came and poured on his head an alabaster jar of expensive perfume as a token of her love and gratitude for his forgiving and saving her soul. It would have cost the woman a lot to purchase this item, and so her action symbolised the giving of her all to Christ. In the same way, the acceptable act of our worship to God should involve all that we have and are (Rom. 12:1–2).

26:8–9 When the disciples saw this, they became indignant and said, "Why this waste? It could have been sold at a high price and the money given to the poor!"

Matthew records that all the disciples were angered that this woman had poured out her expensive gift on Jesus' head; they thought it an extravagant waste. John in his gospel records more specifically that the unrest began with Judas Iscariot. He complained that the perfume should have been sold for a high price and the money given to the poor, not because he cared about the poor but because he loved money. As a thief with access to Jesus' treasury he often helped himself to whatever was put into it (John 12:4–6).

26:10–12 When Jesus learned of this, he said to them, "Why are you bothering this woman? She has done a good service for me. For you will always have the poor with you, but you will not always have me! When she poured this oil on my body, she did it to prepare me for burial.

Jesus rebuked the disciples for their hardness of heart and failure to understand what he had been teaching them, which had resulted in their harsh criticism of this woman. The woman herself had evidently understood Christ's teaching, for Jesus says that her actions were good, and that by them she had prepared his body for burial.

To show love for someone close to you is even more important than showering gifts upon the poor. The disciples would have ample opportunity to show love to the poor, but Jesus would be on earth for just two more days. In the same way we must show our love to our loved ones while they are still here.

26:13 I tell you the truth, wherever this gospel is proclaimed in the whole world, what she has done will also be told in memory of her.

For her demonstration of love to the soon to die Saviour, this woman would be continually remembered wherever the gospel was preached, for her actions teach several important lessons. Firstly, she is a lesson in gratitude and devotion, for she gave all she had to Jesus Christ in gratitude for his salvation, and she was not ashamed to do this in the face of the disciples' criticism. Then secondly she is a lesson in faith, for she believed Christ's words concerning his death and acted upon them. Finally her story teaches that love for Christ must be expressed, for love which is not demonstrated does no good to anyone. Even the love of God for humankind had to be demonstrated; and it was, in the life and ultimately the death of the Lord Jesus.

26:14–15 Then one of the twelve, the one named Judas Iscariot, went to the chief priests and said, "What will you give me to betray him into your hands?" So they set out thirty silver coins for him.

We do not know whether this last disagreement with Jesus had brought to a head a long simmering antipathy in the heart of Judas, but he took this opportunity to strike a bargain with the chief priests about betraying Jesus to them, away from the public eye. His fee was the price of a slave—thirty silver coins; Joseph was sold as a slave for a similar amount, twenty pieces of silver (Gen. 37:28).

26:16 From that time on, Judas began looking for an opportunity to betray him.

From that time on Judas sought opportunity to betray Jesus.

Preparations for the Passover

26:17 Now on the first day of the feast of Unleavened Bread the disciples came to Jesus and said, "Where do you want us to prepare for you to eat the Passover?"

It was customary for the disciples to eat the Passover together with Jesus each year. So they asked him where he would have them to prepare the meal.

26:18 He said, "Go into the city to a certain man and tell him, 'The Teacher says, "My time is near. I will observe the Passover with my disciples at your house." ' "

Luke gives us more detail about this encounter. The disciples were to follow an unnamed man carrying a pitcher of water on his head. They were to approach the house he entered, and say to the owner of the house that Christ would eat his final Passover there (for his time was near). It seems that this man had been prepared by God in some way for this event, possibly through a dream or revelation (Luke 22:7–13).

26:19 So the disciples did as Jesus had instructed them, and they prepared the Passover.

The disciples had come to learn obedience to Jesus, and even as they followed these strange instructions they found things exactly as he had told them. This experience would increase their trust in the Lord, who is always right, down to the tiniest detail.

The Institution of the Communion

26:20–22 When it was evening, he took his place at the table with the twelve. And while they were eating he said, "I tell you the truth, one of you will betray me. They became greatly distressed and each one began to say to him, "Surely not I, Lord?"

As they sat together that evening to eat the Passover meal, Jesus broke the news that one of them would betray him. Since Christ had already revealed something of the sinfulness of their hearts to each of these men, they were not able to entirely trust their own selves. Each of them was distressed to think that it might be him and asks, "surely not I?" We notice that the disciples did not begin to accuse each other. At the Lord's table we are similarly instructed to examine the state of our own hearts before God (1 Cor. 11:28).

26:23 He answered, "The one who has dipped his hand into the bowl with me will betray me.

In literal fulfilment of Psalm 41:9, Jesus shares a sop of bread with Judas on the night in which he was betrayed; this fulfilment of prophecy being intended as a sign to Judas himself.

26:24 The Son of Man will go as it is written about him, but woe to that man by whom the Son of Man is betrayed! It would be better for him if he had never been born."

Although all that was about to happen was in fulfilment of scripture and God's divine purpose, yet no one who participated in the evil about to be done would be excused. This verse clearly portrays God sovereignly working out his own purposes without overruling the free will of men; instead he harnesses their will to accomplish his own ends.

269

26:25 Then Judas, the one who would betray him, said, "Surely not I, Rabbi?" Jesus replied, "You have said it yourself."

Judas is backed into a corner and hypocritically feigns surprise and disbelief. But Jesus is never fooled by such duplicity. He knew who would betray him (John 6:64; John 13:11).

26:26–28 While they were eating, Jesus took bread, and after giving thanks he broke it, gave it to his disciples, and said, "Take, eat, this is my body." And after taking the cup and giving thanks, he gave it to them, saying, "Drink from it, all of you, for this is my blood, the blood of the covenant that is poured out for many for the forgiveness of sins.

Judas having left, Jesus proceeds to institute a new memorial to replace that of the Passover. Just as the Passover involved the death and blood of the lamb, so this act would become a memorial of his broken body and his blood shed on the cross.

As Passover commemorated the Jews deliverance from slavery in Egypt, so the communion pictures the deliverance which Christ provides from the slavery of sin through his death. Christ gave himself that we might be redeemed, purchased for God by his blood. This blessing of redemption is closely related to the forgiveness of sins (Eph. 1:7).

26:29 I tell you, from now on I will not drink of this fruit of the vine until that day when I drink it new with you in my Father's kingdom."

The types and pictures found in the Passover were shortly to be fulfilled by Christ's death and thereafter would no longer be needed. Christ would never take Passover again, but he would share the blessings of the redemption which it symbolised with the believers in his kingdom. Barnes says; "The observance of the Passover, and of the rites shadowing future things, here end. I am about to die. The design of all these types and shadows is about to be accomplished. This is the last time that I shall partake of them with you. Hereafter, when my Father's kingdom is established in heaven, we will partake together of the thing represented by these types and ceremonial observances - the blessings and triumphs of redemption."

26:30 After singing a hymn, they went out to the Mount of Olives.

Before going to face his last and fiercest battle at the cross, Jesus paused to sing hymns of praise to God with his disciples. It is commonly accepted that the hymns sung were the Hallel, or Psalm 113–118. In Christ's singing praise there is a note of the victory which he is about to accomplish. He then sets out to the Mount of Olives, where there is a garden called Gethsemane, to pray there.

Jesus Warns that Self Confidence will Fail

26:31 Then Jesus said to them, "This night you will all fall away because of me, for it is written: 'I will strike the shepherd, and the sheep of the flock will be scattered.

The Lord Jesus Christ knew his disciples better than they knew themselves, so he gave them this penultimate warning (Zech. 13:7). Before the night was over every one of them would desert him. Events were about to happen that the disciples would have no control over and they would not be able to surmount.

26:32 But after I am raised, I will go ahead of you into Galilee."

Jesus gave them a ray of hope that in spite of the fact that they would all desert him, after he was raised from the dead he would go before them into Galilee and meet with them there (Matt. 28:7; Mark 16:7).

26:33 Peter said to him, "If they all fall away because of you, I will never fall away!"

Typically, Peter makes the self-confident boast that even if all the other disciples were made to stumble he would never fail Jesus.

26:34 Jesus said to him, "I tell you the truth, on this night, before the rooster crows, you will deny me three times."

But Jesus told Peter the truth about himself; on that very night he would not only fail his Lord by running away, but before the cock crowed he would deny him three times.

26:35 Peter said to him, "Even if I must die with you, I will never deny you." And all the disciples said the same thing.

Peter ignored what the Lord told him and with great energy and force claimed that he would never deny Jesus even if he had to die with him. All the other disciples made the same commitment. Although they had been with Jesus for so long and knew that every word he said was true, they were blinded by their self-confidence and did not comprehend what he said to them.

Jesus Takes the Cup of Suffering

26:36 Then Jesus went with them to a place called Gethsemane, and he said to the disciples, "Sit here while I go over there and pray.

Jesus then led his disciples to a place called Gethsemane which was an olive grove where he had often met with them (John 18:2).

26:37 He took with him Peter and the two sons of Zebedee, and became anguished and distressed.

As he took Peter, James and John further into the grove than the other disciples, he began to show grief and was deeply troubled.

26:38 Then he said to them, "My soul is deeply grieved, even to the point of death. Remain here and stay awake with me."

He then told the three disciples that he was almost crushed with grief to the point of death. He asked them to remain where they were and stay awake to keep vigilant watch with him. Here he was giving them an opportunity to support him in his time of great need.

26:39 Going a little farther, he threw himself down with his face to the ground and prayed, "My Father, if possible, let this cup pass from me! Yet not what I will, but what you will."

Going a little way from the three disciples, he threw himself face down on the ground and earnestly prayed to his Father that if it was possible the cup of suffering might be taken away from him. Having prayed this Jesus nevertheless submitted himself to the will of his Father, "let your will be done". The cup that Jesus referred to was the death he would suffer on the cross as he bore the sins of the world.

26:40 Then he came to the disciples and found them sleeping. He said to Peter, "So, couldn't you stay awake with me for one hour?

After this he returned to the three disciples and found them asleep. It was to Peter who had boasted that he would die with him that Jesus said "you couldn't even stay awake with me for one hour?" He did not say this contemptuously but with a heart of compassion for he knew the weakness of the flesh.

26:41 Stay awake and pray that you will not fall into temptation. The spirit is willing, but the flesh is weak."

He told them the second time to stay awake and pray so that they would not give in to temptation. Jesus knew that their spirit was willing but that their flesh was weak. We cannot hope to resist temptation or face life's trials victoriously without constant prayer.

26:42 He went away a second time and prayed, "My Father, if this cup cannot be taken away unless I drink it, your will must be done."

Jesus left them for the second time and prayed to his Father that if the cup of suffering could not be taken away unless he drank it, then God's will must be done.

26:43 He came again and found them sleeping; they could not keep their eyes open.

He came again to the disciples and found them sleeping because they could not keep their eyes open.

26:44 So leaving them again, he went away and prayed for the third time, saying the same thing once more.

Leaving them to sleep, he went away and prayed for the third time saying the same things.

26:45 Then he came to the disciples and said to them, "Are you still sleeping and resting? Look, the hour is approaching, and the Son of Man is betrayed into the hands of sinners.

Returning to his disciples he found them still fast asleep. Waking them, he forewarned them that the hour had arrived for the Son of Man to be betrayed into the hands of sinners.

26:46 Get up, let us go. Look! My betrayer is approaching!"

Telling them to get up he went to meet his betrayer.

Jesus' Betrayal and Arrest

26:47 While he was still speaking, Judas, one of the twelve, arrived. With him was a large crowd armed with swords and clubs, sent by the chief priests and elders of the people.

As he was speaking Judas Iscariot arrived with a large crowd armed with swords and clubs who were sent by the chief priests and elders. The chief priests were taking no chances in case the followers of Jesus rose up with weapons to protect him.

26:48–49 (Now the betrayer had given them a sign, saying, "The one I kiss is the man. Arrest him!") Immediately he went up to Jesus and said, "Greetings, Rabbi," and kissed him.

Judas had already arranged with the leader of this crowd that the man whom he greeted with a kiss would be the one to arrest. So he went straight up to Jesus, greeted him as Rabbi and kissed him.

26:50 Jesus said to him, "Friend, do what you are here to do." Then they came and took hold of Jesus and arrested him.

Jesus knew why Judas was there. Was it to challenge Judas to confess that he asked him "friend, why are you here" (AV)? After this they took hold of Jesus and arrested him.

26:51 But one of those with Jesus grabbed his sword, drew it out, and struck the high priest's slave, cutting off his ear.

John 18:10 tells us that it was Peter who took hold of his sword and cut off the ear of the chief priest's servant, probably the one nearest to him.

26:52 Then Jesus said to him, "Put your sword back in its place! For all who take hold of the sword will die by the sword.

Jesus told Peter to put his sword away for those who take up the sword would die by the sword. The apostle John further records that Jesus rebuked Peter for resisting the will of his Father, as he tried to prevent Christ from drinking the cup of suffering (John 18:11). Only Luke tells us that Jesus touched the servant's ear and healed him (Luke 22:51).

26:53 Or do you think that I cannot call on my Father, and that he would send me more than twelve legions of angels right now?

If he wanted to, Jesus could have called upon a greater force than any human army to deliver him from his enemies. If he called on his Father to send twelve legions of angels (over 80,000) to his aid, God would have done so immediately.

26:54 But how then would the Scriptures be fulfilled, that it must come about this way?

But if he did so, then the Scriptures would not be fulfilled (Isaiah 53:4–8), and our salvation could not be accomplished.

26:55 At that moment Jesus said to the crowd, "Have you come out with swords and clubs to arrest me like you would an outlaw? Day after day I sat teaching in the temple courts, yet you did not arrest me.

Turning to the crowds, Jesus asked why they had come with swords and clubs to arrest him as if he were a criminal. He had been in the temple courts openly teaching the people and they had not arrested him then. Of course, he knew that they feared the people too much to arrest him in the day time in a public place.

26:56 But this has happened so that the scriptures of the prophets would be fulfilled." Then all the disciples left him and fled.

As he spoke these words all his disciples fled for their lives, leaving him alone with the hostile crowd, just as he had told them they would (Matt. 26:31).

Trial Before Caiaphas

26:57–58 Now the ones who had arrested Jesus led him to Caiaphas, the high priest, in whose house the experts in the law and the elders had gathered. But Peter was following him from a distance, all the way to the high priest's courtyard. After going in, he sat with the guards to see the outcome.

Although Peter had failed Christ by fighting and then forsaking him in the garden, he returned close enough to see where he was being taken and to follow him. He entered the high priest's residence and sat among the temple guards to see what would happen to Jesus. At first sight, this seems a very brave thing to do; but Peter was not relying on God but on his natural courage, and this would fail him later that evening.

26:59–61 The chief priests and the whole Sanhedrin were trying to find false testimony against Jesus so that they could put him to death. But they did not find anything, though many false witnesses came forward. Finally two came forward and declared, "This man said, 'I am able to destroy the temple of God and rebuild it in three days.'"

According to the Law of Moses, an Israelite was not to be put to death except on the evidence of two or three witnesses. In order to feign obedience to this law, the council deliberately sought men who would testify falsely against Christ.

The remarkable thing was that although many of them could consent to lie about Christ, no two of their testimonies could agree. God had confused their plans, for since Christ was without sin it would be impossible to convict him on the basis of the law.

Finally, two were found who had heard Christ say "destroy this temple and in three days I will raise it up"; but like the other Jews, they mistakenly thought that he was referring to the temple in Jerusalem.

John clarifies that he had actually been speaking of his own body (John 2:19–22).

26:62–63 So the high priest stood up and said to him, "Have you no answer? What is this that they are testifying against you?" But Jesus was silent. The high priest said to him, "I charge you under oath by the living God, tell us if you are the Christ, the Son of God."

Throughout this procedure, Jesus had remained silent in fulfilment of Isaiah 53:7. He neither needed to defend his sinless self nor wanted to testify further before hardened unbelievers. In fact, as the High Priest put him under oath to the Living God to tell the truth as to whether he was the Christ, the Son of God, he had just one more thing to say.

26:64 Jesus said to him, "You have said it yourself. But I tell you, from now on you will see the Son of Man sitting at the right hand of the Power and coming on the clouds of heaven."

Jesus replied that Caiaphas and the whole Sanhedrin had already articulated that he was the son of God, and that their confession was correct. It was their failure to believe this true report that led to their condemnation; and in the future, they would be on trial and Jesus would be their judge. Christ was to be exalted to the highest place of authority in the universe—the right hand of God—and would come again to judge the ungodly; "coming on the clouds of heaven", as Daniel's son of man (Dan. 7:13). Since by the time that these words of Jesus reach their fulfilment, all the Sanhedrin would be dead, it appears that the manifestation of Christ's universal rule will be universally known (Rev. 1:7).

26:65 Then the high priest tore his clothes and declared, "He has blasphemed! Why do we still need witnesses? Now you have heard the blasphemy!

The high priest tore his robes as a sign of his disgust and outrage that Jesus should speak such words (as he thought) of blasphemy. It was unfortunate for Caiaphas that it was his robe and not his heart that was broken, or else he might have realised the simple truth of Jesus' words (Joel 2:13).

26:66 What is your verdict?" They answered, "He is guilty and deserves death."

Christ was convicted by the council of the sin of blasphemy and condemned to death. However, the high priest would have realised that this trial and verdict were merely for show; since Israel's religious power had no right to carry out the death penalty under Roman law. Moreover, the secular power would not recognise their charge of blasphemy in the courts.

26:67 Then they spat in his face and struck him with their fists. And some slapped him,

Yet having convicted him wrongfully of blasphemy, they proceeded to spit at and strike the Lord Jesus with their fists. This was the first time any blows had landed on Christ, and they came from his own people, the supposed custodians of his word (John 1:11). These blows could be taken as representative all the violence of the world. If all people would think that whenever they hit someone they are actually hitting Christ, then they might not be so quick to lose their tempers, fight or make war.

26:68 saying, "Prophesy for us, you Christ! Who hit you?"

The leaders blasphemed and tempted Christ in the very same way that Satan had in the desert; that is, their slander and hatred was not directed at Christ in his humanity but against his deity. It was the God-man whom they hated, as they hated the God whom he revealed (John 15:23).

Peter Denies Christ

26:69 Now Peter was sitting outside in the courtyard. A slave girl came to him and said, "You also were with Jesus the Galilean."

As Jesus began to suffer his humiliation, the writer of this account returns our attention to Peter in the adjacent courtyard. A slave girl had recognised him as a follower of Jesus and identified him to all who were present.

26:70 But he denied it in front of them all: "I don't know what you're talking about!"

With all his previous bravery gone, Peter denied any knowledge of Jesus and of ever being his disciple.

26:71–72 When he went out to the gateway, another slave girl saw him and said to the people there, "This man was with Jesus the Nazarene." He denied it again with an oath, "I do not know the man!"

He was similarly recognised by a different a slave girl near the exit. Perhaps Peter had thought, having been recognised, that he should get away as quietly as possible with no one else noticing; but on being confronted again, he once more denied any acquaintance with Jesus.

26:73 After a little while, those standing there came up to Peter and said, "You really are one of them too — even your accent gives you away!"

Recognising his Galilean accent, others standing nearby took up the accusation—"you really are a follower of Jesus!" they cried.

26:74 At that he began to curse, and he swore with an oath, "I do not know the man!" At that moment a rooster crowed.

At this point Peter caved in completely; his pious oaths were mingled with impious cursing (swear words) as he denied ever knowing Jesus at all. It was at that precise moment that a rooster began to crow for the morning.

26:75 Then Peter remembered what Jesus had said: "Before the rooster crows, you will deny me three times." And he went outside and wept bitterly.

Then Peter remembered how Jesus, following his bold declaration of love and loyalty, had said "the rooster will not crow before you have denied me three times" (Matt. 26:33–35). Peter was completely devastated by the realisation that his own strength was insufficient to fulfil his boasting. He was heartbroken by the fact that his only Lord and Saviour had been condemned to die whilst he was powerless to save him. Perhaps he was also terrified by the knowledge that whoever denied Christ before men would be denied before God (Matt. 10:33).

No doubt, as Satan sifted Peter like wheat, all these thoughts and many others would have gone through his mind (Luke 22:31–32). Yet throughout this experience, Christ kept Peter by his own power; and Peter, following his restoration, would not be so quick to depend on his own ability (1 Peter 4:11). Furthermore, although he had left the courtyard, Peter later returned to be present at the cross, as an eyewitness of the sufferings of Christ (1 Peter 5:1).

Discussion Questions for Chapter 26

1. vv. 1–16. Why do you think Judas betrayed Jesus?

2. vv. 17–30. Describe the significance of Jesus changing the Passover meal into what we now call the communion service.

3. vv. 31–35. Why do you think Peter was unable to keep his promise not to deny Jesus?

4. vv. 36–46. From his prayer in the garden, what can you learn about Jesus' relationship with God his father?

5. vv. 47–61. What impresses or moves you most about the account of Jesus arrest in the garden?

You will find suggested answers to these questions on pages 306–323.

Matthew Chapter 27

Jesus Handed over to Pilate

27:1 When it was early in the morning, all the chief priests and the elders of the people plotted against Jesus to execute him.

Very early in the morning following his arrest, the chief priests and elders met together to consult how they could bring about the death of Jesus. They had already decided that he should die, so they brought a charge against him before the Roman governor, who would take the responsibility of ordering his execution (Luke 22:2).

27:2 They tied him up, led him away, and handed him over to Pilate the governor.

They must have still feared Jesus, or perhaps an attempt by his followers to free him, for they had him tied up. They then led him away to Pontius Pilate the governor of Judea.

The End of Judas

27:3–4 Now when Judas, who had betrayed him, saw that Jesus had been condemned, he regretted what he had done and returned the thirty silver coins to the chief priests and the elders, saying, "I have sinned by betraying innocent blood!" But they said, "What is that to us? You take care of it yourself!"

From the narrative it would appear that although Judas knew the Jewish rulers were plotting to kill Jesus he had deliberately banished this thought from his mind. He must have been nearby when the Sanhedrin met to decide Jesus' fate, for he knew almost immediately that they had condemned him to death. For the first time Judas' conscience troubled him and the full extent of what he had done convicted him. Returning the thirty pieces of silver and confessing his sin was a vain attempt to ease his conscience; he had gone too far and it was too late. The chief priests wiped their hands of him and told him that what he had done his own problem.

27:5 So Judas threw the silver coins into the temple and left. Then he went out and hanged himself.

As they would not take the money from him, Judas threw it into the temple and went out to hang himself.

27:6 But the chief priests took the silver pieces and said, "It is not lawful to put them into the treasury, because they are the price of blood."

By their actions and words the chief priests condemned themselves. They acknowledged that the money they had given to Judas was unclean, having been given for a sinful purpose, and so could not be put into the temple treasury.

27:7 After consulting together they bought the Potter's Field with it, as a burial place for foreigners.

After some discussion they decided to use the money to buy a piece of land called the Potter's Field and use it as a burial place for foreigners.

27:8 For this reason that field has been called the "Field of Blood" to this day.

The general public must have heard about this, for they changed the name of the field to "field of blood" and it was still called by that name at the time Matthew wrote his account (Acts 1:19).

27:9–10 Then what was spoken by Jeremiah the prophet was fulfilled: "They took the thirty silver coins, the price of the one whose price had been set by the people of Israel, and they gave them for the potter's field, as the Lord commanded me."

Matthew says that all this happened in fulfilment of the prophecy of Jeremiah. In actual fact, in our Bibles these words are written in the book of Zechariah 11:12–13:

> Then I said to them, "If it seems good to you, pay me my wages, but if not, forget it." So they weighed out my payment -- thirty pieces of silver. The LORD then said to me, "Throw to the potter that exorbitant sum at which they valued me!" So I took the thirty pieces of silver and threw them to the potter at the temple of the LORD.

Jesus before Pilate

27:11 Then Jesus stood before the governor, and the governor asked him, "Are you the king of the Jews?" Jesus said, "You say so."

Pontius Pilate could not have been unaware of the activities of the Lord Jesus Christ as the whole of Jerusalem and beyond had been stirred and affected by his ministry. Pilate asked Jesus a question based on the accusation of the Jewish leaders: "are you the king of the Jews?" Jesus answered simply, "What you have said is right".

27:12 But when he was accused by the chief priests and the elders, he did not respond.

However, when the Jewish rulers made their accusations against him, he did not answer them (Isaiah 53:7).

27.13–14 Then Pilate said to him, "Don't you hear how many charges they are bringing against you?" But he did not answer even one accusation, so that the governor was quite amazed.

Pilate was completely taken aback by Jesus' refusal to answer the charges that were being made against him. As governor, many had been brought before him for judgment and he had heard and expected them to give some answer in their defence. But Jesus did not answer even one accusation.

Barabbas Chosen Rather than Jesus

27:15 During the feast the governor was accustomed to release one prisoner to the crowd, whomever they wanted.

During the feast of the Passover it was customary for the governor to release one prisoner of the people's choice.

27:16 (NKJV™) And at that time they had a notorious prisoner called Barabbas.

At this time the Romans held in custody a notorious prisoner named Barabbas. He was a thief and had committed murder in an uprising against Rome (Mark 15:7).

27:17 (NKJV™) Therefore, when they had gathered together, Pilate said to them, "Whom do you want me to release to you? Barabbas, or Jesus who is called Christ?"

So after he had called together a crowd of Jews, Pilate asked them who they wanted him to set free, giving them a choice of Barabbas or Jesus. In presenting the thief and murderer Barabbas in contrast with the innocent Jesus Christ, Pilate was hoping that the crowd would choose Jesus, whom he perceived to be innocent.

27:18 (For he knew that they had handed him over because of envy.)

Pilate knew that the only reason the chief priests and elders had handed Jesus over to him to put to death was because of envy.

27:19 As he was sitting on the judgment seat, his wife sent a message to him: "Have nothing to do with that innocent man; I have suffered greatly as a result of a dream about him today."

While Pilate was sat on the judgment seat, his wife sent a message to warn him to not to condemn the innocent man who stood before. Adam Clarke insists that God had spoken to this woman through a dream. If such were the case then the dream was entirely for Pilate's benefit. It was in God's plan of salvation that Jesus Christ should be crucified, not released. Perhaps it was because of this warning that Pilate washed his hands in water in verse 24.

27:20 But the chief priests and the elders persuaded the crowds to ask for Barabbas and to have Jesus killed.

The chief priests and elders who were amongst the crowd persuaded them to ask for the release of Barabbas and to have Jesus executed. Let us keep in mind that the chief priests and elders had a great influence over the lives of the people and many of them would fear the consequences of not obeying them.

27:21 The governor asked them, "Which of the two do you want me to release for you?" And they said, "Barabbas!"

The governor asked them again which of the two they wanted him to set free and they cried out for Barabbas.

27:22 Pilate said to them, "Then what should I do with Jesus who is called the Christ?" They all said, "Crucify him!"

Pilate had expected them to shout for Jesus, but when they did not, he still tried to set Jesus free. So he asked the crowd (who had been worked up by the Jewish leaders) what they wanted him to do with Jesus. At this point he allowed the authority of Caesar to be over-ruled by a mob of unruly people. With one voice they cried "crucify him!"

27:23 He asked, "Why? What wrong has he done?" But they shouted more insistently, "Crucify him!"

Still wanting to set Jesus free, Pilate asked them why he should put someone to death who had done nothing wrong. Still they insistently cried "crucify him!"

27:24 When Pilate saw that he could do nothing, but that instead a riot was starting, he took some water, washed his hands before the crowd and said, "I am innocent of this man's blood. You take care of it yourselves!"

However, having once let go of his power there was no way he could regain it. The crowd began to riot. So Pilate took water and washed his hands before them, signifying that he had not condemned Jesus and was not guilty or responsible for the death of this righteous man. They were to be guilty and responsible if they put him to death.

27:25 In reply all the people said, "Let his blood be on us and on our children!

All the people shouted back that they were willing take the responsibility for his death.

In reality it was not the chief priests, the elders or Pilate that was responsible for the crucifixion of the Lord Jesus Christ; it was all people. Jesus was about to die for the sin of the world, and we have all sinned and fall short of the glory of God (Rom. 3:23; Isaiah 53:5).

27:26 Then he released Barabbas for them. But after he had Jesus flogged, he handed him over to be crucified.

Accordingly, Pilate released Barabbas; and as was the Roman custom before crucifixion, Jesus was flogged with a lead tipped whip before being handed over to the Roman soldiers for execution (Isaiah 50:6).

A Parody of the Truth

27:27 Then the governor's soldiers took Jesus into the governor's residence and gathered the whole cohort around him.

The governor's soldiers then brought Jesus into the common hall of the governor's palace and gathered the whole battalion around him.

27:28 They stripped him and put a scarlet robe around him,

They stripped him of his own clothes and put on him the scarlet robe of one of their officers.

27:29 and after braiding a crown of thorns, they put it on his head. They put a staff in his right hand, and kneeling down before him, they mocked him: "Hail, king of the Jews!"

They then wove a crown from thorn branches and thrust it on his head (the word used *"epitithemi"* can mean to impose in a hostile manner). They put in his right hand a stick and kneeling down before him they pretended to worship him and hailed him as "king of the Jews!"

27:30 They spat on him and took the staff and struck him repeatedly on the head.

They spat in his face and snatched the stick from his hand, repeatedly hitting him on the head with it. This would have pressed the crown of thorns further on his head (Isaiah 50:6).

27:31 When they had mocked him, they stripped him of the robe and put his own clothes back on him. Then they led him away to crucify him.

When they had finished mocking him they took the robe off him and put his own clothes back on him. To the soldiers it was just a game of mockery, a parody of worship; yet they did not realise that he was truly king of kings and lord of lords. They then led him away to be crucified.

The Crucifixion

27:32 As they were going out, they found a man from Cyrene named Simon, whom they forced to carry his cross.

The gospels record that Jesus was taken from Pilate's palace carrying his own cross, but following the severe flogging which he suffered he became too weak to carry it further. Collapsing under its weight, the Roman soldiers conscripted a bystander, a Jew named Simon from Cyrene who would have been in the city to observe Passover, to carry the cross for Jesus as he walked the hill to his execution.

27:33 They came to a place called Golgotha (which means "Place of the Skull")

Golgotha was a hill outside the Jerusalem wall and was so named because it resembled a skull and because of the executions regularly performed on it. Golgotha is a local, Aramaic word; the Latin name is often used instead, Calvaria or Calvary.

27:34 and offered Jesus wine mixed with gall to drink. But after tasting it, he would not drink it.

Immediately prior to his hands and feet being nailed to the cross, the Roman soldiers offered Christ a painkiller or sedative. This gall is thought by some to have been an opiate (related to morphine). Christ tasted but refused this bitter drink, realising the necessity of his being fully conscious throughout his time on the cross; not least in order to lead at least two penitent souls to salvation, to comfort his mother and disciples at the foot of the cross and to announce his ultimate victory.

27:35 When they had crucified him, they divided his clothes by throwing dice.

The callous nature of the Roman soldiers, so inured to the suffering they inflicted, is here emphasised. Rather than return his clothing to his family, who were present, they gambled over which of them should have it as a bonus for the day's gruesome work.

27:36 Then they sat down and kept guard over him there.

The crucifixion having been effected, the job of the Roman garrison was to ensure no one would try to take the condemned off the cross and save their lives from Roman justice.

27:37 Above his head they put the charge against him, which read: "This is Jesus, the king of the Jews."

It was customary to place the crime of which the condemned was guilty above them on the cross to act as a deterrent to others. By the express order of Pilate, the charge was "king of the Jews"; a charge with which Pilate taunted the Jewish leaders in return for backing him into a corner and forcing him to have Jesus executed.

27:38 Then two outlaws were crucified with him, one on his right and one on his left.

Matthew does not provide us with all the details concerning the crucifixion. To get a fuller picture, one must compare all the gospel accounts. Of the two outlaws crucified with him, we may assume that they had been taken in the insurrection (Luke 23:25). Luke tells us of the repentance and salvation of one, but not the other (Luke 23:42–43).

27:39–40 Those who passed by defamed him, shaking their heads and saying, "You who can destroy the temple and rebuild it in three days, save yourself! If you are God's Son, come down from the cross!"

Those who came out from Jerusalem to see the crucifixion cursed and taunted Jesus, as did the chief priests. It is of note that their taunts bear a striking resemblance to the temptations Jesus endured from Satan in the wilderness, in that once again his deity is tempted rather than his humanity. If you are the Son of God, come down! No doubt the spite of the crowd was influenced by more than mere human enmity against God.

27:41 In the same way even the chief priests -- together with the experts in the law and elders -- were mocking him:

One might have thought the religious rulers of the people to be above such taunting of a condemned Jew, but if they were not above his murder, nor were they above gloating over his murder. They considered, vainly, that they could rid themselves of the Son of God who deserved their obedience (Psalm 2:1–4).

27:42–43 "He saved others, but he cannot save himself! He is the king of Israel! If he comes down now from the cross, we will believe in him! He trusts in God -- let God, if he wants to, deliver him now because he said, 'I am God's Son'!"

They heaped insults on Jesus by implying that God would not hear him or want him, for he had blasphemed God by claiming to be his son. In reality, Jesus, the beloved son, was returning to his father (John 16:28).

27:44 The robbers who were crucified with him also spoke abusively to him.

This verse clarified that both robbers initially cursed the Lord Jesus, and so it must have been at some point as they hung on the cross that one of them repented and turned to him for forgiveness. Even then, after this cursing of the dying Son of God, instant, full and everlasting forgiveness was available for this man.

27:45 Now from noon until three, darkness came over all the land.

A short while into the crucifixion, the sun refused to shine and the whole land was plunged into darkness for approximately three hours. That this was a preternatural event was evident since it was Passover time, when the moon was full and so a solar eclipse was impossible. The times on the cross are not definite, John places the crucifixion later than "the sixth hour" but some commentators suggest he was using Roman time, whilst the other gospel writers used Jewish time. More modern commentators suppose that the times are approximate and the truth could be a little in between. Wesley says that by this darkness, God was testifying to his abhorrence of the wickedness which was bring committed; "it likewise intimated Christ's sore conflicts with the divine justice and with all the powers of darkness".

27:46 At about three o'clock Jesus shouted with a loud voice, "Eli, Eli, lama sabachthani?" that is, "My God, my God, why have you forsaken me?"

Gill says "the meaning is not, that the hypostatical union was dissolved, which was not even by death itself; the fullness of the Godhead still dwelt bodily in him", but as the Son of God became sin for us, he experienced the awful and eternal result of sin on our behalf, and tasted that death which is separation from God during those hours on the cross.

27:47–49 When some of the bystanders heard it, they said, "This man is calling for Elijah." Immediately one of them ran and got a sponge, filled it with sour wine, put it on a stick, and gave it to him to drink. But the rest said, "Leave him alone! Let's see if Elijah will come to save him."

The superstitious standing nearby either knew no Aramaic or little scripture; or more likely they turned Christ's words into an opportunity for deriding him. They said that Christ's cry was a cry for Elijah to come and same him.

One of the bystanders is unwittingly used in the fulfilment of scripture "they gave me vinegar for my thirst" (Psa. 69:21). What motivated this individual to do this is unclear. Perhaps he wanted Christ to wet his lips so that he could hear his dying words more clearly. Whatever the case, God was sovereignly overruling even the derision of these bystanders for his own glory. And so the scripture was fulfilled.

27:50 Then Jesus cried out again with a loud voice and gave up his spirit.

Matthew does not articulate the loud cry which Jesus uttered, which John informs us was "it is finished" (John 19:30). Then bowing his head, Jesus gave up his spirit. He had given his all, made his soul and offering for sin, and gave up his life in triumph; the work of redemption had been fully accomplished.

27:51–53 Just then the temple curtain was torn in two, from top to bottom. The earth shook and the rocks were split apart. And tombs were opened, and the bodies of many saints who had died were raised. (They came out of the tombs after his resurrection and went into the holy city and appeared to many people.)

The death of Christ, like his birth and resurrection, was accompanied by fearful and miraculous signs. The huge curtain which separated the holy place from the holy of holies in the temple was ripped by an invisible hand from top to bottom. The curtain had stood as a reminder that until then the way into God's immediate presence had not been revealed or opened (Heb. 9:8). Only one man, the high priest, and he only once a year, was allowed to enter into the holy place, taking with him the blood of a sacrifice. Outside the Jerusalem wall, a sacrifice had been offered which would forever remove sin, and the event of the torn curtain revealed that through the death of Christ the way into God's presence had been made open to every believer for all time.

Not only symbolic manifestation, but seismic activity accompanied Christ's death. As if groaning under the weight of the sin which had been committed, the earth quaked and the rocks were split. At the same time, as if to show the absolute victory of Christ's death, the tombs of the dead holy people were opened, ready for the events of Easter Sunday, when the dead bodies were raised, and after his resurrection went into the city and appeared to (and were recognised by) many people.

27:54 Now when the centurion and those with him who were guarding Jesus saw the earthquake and what took place, they were extremely terrified and said, "Truly this one was God's Son!"

Perhaps the dignified way in which Christ died, the love and forgiveness which he displayed to his murderers, and his evident fear of God had already affected the centurion and his soldiers deeply. But at the sign of the earthquake, and the midday darkness, they were terrified, and realising these signs as omens from God, they exclaimed "truly this was the Son of God". What this title meant to them is not clear. Romans would have been familiar with stories of their "gods" becoming like men or living in disguise among men. They certainly believed Christ to be more than an ordinary mortal.

27:55–56 Many women who had followed Jesus from Galilee and given him support were also there, watching from a distance. Among them were Mary Magdalene, Mary the mother of James and Joseph, and the mother of the sons of Zebedee.

From John's account it appears that some women and disciples, including his mother and John the apostle, were near to the cross at the time of Jesus death (close enough to hear a dying man speak—John 19:26–27). Others stood at a respectful distance, but were witnesses of his death and of the place of his burial.

Christ's Burial

27:57–58 Now when it was evening, there came a rich man from Arimathea, named Joseph, who was also a disciple of Jesus. He went to Pilate and asked for the body of Jesus. Then Pilate ordered that it be given to him.

Joseph of Arimathea was not ashamed of the fact that he had become a disciple of Jesus, and being rich he realised he was in a position to help with the burial of Jesus' body. He went boldly to Pilate to request permission to carry out this service. Pilate was surprised that Jesus was already dead and first verified with the centurion before granting permission for Joseph to remove the body (Mark 15:44).

27:59–60 Joseph took the body, wrapped it in a clean linen cloth, and placed it in his own new tomb that he had cut in the rock. Then he rolled a great stone across the entrance of the tomb and went away.

Joseph prepared Jesus for burial according to the custom which the Jews followed for their kings and all their important men. He then laid Jesus' body in an expensive tomb which he had prepared for himself; hewn out of solid rock near to the city wall. Joseph (together with Nicodemus) rolled a great stone to seal the entrance of the tomb before hurrying to return home, for it was evening and the Sabbath was beginning.

27:61 (Now Mary Magdalene and the other Mary were sitting there, opposite the tomb.)

The two Marys observed the place of Christ's burial; and it was their intention, together with the other women, to return after the Sabbath and show their love and grief by anointing the body of Jesus with even more fresh spices.

27:62–64 The next day (which is after the day of preparation) the chief priests and the Pharisees assembled before Pilate and said, "Sir, we remember that while that deceiver was still alive he said, 'After three days I will rise again.' So give orders to secure the tomb until the third day. Otherwise his disciples may come and steal his body and say to the people, 'He has been raised from the dead,' and the last deception will be worse than the first."

On the Sabbath itself, the chief priests and Pharisees were prepared to defile themselves by standing before the Roman governor to request that a guard be placed at Jesus' tomb. They wished it to be secured by soldiers so that the disciples could not steal the body and invent a story about Christ being raised from the dead. Their comments reveal that they had all along understood the words of Jesus when he said he would rise again after three days. Were they in fact afraid that this would really happen?

27:65 Pilate said to them, "Take a guard of soldiers. Go and make it as secure as you can."

Pilate was willing to placate them in this, and gave them a detachment of soldiers; the number of which is not specified.

27:66 So they went with the soldiers of the guard and made the tomb secure by sealing the stone.

These guards sealed the stone by placing a wax seal (probably Pilate's own) over the gap between the stone and the rock. This would provide an authoritative warning to any who dared to disturb the tomb, and furthermore a break in this seal would provide evidence of the tomb having been tampered with.

Discussion Questions for Chapter 27

1. vv. 1–10. Explain why the Pharisees would not take the thirty pieces of silver back from Judas.

2. vv. 11–26. Why did Pilate try to set Jesus free?

3. vv. 27–44. Describe the insulting behaviour which Jesus suffered both before and during his crucifixion.

4. vv. 45–54. Describe the miraculous events which accompanied Jesus death.

5. vv.54–58. In these verses, Matthew describes those who were sympathetic to Jesus. Which one of these people impresses you the most and why?

You will find suggested answers to these questions on pages 306–323.

Matthew Chapter 28

The Resurrection

28:1 Now after the Sabbath, at dawn on the first day of the week, Mary Magdalene and the other Mary went to look at the tomb.

When the Sabbath was over, on the first day of the week as it was beginning to get light, Mary Magdalene and the other Mary (the mother of James) and also Salome (not mentioned here) came to look at the tomb (Mark 16:1).

28:2 Suddenly there was a severe earthquake, for an angel of the Lord descending from heaven came and rolled away the stone and sat on it.

As they approached the tomb there was a severe earthquake as an angel of the Lord descended from heaven. He rolled the stone away from the mouth of the tomb and sat on it.

28:3 His appearance was like lightning, and his clothes were white as snow.

The angel shone as bright as lightning and his clothes were as white as snow.

28:4 The guards were shaken and became like dead men because they were so afraid of him.

On seeing the angel, the soldiers who had been placed there to guard the tomb shook with fear and became like paralyzed men, unable to speak or move, although they could still hear and see!

28:5–6 But the angel said to the women, "Do not be afraid; I know that you are looking for Jesus, who was crucified. He is not here, for he has been raised, just as he said. Come and see the place where he was lying.

The angel told the women not to fear; for he knew that they had come looking for Jesus, who had been crucified. He was no longer in the tomb, for he had been raised from the dead, just as he said he would be. The angel invited the women to observe the place where Jesus had been lying, to prove that he was no longer there. Jesus had already risen from the dead before the angel rolled the stone away.

28:7 Then go quickly and tell his disciples, 'He has been raised from the dead. He is going ahead of you into Galilee. You will see him there.' Listen, I have told you!"

The women, having entered the tomb, saw that Jesus was not there. The angel told them to go quickly and tell Jesus' disciples the good news. Jesus had risen from the dead and would reveal himself to them in Galilee as he had promised (Matt. 26:32).

28:8 So they left the tomb quickly, with fear and great joy, and ran to tell his disciples.

They quickly left the tomb, filled with fear and yet a great joy, running to tell the disciples what the angel had commanded them.

28:9 But Jesus met them, saying, "Greetings!" They came to him, held on to his feet and worshiped him.

However before they reached their destination they received another sudden surprise: Jesus met them! His greeting, "all hail" is defined by Thayer as meaning to rejoice and be glad. They immediately recognized him and falling before him, they held on to his feet and worshipped him.

28:10 Then Jesus said to them, "Do not be afraid. Go and tell my brothers to go to Galilee. They will see me there."

Although they most probably would have liked to stay with him, he tells them to go and tell "my brothers" to go to Galilee where they would see him. In Matthew 12:50 Jesus said "whoever does the will of my Father in heaven is my brother and sister". In John 15:14 he says "you are my friends if you do whatever I command you", but this is the first time that Jesus called his disciples brothers. Through the resurrection, this is the relationship that all believers have with him (Heb. 2:11).

A Conspiracy to Conceal the Truth

28:11 While they were going, some of the guard went into the city and told the chief priests everything that had happened.

While the women were on their way to the disciples some of the guard went into Jerusalem and told the chief priests everything that happened. This is proof that although they were paralyzed with fear they heard and saw everything that went on. These soldiers knew that when the women arrived at the tomb the stone was still in its place and the seals had not been broken. They saw the angel roll the stone away and reveal that Jesus was not inside!

28:12–13 After they had assembled with the elders and formed a plan, they gave a large sum of money to the soldiers, telling them, "You are to say, 'His disciples came at night and stole his body while we were asleep.'

The chief priests called the elders together and formulated a plan to conceal the truth. They paid a large sum of money to the soldiers and told them that they were to say that Jesus' disciples came during the night and stole the body away while they were asleep. It would have been extremely unlikely that the disciples, being Jews, would have come to the tomb during the Sabbath and it is clearly recorded that as soon as the Sabbath was over the women came. These Roman soldiers knew what the penalty would have been if they had all been sleeping on duty;

but if they had all been asleep how could they have known that the disciples stole the body?

28:14 If this matter is heard before the governor, we will satisfy him and keep you out of trouble."

The chief priests and elders were confident that they could easily satisfy Pilate with the story and save the soldiers from being punished. Why were they so confident? They knew very well that Pilate had washed his hands of the whole affair. He would not be the least interested in what had happened to Jesus' body.

28:15 So they took the money and did as they were instructed. And this story is told among the Jews to this day.

The soldiers were convinced, took the money and did as they were instructed. At the time Matthew was writing, this story was still being told among the Jews.

The Great Commission

28:16 So the eleven disciples went to Galilee to the mountain Jesus had designated.

Matthew omitted many of the appearances of the Lord Jesus Christ that are recorded in the other gospels, going straight to the main Galilee appearance.

28:17 When they saw him, they worshiped him, but some doubted.

Gill says they worshiped him "with divine adoration, as the eternal Son of God; for so he was now declared to be by his resurrection from the dead" (Rom. 1:4). The next part of the verse is difficult to understand "but some doubted". The reference would include more than just Thomas, as it says "some" not one. As all the disciples present had already seen Jesus, including Thomas, after the resurrection, so it is hard to believe that any of them at this meeting with Jesus in Galilee had any doubts to the fact that he was alive. Young's Literal Translation has "but some wavered" which might imply that although none of the eleven disciples had any further doubts that Jesus had risen from the dead, some hesitated to completely surrender themselves to him. Later events demonstrate that this holding back was only short lived.

28:18 Then Jesus came up and said to them, "All authority in heaven and on earth has been given to me.

Jesus approached them and declared that all authority, power, right and strength had been given to him in heaven and on earth (Eph. 1:20–22; 1 Peter 3:22; 1 Cor. 15:25–28).

28:19 Therefore go and make disciples of all nations, baptizing them in the name of the Father and the Son and the Holy Spirit,

The so-called *great commission* that Jesus gave to his disciples is relevant to all believers in every age and will be until he comes again. Go to all the people in every nation and make disciples; that is, proclaim the gospel message of salvation. It is a complete message that must be made known, that Jesus died for our sins and was buried and rose again (1 Cor. 15:3–4). Those who believe should be baptized in water in the name of the Father, Son and Holy Spirit.

28:20 teaching them to obey everything I have commanded you. And remember, I am with you always, to the end of the age."

New disciples are to be taught the word of God and to obey everything that the Lord Jesus Christ has commanded. As we fulfil this commission, Jesus promises that there will never be a time that he will not be with us, until he comes again and we shall be forever with him. Amen.

Discussion Questions for Chapter 28

1. vv. 1–10. Briefly describe what happened when the women came to the garden tomb.

2. vv. 11–15. Why do you think the chief priests tried to conceal the events which the soldiers reported?

3. vv. 16–17. Why do you think that some of the disciples wavered in their faith or commitment?

4. vv. 18–20. What commission did Jesus give to his disciples after his resurrection?

5. vv.18–20. What promise does Jesus leave with those who are carrying out his great commission?

You will find suggested answers to these questions on pages 306–323.

Bibliography

1. Albert Barnes *Notes on the Bible* (Taken from e-Sword. Rick Meyers, 2000)

2. Robert Jamieson, A.R. Fausset and David Brown *Commentary Critical and Explanatory on the Whole Bible* (Taken from e-Sword. Rick Meyers, 2000)

3. Matthew Henry *Concise Commentary on the Whole Bible* (Taken from e-Sword. Rick Meyers, 2000)

4. A.T. Robertson *Word Pictures in the New Testament* (Taken from e-Sword. Rick Meyers, 2000)

5. M.R. Vincent D.D. *Vincent's Word Studies* (Taken from e-Sword. Rick Meyers, 2000)

6. W.E. Vine *Expository Dictionary of New Testament Words* (Oliphants, 1940)

7. John Wesley *Explanatory Notes on the Whole Bible* (Taken from e-Sword. Rick Meyers, 2000)

8. Amplified New Testament (Amp. N.T.) (Zondervan, 1987)

9. The Living Bible (Taken from e-Sword. Rick Meyers, 2000)

10. The King James Version of the Bible (KJV) (Taken from e-Sword. Rick Meyers, 2000)

11. The Annotated paragraph Bible (Taken from e-Sword. Rick Meyers, 2000)

12. The New Living Testament (Taken from e-Sword. Rick Meyers, 2000)

13. The Contemporary English Version (Taken from e-Sword. Rick Meyers, 2000) American Bible Society, 1995

14. John Gill's Exposition of the Entire Bible (Taken from e-Sword. Rick Meyers, 2000)

15. Thayer's Greek Definitions (Taken from e-Sword. Rick Meyers, 2000)

Sample answers for discussion questions

*These answers are not intended to be thought of as the only "correct" answers. They are a guide to help your study using the discussion questions. You may find that you see more or less detail in the text than is written in these answers; don't worry—it is what **you personally** get out of the passage that is the most important part of the study process.*

Chapter 1

1. The genealogy of Jesus demonstrates that as well as being God, he is also a human being, with his family history rooted in the history of Israel; showing Jesus as part of God's own "salvation history". It demonstrates also: His royal lineage (a descendent of King David) and his role as someone under the law (Gal. 4), who had come to redeem those under the law. Matthew's record of the genealogy also highlights the role of Gentiles in Jesus' family history—pointing to the fact that he is a Saviour for the whole world and not only for Jews.

2. The birth of Jesus was unlike that of any other man. Mary was a virgin, and the child Jesus was conceived within her by the Holy Spirit, without a human father. God was breaking into time; the God-man was being born.

3. Events like these had never happened before, they were incredible, and yet both Mary and Joseph responded with total faith and obedience to the message of God given to them by the angel.

4. In the genealogy of Christ we see many whose life story (recorded in various parts of the Old Testament) was far from perfect. Yet God used these people in fulfilling his plans and purposes for Christ to enter the world. Moreover, other than that they were devout, obedient and faithful, there was nothing remarkable about either Mary or Joseph in these accounts. Only God could accomplish such tremendous things with such ordinary people.

5. The God whom we worship is forgiving—we read in the Old Testament of some of the failings of men like David who are in Jesus' family tree. He is the God who loves the entire world, as we may see from the inclusion of Gentiles in the genealogy. He is the God who acts under his own initiative to save sinners. No one was asking God to do this—He did so of his own accord for the good of mankind

Chapter 2

1. The wise men believed the message of the star and acted in faith, seeking the Lord Jesus. They are examples to us in their faith and desire to seek the Lord. Also, they were prepared to put themselves out to seek him—it was a long way to travel. When they came they were not empty handed, they brought gifts to the Lord. We too should bring our lives, our wealth and our talent and give it all to Jesus.

2. Some suppose that Herod did not want another king to rival him in Israel, but I think it more likely that Herod rejected Christ because he was a sinner who did not want God ruling in his life; he saw Christ as a threat to his sinful way of life.

3. God is never taken by surprise about world events, for he knows the hearts of all people. He is able to keep his own people safe in the midst of an evil world.

4. Not only was Herod's rejection of Christ reflected by all the people of Judea, it resulted in the death of all the young children of Bethlehem and the surrounding region, and the grief this brought to all their families.

5. From a human perspective, Jesus Christ was forced to become a refugee in a foreign land, fleeing the threat of death in his own country.

Chapter 3

1. John the Baptist prepared the people to meet with Jesus by calling them to repent of their sin and turn back to God. He told them that the kingdom of heaven was near, and that they should be genuinely ready for it, not just trusting in the fact that they were Jews. He told them that someone greater than he was coming—meaning Jesus.

2. In his baptism Jesus is identified by God (and John) as his only begotten son, and this is the beginning of his ministry.

3. Jesus was greater than John in that he was more than human, but God in human form. He had existed before John and was his creator.

4. The Holy Spirit came on the Lord Jesus Christ as a person, in complete fullness. This was not an anointing like that received by an Old Testament prophets, it was a complete residing of the Spirit of God in a man. This denotes the divinity of Christ—only the Son of God could receive the Spirit without limit.

5. Yes, I was baptised in water at the age of seventeen in the church where I became a Christian. The pastor asked me to confess publicly that I believed in the Lord Jesus Christ as my Saviour with all my heart, and then he immersed me in the pool of water, baptising me "in the name of the Father, the Son and the Holy Spirit".

Chapter 4

1. The devil tempted Jesus' divinity; insinuating that he was not God's Son whilst asking him to demonstrate that he was God's Son. He tempted him to satisfy his hunger by supernaturally producing bread, to tempt God by leaping off the temple, and to be unfaithful to God by worshipping him (Satan) in return for power and fame.

2. On each occasion Jesus responded to the temptation by quoting and obeying the word of God, submitting to God's revealed will and resisting the devil.

3. A disciple is someone who learns what to do from a master, like an apprentice. Only if they first followed Jesus could they learn his ways and so become like him to share his ministry of reaching the lost.

4. Jesus moved to Capernaum to commence his ministry. It was away from the unbelief of his hometown and family, yet still a strategic base, a significant fishing port, from which to reach out into Galilee, travelling on foot and by boat.

5. For me, before I became a Christian, "repent" meant turn to God and believe on the Lord Jesus Christ. As a Christian, it tells me to turn from known sins in my life, trusting God for forgiveness and help to walk in holiness.

Chapter 5

1. *"Blessed are those who hunger and thirst for righteousness, for they will be satisfied."* I would like to be more hungry and thirsty for God, being filled with more of God; his will be done in my life (righteousness).

2. My own views are close to Christ's own teaching, and influence me to make efforts in remaining faithful to my wife so we do not divorce.

3. I recall promising God that the money I made from my first book sales would be devoted to missions and so far I have been enabled to keep this "vow".

4. The standards of behaviour described by Jesus as God's will for his disciples stand in stark contrast to those of the world, and are a revelation of God and his light to those in darkness.

5. Bitterness, anger and hate against those who speak and do evil things against us is difficult to overcome, and can only be conquered by our receiving the love and grace of God in our hearts.

Chapter 6

1. Jesus wants us to give in secret, for only God to see and not people; seeking the approval of the Lord and not of people.

2. Jesus teaches us to pray privately, for God's ears only. We are to pray simply, asking for our needs to be met, not with vain repetition of religious phrases. We are to honour God as holy in our prayers, forgiving others and praying for his will to be done and his kingdom to come.

3. I think the discipline of fasting takes away distractions so that we can concentrate more on God and on obtaining answers to our prayers.

4. It is foolish to worry because we can do nothing to change our situations, not even our height or hair. Also, it is God who rules our world, even clothing flowers and feeding birds. Worry is the opposite of trust, and if we are not trusting God, we are foolish.

5. Jesus would have us seek the things of God and his kingdom—spiritual things—and focus our affections on things above.

Chapter 7

1. We should not judge others because we ourselves are sinners. Where would we be if God judged us in the same way as we judge others? Yet Jesus says that this is exactly what will happen if we judge.

2. Jesus encourages us to pray by promising that God is good and willing to give good things. Those who ask, seek and knock shall receive, find and have the door of answered prayer opened to them.

3. Everyone is by nature on the wide road away from God, for all are sinners. During this life, the wide way appears to be the easy way, for there are no rules—yet in the end it leads to hell. Only those who receive the Lord Jesus Christ as Saviour enter the narrow way. This way of following Christ is hard and difficult, yet leads to eternal life.

4. We will tell the difference between a true servant of Christ and a false prophet, not so much by their words but by their behaviour. A true servant of Christ brings forth good fruit, the fruit of the Holy Spirit, love joy and meekness etc.

5. I am building my life on Jesus and by God's grace trust to stand the test of God's righteousness and by his gift of grace enter into life.

Chapter 8

1. Like the leper we can approach Jesus in humility, with confidence that he will hear us. The leper believed Jesus could heal him, and we learn from the incident that Jesus is willing as well as able to heal.

2. The Centurion did not consider himself worthy to come to Christ, but showed great faith as well as humility, believing that Jesus could heal simply by his word without being present. In addition, he was a Gentile, and showed that Gentiles as well as Jews could approach the Lord in faith; indeed, Jesus said his faith was greater than any in Israel.

3. Commitment to Jesus might well mean leaving everything, even our homes and comforts and families behind, should he call us to do so.

4. We learn to have faith and to trust in Jesus who is with us in all of our difficult times.

5. I think the towns-people initially rejected Jesus because they were afraid of the awesome demonstration of his power—a supernatural power they could not understand.

Chapter 9

1. Healing is for the body, which will one day return to dust, but the forgiveness of sins saves our souls which last forever.

2. Matthew and his friends are sinners, and Jesus came to seek and to save sinners.

3. To get nearer to God and receive his blessings—perhaps healing for himself or others, or perhaps for a loved one; for the salvation of a loved one; or to receive the baptism of the Holy Spirit; or when under attack from Satanic forces

4. Clearly, the spirit of the girl was somewhere when Jesus called her, and so death is not the end. Jesus who reunited the girl with her family will one day reunite all believers with their fellow believers who have died.

5. Jesus wants to send the kind of workers into his harvest field who share his shepherd's heart of love and concern for the peoples' spiritual condition.

Chapter 10

1. Jesus gave his disciples power to perform miracles, instructed them in what to preach, and how to conduct themselves on their mission. He warned them about opposition and persecution and told them not to fear men; encouraging them to know God was with them, who would one day reward their faithfulness.

2. They would be given the words to speak by the Holy Spirit, and would be saved eternally by enduring in their faith. The God who cares for the sparrows would much more take care of them.

3. I have known many in my family reject the gospel; they have not ill-treated me, but we have little contact with each other.

4. Being fully committed to Jesus may involve persecution and opposition, even from within one's own family.

5. It is not what we give or do, but why we do it that God rewards. If we give of a cup of cold water out of love to Him, God will reward our show of love.

Chapter 11

1. John the Baptist was the greatest of all prophets because of the privilege he had to proclaim the coming of Christ. No other prophet had actually lived to see and preach about Jesus in this way.

2. In Jesus' ministry the blind were made to see, the lame walked, many lepers were made clean, the deaf heard, and the dead were raised.

3. The people were like children in a market who did not want to play no matter what game was being played; or sing or dance whatever song was being played – they would not respond to any approach from God; there was no pleasing them.

4. Christ denounced many of the cities in which he had performed miracles because although they had seen evidence of his power and of his position as God's son, they still refused to repent and believe.

5. Jesus offers the weary lasting spiritual rest from the burden of sin. He gives us the eternal rest of having peace with God and a home in heaven.

Chapter 12

1. Christ created humankind in the beginning, and appointed the days of the week, months and seasons. It was he who gave the laws concerning the Sabbath and so in every sense as creator and law-giver he is Lord of the Sabbath.

2. In Matthew, Jesus' ministry is mainly to Israel, but the prophecy of Isaiah speaks of a time when Gentiles would place their own hope in Jesus too, and we see this being worked out later in the book of Acts.

3. A house or country divided against itself cannot stay together, it will divide and be brought to ruin. Satan and his demons are on the same side. If they were fighting among themselves they would be defeated. Jesus makes the point that only someone stronger than Satan—God—can cast out Satan.

4. The people of Jesus' time rejected him and his call to repent and believe the gospel. The people of Nineveh, however, repented when Jonah warned them of coming judgment. The fact that the same opportunity was given to both sets of people, and that one accepted the opportunity whilst the other group rejected it, makes the one group guilty—especially since the messenger they rejected was the Son of God and not just a prophet.

5. Jesus said we become part of his family by doing the will of God. In practise this means that we must believe in God's Son Jesus Christ so that we can be born again and share God's nature.

Chapter 13

1. Jesus taught in parables to make his spiritual teaching easier to understand. Even so, the truth of this teaching could only be revealed by the Holy Spirit, and hence could only be received by those with open, spiritually receptive hearts. By using parables, Jesus ensured that it was the faithful (those who believed in him), and not merely the intellectuals, who were given the key of knowledge in the kingdom of heaven.

2. The seed that fell on the path stands for those whose hearts are hardened to the gospel and refuse to believe. Thus the devil snatches away the word from their hearts. The seed that fell on stony ground stands for those who receive the word of God with joy, but a deep work has not been done in their lives, and they have no deep root of commitment to Jesus. So when trouble comes for the sake of Christ they turn away from following him. The seed that fell among thorns stands for those who believe in Christ and make a good start in the Christian life, but who allow their love for worldly things to take the place of their love and commitment for Jesus, and so they too fall away. The seed falling on good soil stands for those who hear, receive and obey the word of God, persevering through problems and difficulties, remaining faithful to Jesus. This last type of person is what Jesus wants us all to be.

3. The people failed to understand the parables because their eyes were not opened to the truth; their eyes could only be opened by God as they put their faith in Jesus and became committed to following him.

4. The seeds of the evil one represent false professors; that is, those who are in the church but who only pretend to be Christians (although many of them actually believe they really are Christians), to bring in false teachings and set bad examples.

5. In Jesus' parable, the good fish are his own children and the bad fish are those who, although they profess to know him, do not. The Lord knows those who are his, and will ensure that all of these are saved, whilst those who are not truly his will perish.

Chapter 14

1. Herod wanted to kill John the Baptist because he had rebuked him for living in sin by marrying his brother's wife while his brother was still living. Herod did not like to hear this and was angry with John for he did not wish to repent.

2. For a time, Herod did not carry out his wish to kill John because he feared the people, who recognised John as a prophet.

3. On hearing of John's death Jesus sought to be in a quiet place alone with his disciples, which implies that he was deeply moved and affected by this event. No doubt Jesus wished to grieve for John.

4. Jesus had already shown them many miracles, and now he wanted to challenge their faith by saying "you give them something to eat". By faith in Jesus anything is possible to God's servants.

5. Jesus again wanted to teach his disciples that not only he but they—by faith in him and in his name—could experience miracles. This would become important when we think that Jesus sent them out to preach and do miracles in his name after he returned to heaven. We too should have faith that Jesus, when it is his time and will, will enable his servants to do impossible things for God's glory.

Chapter 15

1. That which happens to the human body does not affect the human spirit, and Jesus taught that it was within the spirit that people are sinful and only in their spiritual natures (hearts) can they repent, be forgiven and be right with God.

2. Jesus said it was wrong to devote money to God which should have been used to honour, help and care for our parents.

3. Jesus tells his disciples to leave false teachers alone simply because they were wilfully blind and would not listen to the truth of God's word.

4. The Syro-Phoenecian woman teaches us to be persistent in faith, keep asking God and not allow God's seeming silence to put us off until we get what we are asking for.

5. The disciples failed to get the point of the feeding of the 5,000 because their hearts were hardened. Perhaps they had seen so many miracles that they failed to appreciate them properly, familiarity breeding contempt.

Chapter 16

1. Jesus had given the Pharisees ample evidence to show who he was, and their request for a sign came from a stubborn unwillingness to believe.

2. The teaching of the Pharisees is like yeast because, like all hypocrisy, it spreads and infects others who listen to it.

3. Some people said Jesus was like John the Baptist, whom they knew to be a holy man, obedient to God, calling them to repent. Others thought him to be Elijah, a prophet who was powerful in mighty works; still others thought Jesus was like Jeremiah who was the prophet who loved his people even when they rejected and made him suffer. These three elements may have been observed by the people in Jesus' character for them to think this way.

4. The keys of the kingdom which we see Peter later using in the book of Acts are prayer and the preaching and teaching of God's word. They may also include the miracle-working gifts of the Spirit which opened doors to many hearts for faith and the gospel message.

5. Peter was rebuked because he allowed his own worldly perspective to get in the way of what God wanted to do in his life. His opposition to Christ's dying on a cross revealed his refusal at that time to take up his own cross and follow Jesus.

Chapter 17

1. As Jesus was transfigured, the glory of his divine nature was no longer concealed by his body, but shone out in fullness of glory.

2. Moses stood for the law and Elijah for the prophets. The fact that they appeared to talk with Jesus, and were declared by God to be subservient to him, indicate that Christ and the new covenant he was introducing would be greater than the old covenant. A new relationship with God would be introduced by Jesus, which was greater than the law or the prophets.

3. Prayer and fasting was necessary to focus the disciples' minds on seeking God for the power to deliver the demon possessed boy.

4. By paying taxes the Christian shows that he or she is willing to live honestly and in this way gives a witness for the validity of the gospel. A Christian knows that a state's taxes are used for the benefit of all its citizens.

5. Our honest living should attract unbelievers to the truth. Jesus was eager to pay his tax "lest we offend them", that is, so that we do not put them off listening to the truth by our unworthy actions.

Chapter 18

1. Those who are least, and most humble, are more like Jesus who is meek and lowly. I think this is why the least shall be called great in the kingdom of heaven. To be great is to be like Jesus.

2. To cause a believer to turn from Jesus is to cause him or her to lose their own souls, and this is a very serious matter indeed.

3. We are not to take Jesus' statements about cutting off hands and feet literally. He refers to the putting to death of sin in our lives; reckoning ourselves as being made dead to sin but alive to God.

4. Putting things right with other believers and forgiving those who wrong us is one way to mitigate the effects of causing offense, and is a safeguard to prevent believers from going back from following Jesus.

5. As believers we should forgive someone who wrongs us for three reasons. Firstly, because God has forgiven us so much, we should forgive others. Secondly, how can we expect God to forgive if we will not? And thirdly, forgiving others keeps our own spirits right with God, and prevents us becoming offended.

Chapter 19

1. Jesus taught that marriage was ordained by God in the beginning and was to be between one man and woman till parted by death. Jesus did not accept that divorce was any part of God's original plan for humankind. Those who married a divorcee or who divorced and then remarried were committing adultery.

2. Children were so important to Jesus because they too could believe on him and enter God's kingdom. Children have living souls, and can inherit eternal life just as adults.

3. The rich young ruler was sad when Jesus challenged his commitment because he was unwilling to part with his wealth, revealing that he loved his money more than God.

4. A rich person can be saved if they do not trust or hold on to their riches, but instead see salvation through faith in Jesus as far more important than their wealth.

5. Those who have left everything to follow Christ will not only gain the eternal life which comes as a gift to those who follow him, but will also be given the shared possession of all that is his, the whole church is available to serve those who serve Christ.

Chapter 20

1. The landowner gave the same money to those who worked for one hour as he did for those who had worked all day, and this appeared unfair. The landowner explained his behaviour by insisting that since it was his money, he had a right to do with it as he saw fit. Every man hired had agreed to his pay, and that agreement was kept.

2. James and John were thinking of Jesus' kingdom as if it were a human or earthly kingdom, where there would be a hierarchy of authority; something which Jesus denies will be in the kingdom of heaven.

3. Only those who receive God's kingdom in simple faith and humility like a trusting little child are able to enter it.

4. Rather than seek greatness, the disciples were to love and serve each other, as Christ had come to love and serve them. Following the example of Jesus was a far greater prize than becoming important.

5. It may be that Matthew inserted the story of the two blind men at this particular point to illustrate how those who are lowly are called by Jesus and given a place in his kingdom based on God's generosity and love, and not their own merit.

Chapter 21

1. Jesus was able to commandeer someone else's donkey because he is the creator of all things; who could resist him? Ultimately everything belongs to him and he has lent all things to us for our use.

2. Jesus was angered when he saw the temple being used as a common market instead of a holy place in which to worship God his father. The actions of the sellers and buyers were robbing Israel of its spiritual life-line to God.

3. The parable of the fig tree can speak to us of the people of Jerusalem at Jesus time. The time should have been right for them to show the fruit of love and obedience to God—for Christ was among them—but instead Jesus found the dead leaves of unbelief and disobedience. The result for Jerusalem would be the same as it was for the fig tree—destruction. It was also used by Jesus to illustrate that all things are possible when we believe in God.

4. The tax collectors and prostitutes were doing the will of God by repenting of their sin and putting their faith in Jesus. The Pharisees and other religious leaders were not.

5. The religious leaders were to be held accountable before God because although he had given them so much (represented by the vineyard) and

expected them to produce fruit (love and obedience) they had not done so. Even when he sent the prophets with his word, urging them to repent, they mistreated and killed them. In Jesus' time they rejected and murdered the Son of God himself. Such a privilege as God sending his son to them brought a great responsibility; a responsibility in which they failed.

Chapter 22

1. Many of those who were invited to the wedding banquet failed to attend because they refused to go; they considered other things such as work and pleasure to be more important than obeying the call of their king. Obviously they did not respect their king very much.

2. The man without wedding clothes was cast out because in those days it was vital to wear the clothes provided by the king—not to wear them was an insult. This illustrates that we can only enter God's kingdom by receiving from God the righteousness which he has provided for us in Christ.

3. If Caesar is the ruling power demanding tax or tribute then as a good citizen I must pay my taxes and fulfil my civil duties. God, on the other hand, owns all that I have and am, so I must give every moment of my life, my abilities and resources to him, making them fully available for his use.

4. According to Jesus the Sadducees got it wrong about there being no resurrection because they did not know the scriptures or the power of God. They should have known from the teachings of Moses that God is the God of the living and not the dead, for all live to him.

5. Jesus explained that since David called the Christ his lord, he was someone greater than David's son.

Chapter 23

1. The scribes and Pharisees were to be obeyed in as much as they were the judiciary who upheld the Law of Moses, which was the civil law in Israel; they were the leadership of the nation.

2. The scribes and Pharisees' example was not to be followed because they were hypocrites. They did not do as they taught others to do. Moreover, they were

hypocritical in their religion, pretending to be pious whilst defrauding widows. Jesus wants us to be genuine in our religion, with respect for God and clean hearts.

3. They opposed the truth which Jesus brought, and by so doing not only failed to enter God's kingdom themselves but were hindering others from entering it.

They pretended to be pious whilst taking advantage of the poor widows.

They made their religious converts worse than themselves.

They gave false teaching about oaths.

Although they tithed, they did not heed the more important commands of the law concerning love and justice.

They kept a number of outward food and ceremonial cleansing laws, looking outwardly righteous, but within their hearts were greedy and disobedient to God.

They would kill and persecute God's true messengers.

4. Punishment was about to come on the people of Jerusalem because they would not heed God's word through the prophets and would not respond to his calling them to himself.

5. Jesus seems sad that it should come to this. He had longed to gather the people in his arms, but it was impossible, not because he was not willing, but because they were not. I think Jesus was very disappointed.

Chapter 24

1. The beautiful temple seemed unimportant to Jesus because his mind and heart were set on eternal things. The temple and even the world itself will not endure forever. Jesus saw temple worship as important, but not as important as obedience to God.

2. Wars, rumours of wars, earthquakes, famines, persecution of the church, false prophets, and the gospel preached in the entire world.

3. The "antichrist" will sit in the temple of God proclaiming that he is God, and demanding worship from all nations of the earth, setting set up a statue of himself in the temple of God. This is the abomination that will lead to desolation. At this time true believers (from the Jewish nation and living in Judea) will flee into the mountains as a time of terrible persecution erupts. God will protect the faithful, and limit the time of persecution so that many might survive. Many false Christs and prophets will perform satanic miracles and they will be days of unimaginable evil.

4. Jesus said he would come suddenly and unexpectedly in power and great glory, with all the holy angels, and that his coming would be visible to the entire cosmos. His enemies will mourn, but his people will be gathered together to him.

5. A faithful and wise servant of Christ will be doing what God has commanded every day, because he knows that each day might be the one in which Christ will come again.

Chapter 25

1. The foolish virgins were foolish because although they knew the bridegroom would come at an unspecified time, they did not make sure they were ready for his coming—they had no oil with which to refill their lamps.

2. The wise virgins, on the other hand, realising that the bridegroom might come at any time prepared for this eventuality; they were ready for his coming. They took enough oil to refill their lamps.

3. The servant with one talent did not use what his lord had given him and so was deprived of his talent, whilst the others did use their lord's money and so were rewarded.

4. They fed him when he was hungry, gave him drink when he was thirsty, took him in when he was a stranger, clothed him when he was naked, cared for him when he was sick and visited him in prison.

5. The sheep are God's people who showed their love for Jesus by demonstrating their love for his church in practical ways. The goats were not God's people and demonstrated this by having no concern for Christ's church, not having any love for God's people to spur them to action.

Chapter 26

1. I think Judas hardened his heart and was not prepared to take up his cross and follow Jesus. He loved the world, and so betrayed Jesus for money, which he thought more important than the salvation of his soul.

2. The Passover symbolised the deliverance of Israel from slavery in Egypt by the blood of an unblemished lamb. Jesus changed this meal into the communion service which is a memorial of his delivering us from the slavery of sin by his own blood shed on the cross.

3. Peter was unable to keep his promise not to deny Jesus because he was relying on his own strength whilst up against satanic power. Only the strength of Jesus living in him would, in later life, prove sufficient for Peter to overcome such temptation and attack of the enemy.

4. From his prayer in the garden, I can see that God did not *make* Jesus obey his will, but that Jesus had to be *willing* to obey, which he was. Jesus must have loved God completely to obey him so fully.

5. Jesus did not resist arrest, for he knew that the scripture must be fulfilled, and he will willingly gave his life for sinners

Chapter 27

1. The Pharisees would not take the thirty pieces of silver back from Judas because it was the price of blood, and would make them unclean. Hypocrites, they were already unclean for condemning Jesus.

2. Pilate knew Jesus was innocent and that the chief priests only wanted him dead because they were envious of him. It is possible that he also feared the "gods" which (as he believed), according to the charges against Jesus and his wife's dream seemed to be on Jesus' side.

3. The soldiers stripped and beat Jesus, putting on him a purple robe and a crown of thorns, paying mock homage to him as king. As he was crucified, the soldiers callously gambled for his clothes, whilst the chief priests and the people tempted him to come down from the cross, saying that God would not welcome him.

4. The miraculous midday darkness, the tearing of the temple curtain, an earthquake and the opening of the tombs and the resurrection of the dead saints.

5. I am impressed by the love and devotion of the women, who were with him, albeit helplessly, throughout his terrible ordeal.

Chapter 28

1. When the women came to the garden tomb they saw an angel roll away the stone. The guards shook and became like dead men, but the angel told them not to fear, since they were looking for Jesus who was crucified and that he was risen from the dead. The angel told them to go and tell the disciples, which they began to do, but as they went, Jesus himself met them and spoke to them.

2. I think the chief priests tried to conceal the events which the soldiers reported because they remained opposed to Jesus whether he was risen from the dead or not!

3. I am not sure why the disciples wavered in their commitment; but I know that it can be a difficult or frightening thing to commit yourself unreservedly to anything. I suppose this difficulty had to be overcome, and it must also be overcome by every follower of Jesus.

4. Jesus told his disciples to go into all the world and preach the gospel to every creature; teaching them to obey all of his commands, and to be baptised in the name of the Father, the Son and the Holy Spirit.

5. Jesus promises those who are carrying out his great commission that he will be with them at all times in every place until the world ends.

Appendix – How to Use this Study Guide

Good Bible study takes time. Set aside a sufficient time to study the chapter on your own—or divide the chapter into two parts. Allow an hour if possible or at least half an hour for your study.

We recommend that you photocopy the discussion questions (or print them from www.biblestudiesonline.org.uk). Use one for yourself, and distribute one each to every member of your study group. Having studied the verses on your own, arrange a meeting so you can join together and compare notes.

Always pray before you begin your study, that God will give you understanding. Then read the chapter itself, from whichever Bible version you prefer. Then sit down, in a quiet place, and read through each verse again together with the guide notes, taking time to reflect and think upon what you read. Make your own notes if possible; recording what God is showing you through the chapter, which might be somewhat different to the guide notes, especially if something is speaking to you personally from a certain verse or chapter. Be sure to share these insights later with your Bible study group. Again, close your study time with a short prayer. Remember that God himself is your greatest teacher, so you need to spend time with him if you wish to understand his word.

We recommend that you concentrate on no more than one chapter at a time. Reading the verses through again will help to ensure that what you have learned will stay in your heart and become part of your life.

Remember—God's word is not an academic textbook to be learned by rote. It is a living word to be hidden in your heart and obeyed in your life. May God bless you as you seek to follow him, employing the best method for spiritual growth which has ever been known to humankind—Bible study!